# HIDDEN®
# Big Island
# of Hawaii

D0324966

# HIDDEN ®

# Big Island of Hawaii

Including the Kona Coast, Hilo, Kailua and Volcanoes National Park

### Ray Riegert

Ulysses Press ®
BERKELEY, CALIFORNIA

Published by:
ULYSSES PRESS
P.O. Box 3440
Berkeley, CA 94703
www.ulyssespress.com

ISSN 1544-1385
ISBN 1-56975-341-5

Printed in Canada by Transcontinental Printing

10 9 8 7 6 5 4 3 2 1

CONTRIBUTING AUTHORS: Leslie Henriques, Allan Seiden, Richard Harris
EDITORIAL DIRECTOR: Leslie Henriques
MANAGING EDITOR: Claire Chun
COPY EDITOR: Lily Chou
EDITORIAL ASSOCIATES: Kate Allen, Laura Brancella, Caroline Cummins, Marin Van Young
CARTOGRAPHY: Pease Press
COVER DESIGN: Sarah Levin, Leslie Henriques
INDEXER: Sayre Van Young
COVER PHOTOGRAPHY: Doug Peebles (Kilauea erupting)
ILLUSTRATOR: Doug McCarthy

Distributed in the United States by Publishers Group West and in Canada by Raincoast Books

# Acknowledgments

First and foremost, I want to thank my wife, Leslie Henriques, who has been with me for all my research trips to the Big Island and did a lot of research and writing of her own for this book. Allan Seiden and Richard Harris, who also helped with the research and writing, were invaluable contributors. I also want to thank Claire Chun for coordinating the project, copy editor Lily Chou, typesetter Lisa Kester and indexer Sayre Van Young. Mahalo to everyone.

# Write to us!

If in your travels you discover a spot that captures the spirit of Wyoming, or if you live in the region and have a favorite place to share, or if you just feel like expressing your views, write to us and we'll pass your note along to the author.

We can't guarantee that the author will add your personal find to the next edition, but if the writer does use the suggestion, we'll acknowledge you in the credits and send you a free copy of the new edition.

Ulysses Press
P.O. Box 3440
Berkeley, CA 94703
E-mail: readermail@ulyssespress.com

# What's Hidden?

At different points throughout this book, you'll find special listings marked with a hidden symbol:

◄ HIDDEN

This means that you have come upon a place off the beaten tourist track, a spot that will carry you a step closer to the local people and natural environment of the Big Island of Hawaii.

The goal of this guide is to lead you beyond the realm of everyday tourist facilities. While we include traditional sightseeing listings and popular attractions, we also offer alternative sights and adventure activities. Instead of filling this guide with reviews of standard hotels and chain restaurants, we concentrate on one-of-a-kind places and locally owned establishments.

Our authors seek out locales that are popular with residents but usually overlooked by visitors. Some are more hidden than others (and are marked accordingly), but all the listings in this book are intended to help you discover the true nature of the Big Island of Hawaii and put you on the path of adventure.

# Contents

# Maps

## OUTDOOR ADVENTURE SYMBOLS

The following symbols accompany national, state and regional park listings, as well as beach descriptions throughout the text.

| | | | |
|---|---|---|---|
| ▲ | Camping | | Waterskiing |
| | Hiking | | Windsurfing |
| | Biking | | Kayaking/Canoeing |
| | Swimming | | Boating |
| | Snorkeling or Scuba Diving | | Boat ramps |
| | Surfing | | Fishing |

# The Orchid Isle

 The Big Island, they call it, and even that is an understatement. Hawaii, all 4030 square miles, is almost twice as large as all the other Hawaiian islands combined. Its twin volcanic peaks, Mauna Kea and Mauna Loa, dwarf most mountains. Mauna Loa, the world's largest active volcano, which last erupted in 1984, looms 13,677 feet above sea level. Mauna Kea, rising 13,796 feet, is the largest island-based mountain in the world. It is actually 32,000 feet from the ocean floor, making it, by one system of reckoning, the tallest mountain on earth, grander even than Everest. And in bulk Mauna Loa is the world's largest. The entire Sierra Nevada chain could fit within this single peak.

Kilauea, a third volcano whose seething firepit has been erupting with startling frequency, is one of the world's most active volcanoes. Since its most recent series of eruptions began in 1983, Kilauea has swallowed almost 200 houses. In 1990 it completely destroyed the town of Kalapana, burying a once lively village beneath tons of black lava; then in 1992 it destroyed the ancient Hawaiian village of Kamoamoa and the *heiau* at Wahaula. There is little doubt that the Big Island is a place of geologic superlatives.

But size alone does not convey the Big Island's greatness. Its industry, too, is expansive. Despite the lava wasteland that covers large parts of its surface, and the volcanic gases that create a layer of "vog" during volcanic eruptions, the Big Island is the state's greatest producer of coffee, papayas, vegetables, anthuriums, macadamia nuts and cattle. Its orchid industry, based in rain-drenched Hilo, is the world's largest. Over 22,000 varieties grow in the nurseries here.

Across the island in sun-soaked Kona, one of the nation's only coffee industries operates. Just off this spectacular western coast lie some of the finest deep-sea fishing grounds in the world. Between Hilo and Kona, and surrounding Waimea, sits the Parker Ranch. Sprawling across 225,000 acres, it is one of the world's largest independently owned cattle ranches.

Yet many of these measurements are taken against island standards. Compared to the mainland, the Big Island is a tiny speck in the sea. Across its broadest reach it measures a scant 93 miles long and 76 miles wide, smaller than Connecticut. The road around the island totals only 300 miles, and can be driven in a day, though I'd recommend taking at least five. The island's 142,000 population comprises just 8 percent of the state's citizens. Its lone city, Hilo, has a population of only 42,133.

*Ua mau ke o ka aina i ka pono,* the state motto, means "The life of the land is perpetuated in righteousness."

But large or small, numbers cannot fully describe the Big Island, for there is a magic about the place that transcends statistics. Hawaii, also nicknamed the Orchid Island and Volcano Island, is the home of Pele, the goddess of volcanoes. Perhaps her fiery spirit is what infuses the Big Island with an unquantifiable quality. Or maybe the island's comparative youth is what makes the elements seem nearer, more alluring and strangely threatening here. It's still growing in size because of lava flows from Kilauea and Mauna Loa. In fact, recent activity has added more than a square mile to the island. The Big Island is geologically the youngest spot on earth, one million years old. Whatever it might be, the Big Island has always been where I feel closest to the Polynesian spirit. Of all the Hawaiian islands, this one I love the most.

It was here, possibly as early as A.D. 400 or as late as the 9th century, that Polynesian explorers may have first landed when they discovered the island chain. Until the advent of the white man, it was generally the most important island, supporting a large population and occupying a vital place in Hawaii's rich mythology. Little wonder then that Kamehameha the Great, the chief who would become Hawaii's first king, was born here in 1753. He established the archipelago's first capital in Kailua and ruled there until his death in 1819.

Within a year of the great leader's passing, two events occurred in Kailua that jolted the entire chain far more than any earthquake. First the king's heir, Liholiho, uprooted the centuries-old taboo system upon which the native Hawaiian religion rested. Then, in the spring of 1820, the first American missionaries dropped anchor off the coast of Kailua-Kona. It was also near here that Captain James Cook, history's greatest discoverer, was slain in 1779 by the same people who had earlier welcomed him as a god. Across the island another deity, Pele, was defied in 1824 when the high chieftess Kapiolani, a Christian, ate *kapu* (forbidden) fruit on the rim of an active lava lake at Kilauea, and suffered no ill consequence.

As stirring as the Big Island's story might be, much of its drama still awaits the visitor. For the land—the volcanoes, beaches and valleys—is as vital and in-

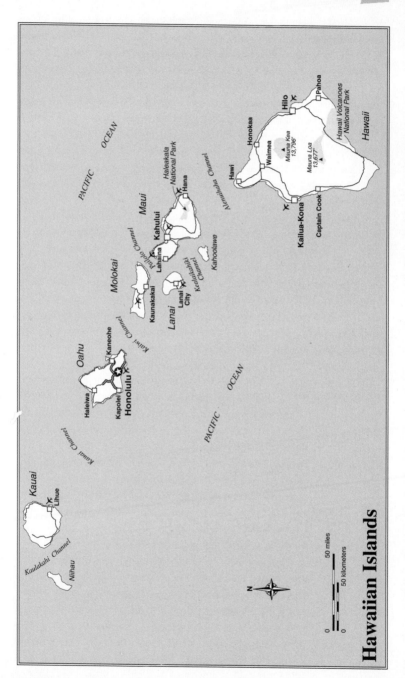

# Hawaiian Islands

triguing today as in the days of demigods and kings. This is a place for the adventurer to spend a lifetime. In the north, from the Hamakua Coast to the Kohala Peninsula, heavy erosion has cut through the volcano to form spectacular canyons such as the Waipio Valley. All along the Hamakua plateau, sugar plantations, fed by waters from Mauna Kea, stretch from the mountains to the surf.

In startling contrast to these verdant mountains is the desert-like Kau district at the southern tip of the island (and, for that matter, the southernmost point in the United States). Along the west coast stretches the Kona district, a vacationer's paradise. Suntan weather, sandy beaches and coral reefs teeming with tropical fish make this an ideal area to just kick back and enjoy. The island's central tourist area is located here in Kailua-Kona, where Hawaiian royalty settled in the 19th century.

And for something unique to the Big Island, there's Waimea with its rolling grasslands, range animals and *paniolos*, or Hawaiian-style cowboys. In fact, one of the biggest Hereford cattle herds is located here in the center of the island.

It's an island I don't think you should miss, an island that offers a string of luxury resorts as well as time-worn tropical retreats hidden along its other shores. To geologists the Big Island is a natural laboratory in which the mysteries of volcanic activity are a fact of everyday life; to many Hawaiians it is the most sacred of all the islands. To everyone who visits it, Hawaii is a place of startling contrasts and unspeakable beauty, an alluring and exotic tropical island.

## Where to Go

History lies half-hidden behind shopping malls, resorts and condominiums in **Kailua-Kona**. The modern-day population center of the Big Island's leeward coast, this town of 10,000 was the site of Hawaiian king Kamehameha's last royal residence and palace, as well as the first Christian missionary church in the Hawaiian Islands. It is also the Big Island's oldest tourist resort area. Sheltered by 8271-foot Hualalai Volcano and taller, more distant Mauna Kea, the area enjoys a relatively dry climate and calm waters year-round, creating ideal conditions for the Kona Coast's two greatest claims to fame—sportfishing and growing gourmet coffee.

The overwhelming impression that strikes travelers as they drive north from Kailua-Kona along the **Kohala Coast** is of a vast, stark black-lava moonscape, set against a backdrop of spectacular Big Island volcano views as well as the soft silhouette of the island of Maui across the water. At the far end of the Kaahumanu Highway lie some of the island's best white-sand beaches. Visitors can see two ancient *heiau* temples—one reputedly dedi-

## Hawaiian Getaway

**Day 1**
- Arrive in **Kailua-Kona** (page 91) and check into a condominium or hotel in town or along the Kohala Coast.

- In the afternoon explore the **Kohala Coast** (page 116) along Route 270, the Akoni Pule Highway, up to the **Pololu Valley Lookout** (page 121).

**Day 2**
- Spend the day snorkeling, swimming, sportfishing, or reading a book.

**Day 3**
- Take Route 190 to the upcountry ranch town of **Waimea** (page 135) and go horseback riding. Or if your rental car company allows, take the Saddle Road up to the road leading to Mauna Kea and the **Onizuka Center for International Astronomy** (page 138). Plan to have dinner in Waimea before heading back.

**Day 4**
- From Kailua-Kona drive around South Point, stopping at **Kealakekua Bay** (page 148) and **Puuhonua o Honaunau National Historical Park** (page 149).

- Continue on Route 11 to Hawaii Volcanoes National Park and spend the night at **Volcano House** (page 169) or a local bed and breakfast. Try to arrive by 4 p.m. so you can see the volcanic activity at dusk, when the glow from the lava is most intense.

**Day 5**
- Explore **Hawaii Volcanoes National Park** (page 164).

**Day 6**
- Head to **Hilo** (page 183) and check in to a hotel or B&B. Explore **downtown** Hilo and the **Liliuokalani Gardens** (page 184). Beach lovers can spend the afternoon at **Richardson Ocean Park** (page 196). Orchid fans should be sure to visit some of the local **flower farms** (page 184).

**Day 7**
- Return to the Kohala Coast via the **Hamakua Coast** (page 197), visiting the **Waipio Valley** (page 200), if time allows, before checking in at the airport.

cated with a human sacrifice—and stop for lunch in Kawaihae, a busy cattle-shipping port, before continuing northward into the luxuriantly tropical region farther up the coast.

Cowboys in paradise? You'll find them riding the range around **Waimea**, the only major town in the Big Island's interior. Along with one of the world's largest cattle ranches, the rustic outskirts of Waimea boast pastoral landscapes and a cool microclimate, complete with bed-and-breakfast inns and gourmet restaurants. Sightseers will find three outstanding museums in the area, and adventurers can discover hiking and horseback riding trails in the nearby volcanic hills with their lush, steep-walled valleys and spectacular waterfalls.

Travelers who drive south, rather than north, along the coast from Kailua-Kona will discover one of the most "hidden" parts of the Big Island—the **Kona/Kau** district. Kona coffee plantations and colorful flowers punctuate the vast black lava flows from Hualalai and Mauna Loa en route to the southernmost point in the United States. Fishing villages unspoiled by tourism dot the Kona/Kau coastline, as do secluded beaches of black sand, beige sand and green—yes, green—sand. As it veers inland on its way toward Hawaii Volcanoes National Park, the highway passes between two dramatically contrasting ecological zones— the lush Kau Forest Reserve and the Kau Desert, the latter so desolate that astronauts practiced there for lunar landings.

A visit to **Hawaii Volcanoes National Park** is the biggest event in any visit to the Big Island. The centerpieces of this 344-square-mile park are two active volcanoes. Motorists can drive all the way around the caldera of Kilauea, the world's most active volcano, which fumes almost continuously. Ambitious hikers can trek to the top rim of 13,679-foot Mauna Loa, the world's tallest volcano. Other trails lead visitors through rain forest, desert and a lava tube. Accommodation options include a unique national park lodge perched on Kilauea's rim.

Due east of the volcanos, the **Puna District** offers another chance to explore the "hidden" Big Island. With its sizeable Native Hawaiian population, the district has been spared from big-resort development because of the red-hot molten lava rivers that occasionally spill down the slopes of Kilauea Volcano, such as the one that destroyed a village in 1991. You can stay in an old sugar plantation house turned bed and breakfast and explore the surrealistic landscape of tropical forest, sea cliffs, lava caves, secluded bays, shell-strewn beaches and steaming volcanic cones.

Though many visitors now fly in to the Big Island's other airports, inevitably their explorations will eventually bring them to **Hilo**, the island's largest "city" by far with a population of over 40,000. Time and money seem to have passed Hilo by as two devastating tidal waves and the collapse of the sugar industry steered recent land development toward sunnier climes on other parts of

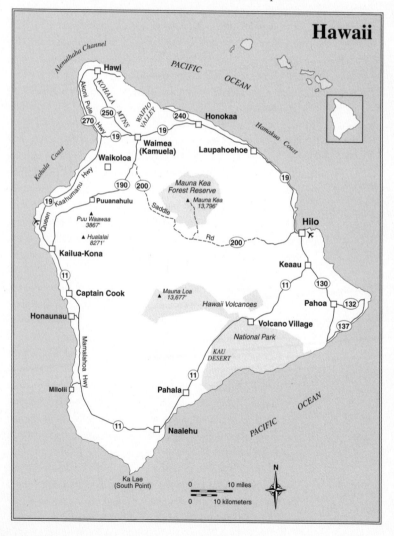

the island. But 140 inches of annual rainfall have helped transform Hilo into a city of tropical foliage, the center of Hawaii's orchid, papaya and macadamia nut production, and the once-busy bayfront port facilities have been replaced by tropical gardens.

Continuing north from Hilo, motorists will encounter more of the rain-drenched windward shoreline with its flowers and macadamia groves along the **Hamakua Coast,** but without Hilo's population. The remnants of former sugar cane plantation towns slumber wrapped in shadowy forests and groves of eucalyptus, ferns, bamboo and birds of paradise and guarded from the outside world by deep canyons and plunging waterfalls. At the end of this spectacularly scenic drive, the Waipio Valley, the largest valley on the island, was once home to thousands of Native Hawaiians; today it has largely reverted to wilderness awaiting adventurous travelers who can explore it on foot or on a four-wheel-drive tour.

## When to Go

### SEASONS

There are two types of seasons on the Big Island, one keyed to tourists and the other to the climate. The peak tourist seasons run from mid-December until Easter, then again from mid-June through Labor Day. Particularly around the Christmas holidays and in August, the visitors centers are crowded. Prices increase, hotel rooms and rental cars become harder to reserve, and everything moves a bit more rapidly. Shop around, however; package deals that include discounts on published rates are available.

If you plan to explore the Big Island during these seasons, make reservations several months in advance; actually, it's a good idea to make advance reservations whenever you visit. Without doubt, the off-season is the best time to hit the island. Not only are hotels more readily available, but campsites and hiking trails are also less crowded.

Climatologically, the ancient Hawaiians distinguished between two seasons—*kau*, or summer, and *hooilo*, or winter. Summer extends from May to October, when the sun is overhead and the temperatures are slightly higher. Winter brings more variable winds and cooler weather.

The important rule to remember about the Big Island's beautiful weather is that it changes very little from season to season but varies dramatically from place to place. The average yearly temperature is about 78°, and during the coldest weather in January and the warmest in August, the thermometer rarely moves more than 5° or 6° in either direction. Similarly, sea water temperatures range comfortably between 74° and 80° year-round.

Crucial to this luxurious semitropical environment is the trade wind that blows with welcome regularity from the northeast, providing a natural form of air conditioning. When the trades stop blowing, they are sometimes replaced by *kona* winds carrying rain and humid weather from the southwest. These are most frequent in the winter, when the island receives its heaviest rainfall.

> The average annual rainfall in Hilo is nearly 130 inches! Kawaihae, on the Kohala Coast, averages a mere 10 inches.

While summer showers are less frequent and shorter in duration, winter storms are sometimes quite nasty. I've seen it pour for five consecutive days, until hiking trails disappeared and streets were awash. If you visit in winter, particularly from December to March, you're risking the chance of rain.

A wonderful factor to remember through this wet weather is that if it's raining where you are, you can often simply go someplace else. And I don't mean another part of the world, or even a different island. Since the rains generally batter the northeastern section of the island, you can usually head over to the south or west coast for warm, sunny weather.

## CALENDAR OF EVENTS

Something else to consider in planning a visit to the Big Island is the lineup of annual cultural events. For a thumbnail idea of what's happening, check the calendar below. You might just find that special occasion to climax an already dynamic vacation. For a comprehensive listing with current updates, check the Hawaii Visitors & Convention Bureau website: www.calendar.gohawaii.com/bigisland.

**Various sites**  The annual **Sanctuary Ocean Count**, a yearly shore-based census taken during the breeding season of the humpback whales, occurs at various sites around the island.     **JANUARY**

**Kohala Coast**  Masters of the ukulele strum their melodies at the **Ukulele Festival** while exhibits display how ancient Hawaiian musical instruments were made in Waikoloa.     **FEBRUARY**

**Waimea**    Waimea honors Japanese culture at the **Waimea Cherry Blossom Heritage Festival** with a parade, craft vendors, food and family events.

**Hilo**    One of Hawaii's myriad cultures is extolled at **Portuguese Day in the Park**, where food and people are the primary draw. In Gilbert Carvalho Park, orchids of every ilk are showcased at the **Hilo Orchid Society's Annual Show and Sale**. One of the most scenic marathons in the United States is the **Big Island International Marathon** that runs along the ocean through tropical rainforests and past waterfalls and finishes at Hilo Bay.

**APRIL**

**Island-wide**    Buddhist temples on all the islands mark **Buddha Day**, the luminary's birthday, with special services. Included among the events are pageants, dances and flower festivals.

**Hilo**    The week-long **Merrie Monarch Festival** pays tribute to David Kalakaua, Hawaii's last king. Festivities include musical performances, pageants and a parade.

**MAY**

**Island-wide**    **Lei Day** is celebrated on May 1 in the islands by people wearing flower leis and colorful Hawaiian garb.

**Kailua-Kona/Kohala Coast**    Challenging themselves on the same course as the famous Ironman Triathlon World Championship, the **Keauhou-Kona Triathlon** athletes run, swim and bike in order to qualify for the Ironman later in the year.

**Hilo**    An umbrella parade kicks off the annual **Hilo Rain Festival**, applauding the wettest city in the state. Food booths, crafts and island entertainment help make merry of this wet venue.

**JUNE**

**Island-wide**    Throughout the islands **King Kamehameha Day** is celebrated with festivities.

**Kohala Coast**    Food, music and three days of fun in the sun are all part of the revelries at **Dolphin Days**, hosted by the Hilton Waikoloa Village.

**Waimea**    The slopes of Mauna Kea are the venue of the **Waikii Music Festival**, held every Father's Day weekend, and features the best of Hawaiian entertainment, food and crafts.

**Kona/Kau**    Canoe rides, arts and crafts, a *hukilau* and other Hawaiian traditions are featured at the Puuhonua O Honaunau National Historical Park's **Cultural Festival**.

**Hilo**    A re-enactment of historical events that took place during the king's reign are presented on Moku Ola (Coconut Island).

**Kohala Coast**   The 4th of July is independence day for green sea turtles nurtured by Sea Life Park and ready to return to the ocean. Sponsored by Mauna Lani Bay Hotel, **Turtle Independence Day** offers live entertainment and children's activities, including educational displays, following the release. **Hawaiian Flag Day** (or **La Hae Hawaii**) is celebrated at Puukohola National Historic Site, one of three locations in the islands where the Hawaiian flag has been allowed to fly alone as a symbol of the Hawaiian people.

**JULY**

**Waimea**   Horse racing, double mugging, roping and other traditional rodeo events are the draw at the **Parker Ranch 4th of July Horse Races and Rodeo**—food and shopping keep you occupied when the *paniolos* take a break from strutting their stuff.

**Island-wide**   Local residents celebrate **Admission Day** on August 21, the date in 1959 when Hawaii became the 50th state.

**AUGUST**

**Kohala Coast**   Spencer Park hosts the Aloha Festival pageantry of **Pikai** and **Hookupu** as the Royal Court visits the ocean, then proceeds into the sea for a "washing" of the Moi and Moi Wahine in preparation for a successful reign.

**Hawaii Volcanoes National Park**   Hula and chants are the highlights of **Ka Hoolaa O Na Alii**, an investiture of the Aloha Festival's Royal Court held on the rim of Halemaumau Crater.

**Kohala Coast**   At the Outrigger Waikoloa the **Annual Clyde Sproat Falsetto and Storytelling Contest** salutes the melodious voices of Hawaiian singers.

**SEPTEMBER**

### A CIRCLE OF ALOHA

The lei—a symbol of Hawaii, along with grass skirts and palm trees. If you're fortunate enough to be met at the airport by someone you know, chances are you'll be wreathed in fragrant blossoms and kissed on both cheeks. But if you come to the island as a stranger, give yourself this aromatic gift. Lei-giving is a tradition that dates back to ancient times, when they were used as head wreaths as well as flower necklaces in religious ceremonies and were presented to the *alii*. The craft of lei-making continues to thrive today. You can still find leis that incorporate ferns, *pukeawe* (red berries), *lehua* blossoms and *maile* leaves into intricate works of art, some having hundreds of blossoms and all made with *aloha*.

**Hilo**    The **Hilo Hoolaulea**, part of the Aloha Festival celebrations, showcases Hawaiian food and cultural activities, including the arrival of the Royal Court by *waa* (canoe), along with a *hookupu* ceremony. The **Hawaii County Fair** features an orchid show, lei contest, steer show and agricultural displays, plus exhibits of Hawaiian arts and crafts. **Queen Liliuokalani's birthday** is celebrated at He Halia Aloha O Liliuokalani Park.

**OCTOBER**    **Kailua-Kona/Kohala Coast**    The **Ironman Triathlon World Championship** tests the stamina of the world's best-conditioned in mid-October.

**NOVEMBER**    **Kona/Kau**    Hundreds of celebrants gather for the harvesting of coffee, the focus of the **Kona Coffee Cultural Festival**, where food is just the side order for the area's famed brew.

**DECEMBER**    **Island-wide**    Buddha's enlightenment is commemorated on all the islands with **Bodhi Day** ceremonies and religious services
**Waimea**    *Paniolo* country hosts the annual **Waimea Christmas Parade**, a colorful way to welcome in the yuletide season.
**Hamakua Coast**    The entire community of Wailea Village comes out for the **Mochi-Zuki Celebration**, the making of traditional rice cakes the old-fashioned way.

▼▼▼▼▼▼▼▼▼▼▼

# Before You Go

**VISITORS CENTERS**

The **Hawaii Visitors & Convention Bureau**, a state-run agency, is a valuable resource from which to obtain free information on the Big Island and the rest of Hawaii. With branches on each of the four largest islands, the Bureau can help plan your trip and then offer advice once you reach the Big Island. The Big Island office is called the **Big Island Visitors Bureau**. ~ 250 Keawe Street, Hilo, 808-961-5797, fax 808-961-2126, www.bigisland.org; or 75-5719 Alii Drive, Suite W, Kailua-Kona, 808-329-7787. You can also contact the main Hawaii Visitors & Convention Bureau office in Honolulu. ~ 2270 Kalakaua Avenue, Suite 801, Honolulu, HI 96815; 808-923-1811, 800-464-2924; www.gohawaii.com.

Another excellent resource is the **Hawaii State Public Library System**. With branches in Holualoa, Kohala, Honokaa, Kailua-Kona, Kealakekua, Laupahoehoe, Naalehu and Kamuela, this government agency provides facilities for residents and non-residents alike. The libraries are good places to find light beach-reading material as well as books on Hawaii. Visitors can check out books by simply applying for a library card with a valid identification card.

## PACKING

When I get ready to pack for a trip, I sit down and make a list of everything I'll need. It's a very slow, exact procedure: I look in closets, drawers and shelves, and run through in my mind the activities in which I'll participate, determining which items are required for each. After all the planning is complete and when I have the entire inventory collected in one long list, I sit for a minute or two, basking in my wisdom and forethought.

Then I tear the hell out of the list, cut out the ridiculous items I'll never use, halve the number of spares among the necessary items, and reduce the entire contents of my suitcase to the bare essentials.

Before I developed this packing technique, I once traveled overland from London to New Delhi carrying two suitcases and a knapsack. I lugged those damned bundles onto trains, buses, jitneys, taxis and rickshaws. When I reached Turkey, I started shipping things home, but by then I was buying so many market goods that it was all I could do to keep even.

> The Big Island's environment is fragile. Part of its natural beauty comes from its geographic isolation from alien ecosystems. Bringing in plants, produce or animals can introduce pests and non-endemic species that could eventually undermine the ecosystem.

I ended up carrying so much crap that one day, when I was sardined in a crowd pushing its way onto an Indian train, someone managed to pick my pocket. When I felt the wallet slipping out, not only was I unable to chase the culprit—I was so weighted down with baggage that I couldn't even turn around to see who was robbing me!

I'll never travel that way again, and neither should you. Particularly when visiting the Big Island, where the weather is mild, you should pack very light. The airlines permit two suitcases and a carry-on bag; try to take one suitcase and maybe an accessory bag that can double as a beach bag. Dress styles are very informal in the islands, and laundromats are ubiquitous, so you don't need a broad range of clothing items, and you'll require very few extras among the essential items.

Remember, you're packing for a semitropical climate. Take along a sweater or light jacket for the mountains, and a poncho to protect against rain. But otherwise, all that travelers on the Big

Island require are shorts, long pants for hiking, bathing suits, lightweight slacks, short-sleeved shirts and blouses, and summer dresses or muumuus. Rarely do visitors require sports jackets or formal dresses. Wash-and-wear fabrics are the most convenient.

For footwear, I suggest soft, comfortable shoes. Low-cut hiking boots or tennis shoes are preferable for hiking; for beachgoing, there's nothing as good as sandals.

There are several other items to squeeze in the corners of your suitcase—sunscreen, sunglasses, a towel and, of course, your copy of *Hidden Big Island of Hawaii*. You might also consider packing a mask, fins and snorkel, and possibly a camera.

If you plan on camping, you'll need most of the equipment required for mainland overnighting. You can get along quite comfortably with a lightweight tent and sleeping bag. You'll also need a knapsack, canteen, camp stove and fuel, mess kit, first-aid kit (with insect repellent, water purification tablets and Chapstick), toilet kit, hat, waterproof matches, flashlight and ground cloth.

**LODGING**   Accommodations on the Big Island range from funky cottages to bed-and-breakfast inns to highrise condos. You will find inexpensive family-run hotels, middle-class tourist facilities and world-class resorts.

Whichever you choose, there are a few guidelines to help save money. Try to visit during the off-season, avoiding the high-rate periods during the summer and from Christmas to Easter. Rooms with mountain views are less expensive than oceanview accommodations. Another way to economize is by reserving a room with a kitchen. In any case, try to reserve far in advance.

To help you decide on a place to stay, I've described the accommodations not only by area but also according to price (prices listed are for double occupancy during the high season; prices may decrease in low season). *Budget* hotels are generally less than $60 per night for two people; the rooms are clean and comfortable, but lack luxury. The *moderately* priced hotels run $60 to $120, and provide larger rooms, plusher furniture and more attractive surroundings. At *deluxe*-priced accommodations you can expect to spend between $120 and $180 for a double in a hotel or resort. You'll check into a spacious, well-appointed room with all modern facilities; downstairs the lobby will be a fashionable affair, and you'll usually see a restaurant, lounge and

# Vacation Rentals on the Big Island

- **Aloha Hawaii Vacation Homes**; 888-822-5642; www.aloha homes.com

- **Aldridge Associates**; 800-662-5642; www.waikoloa.net

- **All Globe Travel and Vacations**—Hawaii; 800-688-2254; www.enjoyhawaii.com

- **Hawaii Vacation Rentals, Inc.**; 800-332-7081; www.bigisland-vacation.com

- **Keauhou Property Management**; 800-745-5662; www.kpmco.com

- **Kona Hawaii Vacation Rentals**; 800-622-5348; www.kona hawaii.com

- **Lehua Properties, Ltd.**; 808-326-1133; www.lehuaproperties.com

- **Marc Resorts Hawaii**; 800-535-0085; www.marcresorts.com

- **Maui & All Islands Condominiums & Cars**; 800-663-6962; www.mauiallislands.com

- **Oceanfront Realty**; 808-826-6585

- **Outrigger Hotels & Resorts**; 800-688-7444; www.outrigger.com

- **Pleasant Hawaiian Holidays**; 800-242-9244; www.pleasant.net

- **Premier Resorts**; 800-367-7052; www.premier-resorts.com

- **Property Network**; 800-358-7977; www.hawaii-kona.com

- **Prosser Realty**; 800-767-4707; www.prosser-realty.com

- **R & R Realty & Rentals**; 800-367-8022; www.r7r.com

- **Suite Paradise**; 800-367-8020; www.suite-paradise.com

- **West Hawaii Property Services**; 800-799-5662; www.kona rentals.com

a cluster of shops. If you want to spend your time (and money) in the island's very finest hotels, try an *ultra-deluxe* facility, which will include all the amenities and price well above $180.

**Bed-and-Breakfast Inns**  The bed-and-breakfast business on the Big Island becomes more diverse and sophisticated every year. Today there are several referral services that can find you lodging on any of the islands. Claiming to be the biggest clearing-house in the state, **Bed and Breakfast Honolulu (Statewide)** represents over 400 properties. ~ 3242 Kaohinani Drive, Honolulu, HI 96817; 808-595-7533, 800-288-4666, fax 808-595-2030; www.hawaiibnb.com.

The original association, **Bed and Breakfast Hawaii**, claims more than 200 locations. This Kauai-based service was founded in 1979 and is well-known throughout Hawaii. ~ P.O. Box 449, Kapaa, HI 96746; 808-822-7771, 800-733-1632, fax 808-822-2723; www.bandb-hawaii.com. For other possibilities, contact **Hawaiian Islands Bed & Breakfast**. ~ 808-261-7895, 800-258-7895, fax 808-262-2181; www.flyhi.com.

You can also try the Maui-based **Affordable Accommodations**, which offers help finding all types of lodging. ~ 2825 Kauhale Street, Kihei, HI 96753; 808-879-7865, 888-333-9747, fax 808-874-0831; www.affordablemaui.com. Or call **All Islands Bed & Breakfast,** an Oahu-based reservation service that represents over 700 bed and breakfasts. ~ 463 Iliwahi Loop, Kailua, HI 96734; 808-263-2342, 800-542-0344, fax 808-263-0308; home.hawaii.rr.com/allislands.

While the properties represented by these agencies range widely in price, **Hawaii's Best Bed & Breakfasts** specializes in small, up-scale accommodations on all the islands. With about 100 establishments to choose from, it places guests in a variety of privately owned facilities; most are deluxe priced. ~ P.O. Box 563, Kamuela, HI 96743; 808-885-4550, 800-262-9912, fax 808-885-0559; www.bestbnb.com.

**Condos**  Many people visiting the Big Island, especially those traveling with families, find that condominiums are often cheaper than hotels. While some hotel rooms come with kitchenettes, few provide all the amenities of condominiums. A condo, in essence, is an apartment away from home. Designed as studio, one-, two- or three-bedroom apartments, they come equipped with full

The Big Island has more ancient petroglyphs—prehistory drawings depicting animals, stick figures, canoes and other intriguing images—than any other island.

kitchen facilities and complete kitchenware collections. Many also feature washer/dryers, dishwashers, air conditioning, color televisions, telephones, lanais and community swimming pools.

Utilizing the kitchen will save considerably on your food bill; by sharing the accommodations among several people, you'll also cut your lodging bill.

A few guidelines will help you chart a course through the Big Island's countless dining places. Each restaurant entry is described as budget, moderate, deluxe or ultra-deluxe in price.

**DINING**

To establish a pattern for the Big Island's parade of dining places, I've described not only the cuisine but also the ambience of each establishment. Restaurants listed offer lunch and dinner unless otherwise noted.

Dinner entrées at *budget* restaurants usually cost $8 or less. The ambience is informal café style and the crowd is often a local one. *Moderately* priced restaurants range between $8 and $16 at dinner and offer pleasant surroundings, a more varied menu and a slower pace. *Deluxe* establishments tab their entrées above $16, featuring sophisticated cuisines, plush decor and more personalized service. *Ultra-deluxe* restaurants generally price above $24.

Breakfast and lunch menus vary less in price from restaurant to restaurant. Even deluxe-priced kitchens usually offer light breakfasts and lunch sandwiches, which place them within a few dollars of their budget-minded competitors. These early meals can be a good time to test expensive restaurants.

Be sure to check the Big Island's newspapers for listings of local luaus. These fundraisers are a great way to mingle with locals while dining on island food at bargain prices.

The Big Island is an ideal vacation spot for family holidays. The pace is slow, the atmosphere casual. A few guidelines will help ensure that your trip to the islands brings out the joys rather than the strains of parenting, allowing everyone to get into the *aloha* spirit.

**TRAVELING WITH CHILDREN**

Use a travel agent to help with arrangements; they can reserve spacious bulkhead seats on airlines and determine which flights are least crowded. They can also seek out the best deals on inexpensive condominiums, saving you money on both room and board.

Planning the trip with your kids stimulates their imagination. Books about travel, airplane rides, beaches, whales, volcanos and

Hawaiiana help prepare even a two-year-old for an adventure. This preparation makes the "getting there" part of the trip more exciting for children of all ages.

And "getting there" means a long-distance flight. Plan to bring everything you need on board the plane—diapers, food, books, toys and extra clothing for kids and parents alike. I found it helpful to carry a few new toys and books as treats to distract my son and daughter when they got bored. When they were young children, I also packed extra snacks.

Allow extra time to get places. Book reservations in advance and make sure that the hotel or condominium has the extra crib, cot or bed you require. It's smart to ask for a room at the end of the hall to cut down on noise. And when reserving a rental car, inquire to see if they provide car seats and if there is an added charge. Hawaii has a strictly enforced car-seat law.

Besides the car seat you may have to bring along, also pack shorts and T-shirts, a sweater, sun hat, sundresses and waterproof sandals. A stroller with sunshade for little ones helps on sightseeing sojourns; a shovel and pail are essential for sandcastle building. Most importantly, remember to bring a good sunscreen. The quickest way to ruin a family vacation is with a bad sunburn. Also plan to bring indoor activities such as books and games for evenings and rainy days.

Some resorts and hotels have daily programs for kids during the summer and holiday seasons. Hula lessons, lei making, storytelling, sandcastle building and various sports activities keep *keikis* (kids) over six happy while also giving Mom and Dad a break. As an added bonus, these resorts offer family plans, providing discounts for extra rooms or permitting children to share a room with their parents at no extra charge. Check with your travel agent.

Most towns have stores that carry diapers, food and other essentials. However, prices are much higher on the Big Island. To economize, some people take along an extra suitcase filled with diapers and wipes, baby food, peanut butter and jelly, etc.

A first-aid kit is always a good idea. Also check with your pediatrician for special medicines and dosages for colds and diarrhea. If your child does become sick or injured on the Big Island, contact **Hilo Medical Center** (808-974-4700) or **Kona Community**

Hospital (808-322-9311). There's also a **Hawaii Poison Center** in Honolulu. ~ 808-941-4411, 800-362-3585.

Hotels often provide access to babysitters for a fee, or check with your concierge for suggestions.

**WOMEN TRAVELING ALONE**

Traveling solo grants an independence and freedom different from that of traveling with a partner, but single travelers are more vulnerable to crime and should take additional precautions. An option for those who are alone but prefer not to be is to join a tour group.

It's unwise to hitchhike and probably best to avoid inexpensive accommodations on the outskirts of town; the money saved does not outweigh the risk. Bed and breakfasts, youth hostels and YWCAs are generally your safest bet for lodging, and they also foster an environment ideal for bonding with fellow travelers.

> A photography hint: Buy your film in the islands and have it developed before you leave to avoid X-ray damage. Never carry undeveloped film in your checked luggage.

Keep all valuables well-hidden and hold on to cameras and purses. Avoid late-night treks or strolls through undesirable parts of town, but if you find yourself in this situation, continue walking with a confident air until you reach a safe haven. A fierce scowl never hurts.

These hints should by no means deter you from seeking out adventure. Wherever you go, stay alert, use your common sense and trust your instincts.

In case of an emergency, the **Sexual Assault Crisis Line** is 808-935-0677.

For more helpful hints, get a copy of *Safety and Security for Women Who Travel* (Traveler's Tales).

**GAY & LESBIAN TRAVELERS**

The *Pocket Guide to Hawaii*, published by **Pacific Ocean Holidays**, is helpful for gay travelers. It comes out three times a year and lists the best and hottest establishments and beaches that Hawaii has to offer. Send $5 per copy (via mail only) if ordering from the mainland; otherwise, it's distributed free by local gay businesses. This outfit can also help book vacation packages. ~ P.O. Box 88245, Honolulu, HI 96830; 808-923-2400, 800-735-6600 reservations only; www.gayhawaii.com.

Based on Maui, **Gay Hawaiian Excursions** offers special tour packages involving a huge scope of outdoor activities (snorkeling, horseback riding, fishing, whale watching, among others). It can also help book accommodations and arrange interisland trips. ~ 800-311-4460, fax 808-891-8307; www.gayexcursions. com, e-mail gaytours@maui.net.

Spanning the entire Hawaiian chain, the Big Island–based **Black Bamboo Guest Services** unearths the best cottages and houses for gay and straight travelers. This service also arranges car rentals, hiking tours, birdwatching trips and other sporting activities for its guests. ~ P.O. Box 211, Kealakekua, HI 96750; 808-328-9607, 800-527-7789; www.blackbamboohawaii.com.

For further information, be sure to look under "Gay-friendly travel" in the index at the end of the book.

**SENIOR TRAVELERS**   The Big Island is a hospitable place for senior citizens to visit. Museums, historic sights and even restaurants and hotels offer senior discounts that can cut a substantial chunk off vacation costs.

The **American Association of Retired Persons** (AARP) offers membership to anyone over 50. AARP's benefits include travel discounts with a number of firms. ~ 601 E Street NW, Washington, DC 20049; 800-424-3410; www.aarp.org.

**Elderhostel** offers reasonably priced, all-inclusive educational programs in a variety of locations throughout the year. One such program explores the culture and natural history of the Big Island. Contact Elderhostel for more information. ~ 11 Avenue de Lafayette, Boston, MA 02111; 877-426-8056, fax 617-426-0701; www.elderhostel.org.

Be extra careful about health matters. Consider carrying a medical record with you—including your medical history and current medical status as well as your doctor's name, phone number and address. Make sure your insurance covers you while you are away

## MADE ON THE BIG ISLAND

You know you have to bring Uncle Joe a present from the islands. And *you* have to have something special to remind you of your days (and nights) on the island. *Hele* on down to the local souvenir shop and bring home some Big Island-made products like island papayas, woodcarvings, Hawaiian heirloom jewelry, a *lauhala hat*, or a pound or two of Kona coffee. For inexpensive used island wear, check out the local thrift shops such as the Salvation Army or the Hospice of Kona Thrift Shop. And if you remember, buy a lei (or two) from a local florist before heading to the airport.

from home. It is wise to have your doctor write out extra prescriptions in case you lose your medication. Always carry your medications on board your flight, not in your luggage.

The **Commission on Persons with Disabilities** publishes a survey of the city, county, state and federal parks in Hawaii that are accessible to travelers with disabilities. In addition, its "Hawaii Travelers Tips" offers information on accessibility features of the airports as well as ground transportation, medical and support services and a fact sheet on civil rights and air travel. This guide is also available on its website. It also provides answers to specific questions by phone and e- mail. ~ 808-586-8121 (V/TTY); www.hawaii.gov/health/dcab, e-mail accesshi@aloha.net.

The **Hele-On Bus** provides accessible transportation for the general public, with discounted tickets available from the County of Hawaii Mass Transit Authority for persons with disabilities. ~ 630 East Lani Kaula Street, Hilo; 808-961-8744, fax 808-961-8745.

You might also want to contact the **Centers for Independent Living**. There are two locations. West Hawaii: 81-6627 Mamalahoa Highway, Suite B-5, P.O. Box 2197, Kealakekua, HI 96750; 808-323-2221, 808-323-2262 (TTY), fax 808-323-2383; e-mail cilwh@haii.net. East Hawaii: 400 Hualani Street, Suite 16 D, Hilo, HI 96720; 808-935-3777 (V/T), fax 808-961-6737; e-mail cileh@interpac.net.

Several car rental companies will install hand controls. Reservations must be made at least two business days in advance. These companies include **Alamo Rent A Car** (800-651-1223), **Avis Rent A Car** (800-321-3712), **Budget Rent A Car** (800-526-6408), **Dollar Rent A Car** (800-367-5171) and **Hertz Rent A Car** (800-654-3011).

The **Society for Accessible Travel & Hospitality** (SATH) offers information for travelers with disabilities. ~ 347 5th Avenue, Suite 610, New York, NY 10016; 212-447-7284, fax 212-725-8253; www.sath.org. **Travelin' Talk**, a network of people and organizations, also provides assistance. ~ P.O. Box 1796, Wheatridge, CO 80034; 303-232-2979; www.travelintalk.net. **Access-Able Travel Source** has worldwide information online. ~ 303-232-2979; www.access-able.com.

Be sure to check in advance when making room reservations. Some hotels feature facilities for those in wheelchairs.

**FOREIGN TRAVELERS**

**Passports and Visas**   Most foreign visitors are required to obtain a passport and tourist visa to enter the United States. Contact your nearest United States Embassy or Consulate well in advance to obtain a visa and to check on any other entry requirements.

**Customs Requirements**   Foreign travelers are allowed to carry in the following: 200 cigarettes (1 carton), 50 cigars or 2 kilograms (4.4 pounds) of smoking tobacco; one liter of alcohol for personal use only (you must be 21 years of age to bring in alcohol); and US$100 worth of duty-free gifts that include an additional quantity of 100 cigars. You may bring in any amount of currency, but must fill out a form if you bring in over US$10,000. Carry any prescription drugs in clearly marked containers. (You may have to produce a written prescription or doctor's statement for the customs officer.) Meat or meat products, seeds, plants, fruits and narcotics are not allowed to be brought into the United States. Contact the **United States Customs Service** for further information. ~ 1301 Constitution Avenue NW, Washington, DC 20229; 202-927-6724; www.customs.treas.gov.

> You might want to add some of the upscale resorts to your sightseeing itinerary. Several of them, especially the Mauna Kea and Hilton Waikoloa Village, display excellent examples of art collections throughout their facilities.

**Driving**   If you plan to rent a car, an international driver's license should be obtained prior to arrival. Some rental car companies require both a foreign license and an international driver's license. Many car rental agencies require that the lessee be at least 25 years of age; all require a major credit card. Seat belts are mandatory for the driver and all passengers. Children under the age of 5 or weighing less than 40 pounds should be in the back seat in approved child safety restraints.

**Currency**   United States money is based on the dollar. Bills come in seven denominations: $1, $2, $5, $10, $20, $50 and $100. Every dollar is divided into 100 cents. Coins are the penny (1 cent), nickel (5 cents), dime (10 cents), quarter (25 cents), half-dollar (50 cents) and dollar (100 cents).

You may not use foreign currency to purchase goods and services in the United States. Consider buying traveler's checks in dollar amounts. You may also use credit cards affiliated with an American company such as Interbank, Barclay Card, VISA, MasterCard and American Express.

**Electricity and Electronics**    Electric outlets use currents of 110 volts, 60 cycles. For appliances made for other electrical systems, you need a transformer or adapter. Travelers who use laptop computers for telecommunication should be aware that modem configurations for U.S. telephone systems may be different from their European counterparts. Similarly, the U.S. format for videotapes is different from that in Europe; U.S. Park Service visitors centers and other stores that sell souvenir videos often have them available in European format.

**Weights and Measurements**    The United States uses the English system of weights and measures. American units and their metric equivalents are as follows: 1 inch = 2.5 centimeters; 1 foot (12 inches) = 0.3 meter; 1 yard (3 feet) = 0.9 meter; 1 mile (5280 feet) = 1.6 kilometers; 1 ounce = 28 grams; 1 pound (16 ounces) = 0.45 kilogram; 1 quart (liquid) = 0.9 liter.

## Transportation

### GETTING TO THE ISLANDS

During the 19th century, sleek clipper ships sailed from the West Coast to Hawaii in about 11 days. Today, you'll be traveling by a less romantic but far swifter conveyance—the jet plane. Rather than days at sea, it will be about five hours in the air from California, nine hours from Chicago, or around 11 hours if you're coming from New York.

Chances are you'll be flying through Honolulu on your way to the Big Island. The **Honolulu International Airport** is served by Air New Zealand, Aloha Airlines, American Airlines, Canada 3000, Canadian Airlines, China Airlines, Continental Airlines, Delta Air Lines, Hawaiian Airlines, Korean Air, Northwest Airlines, Qantas, Philippine Airlines and United.

Visiting the Big Island means flying to one of two airports—Hilo International Airport (General Lyman Field) and Kona International Airport.

The main landing facility is **Kona International Airport**. Many mainland visitors fly here rather than to Honolulu to avoid Oahu's crowds. Aloha Airlines, American Airlines and United Airlines provide service directly to Kailua-Kona from the mainland and Canada 3000 and Japan Airlines fly directly from their respective countries.

This facility has snack bars, cocktail lounges, duty-free shops, a restaurant and souvenir shops, but no lockers or bus service. A ten-mile cab ride into town costs about $30.

**Hilo International Airport** (General Lyman Field), once the island's main jetport, is now more like a small city airport. Here you'll find a cafeteria-style restaurant, cocktail lounge, gift shop, newsstand and lockers, but no bus service. Covering the two miles into town means renting a car, hailing a cab, hitching or hoofing.

Passengers flying between the islands use Aloha Airlines or Hawaiian Airlines. They provide frequent jet service from Oahu and the other islands to both Hilo and Kona. Other inter-island carriers include Island Air, Pacific Wings and Paragon Air.

Whichever carrier you choose, ask for the economy or excursion fare, and try to fly during the week; weekend flights are generally higher in price. To qualify for the lower fares, it is sometimes necessary to book your flight two weeks in advance and to stay in the islands at least one week. Generally, however, the restrictions are minimal. Children under two years of age can fly for free, but they will not have a seat of their own. Each passenger is permitted two large pieces of luggage plus a carry-on bag. Shipping a bike or surfboard will cost extra. (Be sure to check on the size restrictions.)

In planning a Big Island sojourn, one potential moneysaver is the **package tour**, which combines air transportation with a hotel room and other amenities. Generally, it is a style of travel that I avoid. However, if you can find a package that provides air transportation, a hotel or condominium accommodation and a rental car, all at one low price—it might be worth considering. Just try to avoid the packages that preplan your entire visit, dragging you around on air-conditioned tour buses. Look for the package that provides only the bare necessities, namely transportation and lodging, while allowing you the greatest freedom.

However you decide to go, be sure to consult a travel agent. They are professionals in the field, possessing the latest information on rates and facilities, and their service to you is usually free.

**GETTING BETWEEN ISLANDS**

Getting between islands usually means hopping on a plane. There are ferries available between Maui, Molokai and Lanai, but the only commercial transportation to and from the Big Island is by air. **Aloha Airlines** and **Hawaiian Airlines**, the state's major carriers, provide frequent inter-island jet service. If you're looking for smooth, rapid, comfortable service, this is certainly it. You'll be buckled into your seat, offered a low-cost cocktail and whisked to your destination within about 20 minutes.

Without doubt, the best service aboard any inter-island carrier is on Aloha Airlines. They have an excellent reputation for flying on time and offer a seven-day, unlimited travel pass for island-hopping travelers. I give them my top recommendation.

Renting a car is as easy on the Big Island as anywhere. The island supports several rental agencies, which compete fiercely with one another in price and quality of service. So before renting, shop around: check the listings in this book, and also look for special temporary offers that many rental companies sometimes feature.

**CAR RENTALS**

There are several facts to remember when renting a car. First of all, a major credit card is essential. Also, many agencies don't rent at all to people under 25. Regardless of your age, many companies charge several dollars a day extra for insurance. The insurance is optional and expensive, and in many cases, unnecessary (many credit cards provide the same coverage when a rental is charged to the card). Find out if you credit card company offers this coverage. Your personal insurance policy may also provide for rental cars and, if necessary, have a clause added that will include rental car protection. Check on this before you leave home. But remember, whether you have insurance or not, you are liable for the first several thousand dollars in accident damage.

A vigorous agricultural inspection keeps unwanted pests out of Hawaii. If you forgot that apple tucked into your backpack, a sniffing dog inspector may tag you.

Rates fluctuate with the season; slack tourist seasons are great times for good deals. Also, three-day, weekly and monthly rates are almost always cheaper than daily rentals; cars with standard shifts generally cost less than automatics; and compacts are more economical than the larger four-door models.

I don't recommend renting a jeep. They're more expensive and less comfortable than cars, and won't get you to very many more interesting spots. In addition, the rental car collision insurance provided by most credit cards does not cover jeeps. Except in extremely wet weather when roads are muddy, most of the places mentioned in this book, including the hidden locales, can be reached by car, unless otherwise stated.

When choosing a rental agency, check whether they permit driving on the Saddle Road across the island and on South Point Road, both good paved roads with few potholes and many points of interest. I think it's quite unfair, even irrational, that some rental companies revoke insurance coverage if you drive these thoroughfares. But my protests will be of little benefit in case of an accident. So check first or be prepared to take your chances! It's wise to remember that you will be driving farther on the Big Island than on other islands, sometimes through quite rural areas; it may sound obvious, but remember to watch your gas gauge.

Several companies have franchises at the Hilo and Kailua-Kona airports. Among these are **Avis** (808-935-1290, 808-327-3001, 800-331-1212), **Budget Rent A Car** (808-935-6878, 808-329-8511, 800-527-0700), **Dollar Rent A Car** (808-961-6059, 808-329-2744, 800-800-4000), **Hertz Rent A Car** (808-935-2896, 808-329-3566, 800-654-3011), **National Car Rental** (808-935-0891, 808-329-1674, 800-227-7368) and **Thrifty Car Rental** (808-961-6698, 808-329-1339, 800-367-5238).

**Alamo Rent A Car** is located outside the Hilo International Airport and Kona Airport. ~ 808-961-3343, 808-329-8896, 800-327-9633. **Harper Car & Truck Rental** is located inside the Kona airport but you must take a shuttle to reach its Hilo location. ~ 808-969-1478, 800-852-9993.

**JEEP RENTALS**

**Budget Rent A Car** rents four-wheel drives. ~ 808-935-6878, 808-329-8511, 800-527-0700. With offices in Hilo and Kona, **Harper Car & Truck Rental** offers four-wheel-drive vehicles and allows travel on the Saddle Road and Mauna Kea summit road. ~ 808-969-1478, 800-852-9993.

**STAR STRUCK**

A trip to the top of the Big Island's star attraction is offered by **Mauna Kea Summit Adventures**. This outfitter, with 24 years of experience, offers educational tours of the top of this massive volcano, including sunset-watching and evening stargazing tours (including a look through a telescope). Dinner and warm clothing for the chilly air on the 13,000-feet-above-sea-level mountain are provided. ~ P.O. Box 9027, Kailua-Kona, HI 96745; 808-322-2366, 888-322-2366, fax 808-322-6507; www.maunakea.com, e-mail reservations@maunakea.com.

Harleys and scooters are available through **DJ's Rentals**, which rents by the half-day, day and overnight. Some three-day and weekly rentals are also available. ~ 75-5663 Palani Road, Kailua-Kona; 808-329-1700, 800-993-4647, fax 808-329-7575; harleys. com, e-mail info@harleys.com.

**MOPED RENTALS**

The **Hele-On Bus** provides cross-island service Monday through Saturday between Hilo and Kailua-Kona. There are also limited intra-city buses serving Hilo. The Hele-On runs Monday through Saturday; fares range from 75¢ for short rides to $6 for the Hilo–Kailua cross-island run.

**PUBLIC TRANSIT**

The Hilo bus terminal is on Kamehameha Avenue at Mamo Street. You'll see few bus stops indicated on the island. The official stops are generally unmarked, and you can hail a bus anywhere along its route. Just wave your hand. When it's time to get off, the driver will stop anywhere you wish.

For information and schedules, phone the **County Hawaiian Transit**. ~ 808-961-8343.

Thanks to the Kilauea eruption, the Big Island offers a wide variety of flightseeing options. In addition to the lava flows, you'll see remote coastlines, the slopes of Mauna Kea and coffee plantations. Bring your camera because the lava flow is one of Hawaii's greatest sightseeing opportunities.

**AERIAL TOURS**

**Volcano Helitours** offers a narrated 45-minute tour of all active eruptions. ~ Hilo International Airport; 808-967-7578.

At **Blue Hawaiian Helicopter** you have a choice of two flights lasting up to two hours. Passengers view the valleys and waterfalls on the island's northern end, as well as volcanic activity at Kilauea. They fly out of two locations. ~ Hilo International Airport; Queen Kaahumanu Highway, Waikoloa; 808-961-5600, 800-786-2583; www.bluehawaiian.com.

With its small four-seater planes, **Island Hoppers** provides an up-close circle-island look at such sights as the ever-spewing Kilauea Volcano, ancient Hawaiian settlements, waterfalls, black-sand beaches and the remote cliffs of North Kohala. ~ 73-300 Uu Street, Kailua-Kona; Gate 29, Hilo International Airport, Hilo; 808-969-2000; www.hawaii-paradise.com, e-mail info@hawaii-paradise.com.

**Mokulele Flight Service** offers two air tours of the Big Island: the two-hour Kona trip circles the island, while the 45-minute Hilo trip showcases the lava fields of Hawaii Volcanoes National Park and waterfalls outside of Hilo. You are guaranteed a window seat on either their Cessna 206 five-passenger aircraft or their Brittan-Norman Islander nine-passenger aircraft. ~ Commuter Terminal, Kona International Airport, P.O. Box 830, Holualoa, HI 96725; 808-326-7070, 866-260- 7070; www.mokulele. com, e-mail office@mokulele.com.

**Tropical Helicopters** operates several tours of the Big Island's volcanoes, waterfalls and valleys, including an open-door "Feel the Heat" volcano trip. Custom charters are also available. ~ Main Terminal, Hilo International Airport, Hilo; 808-961-6810; www. tropicalhelicopters.com, e-mail info@tropicalhelicopters.com.

Flying out of Hilo, **Safari Helicopters'** two tours both emphasize viewings of the Kilauea Volcanic system, with its lava tubes to the ocean, cinder cones and much more. One tour adds a visit to the waterfalls near Hilo to the itinerary. ~ P.O. Box 1941, Lihue, Kauai, HI 96766; Hilo Commuter Air Terminal, Hilo International Airport, Hilo; 808-969-1259, 800-326-3356; www.safariair.com, e-mail info@safariair.com.

Also flying out of Hilo, **Paradise Helicopters** offers a volcano-and-waterfall tour as well as a longer around-the-island tour. ~ Main Terminal, Hilo International Airport, Hilo; 808-969-7392.

**Big Island Air** takes passengers on a circle island tour featuring Kilauea and the north end valleys and waterfalls. Flights last about 1 hour and 45 minutes. ~ Kona Airport; 808-329-4868.

# TWO

# The Land and Outdoor Adventures

The Big Island is part of the Hawaiian archipelago that stretches more than 1500 miles across the North Pacific Ocean. Composed of 132 islands, Hawaii has eight major islands, including the Big Island, clustered at the southeastern end of the chain. Together these larger islands are about the size of Connecticut and Rhode Island combined. Only seven are inhabited: the eighth, Kahoolawe, once served as a bombing range for the U.S. Navy. Another island, Niihau, is privately owned and is primarily off-limits to the public.

Located 2500 miles southwest of Los Angeles, the Big Island is on the same 20th latitude as Hong Kong and Mexico City. It's two hours earlier on the Big Island than in Los Angeles, four hours earlier than Chicago and five hours earlier than New York. Since Hawaii does not practice daylight saving, this time difference becomes one hour greater during the summer months.

The Big Island, in a sense, is a small continent. Volcanic mountains rise in the interior, while the coastline is fringed with coral reefs and white and black sand beaches. The northeastern face, buffeted by trade winds, is the wet side. The contrast between this side and the island's southwestern sector is sometimes startling. Dense rainforests in the northeast teem with exotic tropical plants, while across the island you'll see cactus growing in a barren landscape!

Although sugar was once a significant part of the island's economy (primarily on the Hamakua coast), it is in decline. But agriculture still plays a major role in the Big Island economy. Coffee farms, flower farms (including anthurium and orchid growers), macadamia nut farms and other produce venues generate one-third of the entire state's vegetables and over three-fourths of the fruit. Herbal remedies and aquaculture are making an impact on the economy as well. And with all of its acres of ranchland, one of the Big Island's main sources of revenue comes from its cattle ranches, which produce over 5 million pounds of beef per year.

Tourism is still the largest industry on the Big Island. About four million Americans and almost seven million travelers worldwide visit the state of Hawaii every year. It's now a $10.9 billion business that expanded exponentially during the 1970s and 1980s, leveled off in the 1990s and was on the rise until September 11, 2001, and the subsequent slow-down in air travel. When the economy on the mainland is poor, the Big Island and the state of Hawaii are generally hit harder than most other areas of the country.

**GEOLOGY**    More than 25 million years ago a fissure opened along the Pacific floor. Beneath tons of sea water molten lava poured from the rift. This liquid basalt, oozing from a hot spot in the earth's center, created a crater along the ocean bottom. As the tectonic plate that comprises the ocean floor drifted over the earth's hot spot, numerous other craters appeared. Slowly, in the seemingly endless procession of geologic time, a chain of volcanic islands, now stretching almost 2000 miles, has emerged from the sea.

The youngest of the Hawaiian islands, the Big Island is the closest to the "hot spot" beneath the earth's surface. Both Mauna Loa and Kilauea volcanoes steadily add more to the land mass of the 50th state.

On the continents it was also a period of terrible upheaval. The Himalayas, Alps and Andes were rising, but these great chains would reach their peaks long before the Pacific mountains even touched sea level. Not until about 25 million years ago did the first of these underwater volcanos, today's Kure and Midway atolls, break the surface and become islands. It was not until about five million years ago that the first of the main islands of the archipelago, Niihau and Kauai, broke the surface to become high islands.

For many millennia, the mountains continued to grow. The forces of erosion cut into them, creating knife-edged cliffs and deep valleys. Then plants began germinating: mosses and ferns, springing from windblown spores, were probably first, followed by seed plants carried by migrating birds and on ocean currents. The steep-walled valleys provided natural greenhouses in which unique species evolved, while transoceanic winds swept insects and other life from the continents.

Some islands never survived this birth process: the ocean simply washed them away. The first islands that did endure, at the northwestern end of the Hawaiian chain, proved to be the smallest. Today these islands, with the exception of Midway, are barren uninhabited atolls. The volcanoes of the Big Island and its sister islands became the mountainous archipelago generally known as the Hawaiian Islands.

Most of the plants you'll see on the Big Island are not endemic, or native. In fact, much of the lush vegetation of this tropical island found its way here from locations all over the world. Sea winds, birds and seafaring settlers brought many of the seeds, plants, flowers and trees from the islands of the South Pacific, as well as from other, more distant regions. Over time, some plants adapted to the Big Island's unique ecosystem and climate, creating strange new lineages and evolving into a completely new ecosystem. This process has long interested scientists, who call the Hawaiian Islands one of the best natural labs for studies of plant evolution.

▼▼▼▼▼▼▼▼▼▼

## Flora and Fauna

### FLORA

Sugar cane arrived on the Big Island with the first Polynesian settlers, who appreciated its sweet juices. By the late 1800s, it was well established as a lucrative crop. The pineapple was first planted during the same century. A member of the bromeliad family, this spiky plant is actually a collection of beautiful pink, blue and purple flowers, each of which develops into a fruitlet. The pineapple is a collection of these fruitlets, grown together into a single fruit that takes 14 to 17 months to mature. Sugar cane and pineapple are still the main crops in Hawaii, although competition from other countries and environmental problems caused by pesticides have taken their toll.

Visitors to the Big Island will find the island a perpetual flower show. Sweetly scented plumeria, deep red, shiny anthurium, exotic ginger, showy birds of paradise, small lavender crown flowers, highly fragrant gardenias and the brightly hued hibiscus run riot on the island and add color and fragrance to the surrounding area. Scarlet and purple bougainvillea vines as well as the aromatic lantana, with its dense clusters of flowers, are also found in abundance.

Known as the "Orchid Isle," the Big Island's nickname derives from the thousands of varieties of this delicate plant that thrive in the tropical heat and humidity of the windward side of the island. The most popular orchids are the *dendrobium*, which can come in white, purple, lavender or yellow hues; the *vanda* (bamboo orchid), which is fuschia and white and often used for making leis; and the popcorn, which has small yellow flowers. The wild *vanda*, with its white and lavender petals, can be spotted along the Hamakua Coast's roadside year-round.

Each Hawaiian island has a specific bloom designated as its island flower; the Big Island's pick is the red *lehua ohia*, a pompom flower with numerous stamens about a half-inch to an inch long that grows on a slow-growing evergreen tree on heights of up to 80 feet. The most prevalent tree on the island, it is one of the first to propogate on lava flows and is tolerant to volcanic fumes. Flowers appear throughout the year.

Although many people equate the tropics with the swaying palm tree, the Big Island is home to a variety of exotic trees. The *koa* tree, endemic to Hawaii, has been endangered by cattle and goats, not to mention human logging. Used for centuries by Hawaiians for making surfboards and canoes, it is still prized for its beauty today. *Koa* is a form of acacia and can grow to heights of over 60 feet. There are reserves of old-growth *koa* that are protected on the island.

The candlenut, or *kukui*, tree, originally brought to the Big Island from the South Pacific islands, is big, bushy and prized for its nuts, which can be used for oil or polished and strung together to make leis. With its cascades of bright yellow or pink flowers, the cassia tree earns its moniker—the shower tree. Covered with tiny pink blossoms, the canopied monkeypod tree has fernlike leaves that close up at night.

A member of the mesquite family, *kiawe* trees were originally thought to have come from Paris, France, and are found in the dry coastal areas. Hearty trees, they were planted on ranches so that cattle could graze on the sugary pods.

Along the coast you'll find the *hala* tree, or the pandanus. Its leaves are used for making rope, baskets, fans, thatching and weavings. The green or green and yellow leaves, which look like thin swords, grow in clusters two to three feet in length and sport little prickles and sharp tips.

Found in a variety of shapes and sizes, the ubiquitous palm does indeed sway to the breezes on white-sand beaches, but it also comes in a short, stubby form featuring more frond than trunk. The fruit, or nuts, of these trees are prized for their oil, which can be utilized for making everything from margarine to soap. The wood (rattan, for example) is often used for making furniture.

**FRUITS AND VEGETABLES**   There's a lot more to the Big Island's tropical wonderland than gorgeous flowers and overgrown rainforests. The island also teems with edible plants. Roots, fruits, vegetables, herbs and spices grow like weeds from the shoreline to the mountains. Following is a list of some of the more commonly found edibles.

*Avocado:* Covered with either a tough green or purple skin, this pear-shaped fruit sometimes weighs as much as three pounds. It grows on ten- to forty-foot-high trees, and ripens from June through November.

*Bamboo:* The bamboo plant is actually a grass with a sweet root that is edible and a long stem frequently used for making furniture. Often exceeding eight feet in height, bamboo is green until picked, when it turns a golden brown.

*Banana:* Polynesians use banana trees not only for food but also for clothing, medicines, dyes and even alcohol. The fruit, which grows upside down on broad-leaved trees, can be harvested as soon as the first banana in the bunch turns yellow.

*Breadfruit:* This large round fruit grows on trees that reach up to 60 feet in height. Like the banana and plantain, the breadfruit may be roasted in an underground oven on preheated rocks or baked with a little water in a pan. Sometimes it is cored and stuffed with coconut before roasting. Breadfruit is also candied, or sometimes prepared as a sweet pickle.

*Coconut:* The coconut tree is probably the most important plant in the entire Pacific. Every part of the towering palm is used. Most people are concerned only with the hard brown nut, which yields delicious milk as well as a tasty meat. If the coconut is still green, the meat is a succulent jellylike substance. Otherwise, it's a hard but delicious white rind.

◆◆◆◆◆◆◆◆◆◆◆◆◆◆◆◆◆◆◆◆◆◆◆◆◆◆◆◆◆◆◆◆◆◆◆◆◆◆◆◆◆◆◆◆◆◆◆◆◆◆◆

### ANOTHER ISLAND IN THE SUN

A mere 3000-plus feet below the water's surface, and 20 miles to the southeast of the Big Island, lies the emerging island of Loihi. Madame Pele's youngest offspring continues to build her land mass with frequent eruptions—unfortunately, scientists estimate it will be another 10,000 to 100,000 years before it reaches the surface and graces the state with another venue to visit. At its highest point, the seamount reaches about 12,500 feet.

*Guava:* A roundish yellow fruit that grows on a small shrub or tree, guavas are extremely abundant in the wild. They ripen between June and October.

*Lychee:* Found hanging in bunches from the lychee tree, this popular fruit is encased in red, prickly skin that peels off to reveal the sweet-tasting, translucent flesh.

*Mango:* Known as the king of fruits, the mango grows on tall shade trees. The oblong fruit ripens in the spring and summer.

*Mountain apple:* This sweet fruit grows in damp, shaded valleys at an elevation of about 1800 feet. The flowers resemble fluffy crimson balls; the fruit, which ripens from July to December, is also a rich red color.

*Papaya:* This delicious fruit, which is picked as it begins to turn yellow, grows on unbranched trees. The sweet flesh can be bright orange or coral pink in color. Summer is the peak harvesting season.

*Passion fruit:* Known as *lilikoi* in the islands, this tasty yellow fruit is oval in shape and grows to a length of about two or three inches. It's produced on a vine and ripens in summer or fall.

*Taro:* The tuberous root of this Hawaiian staple is pounded, then fermented into a grayish purple paste known as *poi.* One of the most nutritious foods, it has a rather bland taste. The plant, called *kalo* in Hawaiian, has wide, shiny, thick leaves with reddish stems; the root is white with purple veins. The Western palate may prefer taro in the form of chips. It can also be baked like a breadfruit.

**FAUNA**

On the Big Island, it seems there is more wildlife in the water and air than on land. A scuba-diver's paradise, the ocean is also a promised land for many other creatures. Coral, colorful fish and migrating whales are only part of this underwater community. Sadly, many of Hawaii's coral reefs have been dying mysteriously in the last several years. No one is sure why, but many believe this is partially due to runoff from pesticides used in agriculture.

Green sea turtles are common on all of the Hawaiian islands, although this was not always the case. Due to the popularity of their shells, they spent many years on the endangered species list, but are now making a comeback. Measuring three to four feet in diameter, these large reptiles frolic in saltwater only, and are often visible from the shore.

Not many wild four-footed creatures roam the island. Deer, feral goats and pigs were brought here early on and have found a home in the forests. Some good news for people fearful of snakes: There is nary a serpent (or a sea serpent) on the Big Island, although lizards such as skinks and geckos abound.

One can only hope that with the renewed interest in Hawaiian culture, and growing environmental awareness, Hawaii's plants and animals will continue to exist as they have for centuries.

**WHALES & DOLPHINS**    Every year, humpback whales converge in the warm waters off the islands to give birth to their calves. Beginning their migration in Alaska, they can be spotted in Hawaiian waters from November through May. The humpback, named for its practice of showing its dorsal fin when diving, is quite easy to spy. They feed in shallow waters, usually diving for periods of no longer than 15 minutes. They often sleep on the surface and breathe fairly frequently. Unlike other whales, humpbacks have the ability to sing.

Loud and powerful, their songs carry above and below the water for miles. The songs change every year, yet, incredibly, all the whales always seem to know the current one. Quite playful, they can be seen leaping, splashing and flapping their 15-foot tails over their backs. The best time for whale watching is from January to April.

Spinner dolphins are also favorites among visitors. Named for their "spinning" habit, they can revolve as many as six times dur-

### A TAIL OF A WHALE

Not only is it possible to see the spectacular humpback whales that migrate in Hawaiian waters from December through April, you can also gaze upon their relatives year-round—including the odd-looking beaked whales, sperm whales, pilot whales, pygmy sperm whales and false killers (where do they come up with these names?). The beaked whale, unsurprisingly, is named for its long, narrow snout. The pygmy sperm whale is—guess what—the smallest (about 13 feet long), and has a very large head and substantial teeth (let's not think about the symbolism here!), while the 20-foot pilot sometimes beaches itself (thank goodness they are not real pilots). The mighty sperm whale averages between 50 to 60 feet in length and weighs in the 15- to 20-ton range. Several outfitters offer year-round whale watching.

ing one leap. They resemble the spotted dolphin, another frequenter of Hawaiian waters, but are more likely to venture closer to the shore. Dolphins have clocked in with speeds ranging from 9 to 25 mph, a feat they often achieve by propelling themselves out of the water (or even riding the bow wave of a ship). Their thick, glandless skin also contributes to this agility. The skin is kept smooth by constant renewal and sloughing. Playful and intelligent, dolphins are a joy to watch. Many research centers are investigating the mammals' ability to imitate, learn and communicate; some believe that dolphin intelligence may be comparable to that of humans.

**FISH** It'll come as no surprise to anyone that the Big Island's waters literally brim with an extraordinary assortment of fish— over 400 different species, in fact.

The goatfish, with more than 50 species in its family worldwide, boasts at least ten in Hawaiian waters. This bottom dweller is recognized by a pair of whiskers, used as feelers for searching out food, that are attached to its lower jaw. The *moano* sports two stripes across its back and has shorter whiskers. The red-and-black banded goatfish has a multihued color scheme that also includes yellow and white markings; its light yellow whiskers are quite long. The head of the goatfish is considered poisonous and is not eaten.

Occasionally found on the sharper end of your line is the bonefish, or *oio*. One of the best game fish in the area, its head extends past its mouth to form a somewhat transparent snout. The *awa*, or milkfish, is another common catch. This silvery, fork-tailed fish can grow longer than three feet and puts up a good fight.

A kaleidoscope of brilliantly colored specimens can be viewed around the reefs of the Big Island; you'll feel like you're in a technicolor movie when snorkeling. Over 20 known species of butterfly fish are found in this area. Highlighted in yellow, orange, red, blue, black and white, they swim in groups of two and three. The long, tubular body of the needlefish, or *aha*, can reach up to 40 inches in length; this greenish, silvery species is nearly translucent. The masked angelfish flits around in deeper waters on the outer edge of reefs. The imperial angelfish is distinguishable by fantastic color patterns of dark blue hues. The Hawaiian fish with the longest name, the colorful *humuhumunukunukuapuaa*, is found in the shallow waters along the outer fringes of reefs.

# The Big Island's
## Big Fish

Deep-sea fishing enthusiasts consider the waters off the Big Island's Kona coast to be one of the world's best sportfishing areas. The water is typically calm year-round, and deep water close to shore means that fishing charter travel time is minimal. The world's record marlin—a 1166-pound Pacific blue marlin—was hooked here in May 1982. Striped marlin and black marlin also frequent the area, along with huge *ahi* (yellowfin) tuna, mahimahi, *ono* (wahoo) and spearfish.

Fishing charter captains encourage clients to tag and release any marlin or other billfish they catch. Consider doing this even if you plan to have your fish mounted as a trophy. Most saltwater fish are not stuffed to mount using the skin. Instead, the charter captain will take measurements and photos, and a taxidermist will use them to make a fiberglass replica for mounting. Keeping other types of fish you catch is less labor intensive. Local restaurants will cook and serve them to you, or charter operators can arrange to have the fish processed and stored so you can ship or carry it back home at the end of your vacation.

Among the many deep-sea fishing charter operators on the Kona coast are: **Legend Sportfishing**, 73-1530 Apela Place, Kailua-Kona, 808-325-5043, fax 808-325-0653, e-mail vidal@aloha.net; **Seastrike**, Kailua-Kona, 808-325-2108, 800-264-4595, e-mail seastrik@gte.net; **Lady Dee Sportfishing**, Kailua-Kona, 808-322-8026, 800-278-7049, fax 808-324-7052; **Captain Jack's Kona Charters**, Kailua-Kona, 800-545-5662, fax 808-322-6507, e-mail laxe87a@prodigy.net; and **Ho'okele Sportfishing**, Kailua-Kona, 808-960-5866, fax 808-329-7360, e-mail 1marlin@gte.net.

Sharks, unlike fish, have skeletons made of cartilage; the hardest parts of their bodies are their teeth (once used as tools by the Hawaiians). If you spend a lot of time in the water, you may spot a shark. But not to worry; Hawaiian waters are just about the safest around. The harmless, commonly seen blacktipped and whitetipped reef sharks (named for the color of their fins) are as concerned about your activities as you are about theirs. The gray reef shark (gray back, white belly with a black tail) and tiger shark, however, are predatory and aggressive, but they are rarely encountered.

At Kona Bowl, the usual rounds of ten-pin are spiffed up Friday and Saturday with "Cosmic Bowl" (rock music, glow-in-the-dark pins and laser lights). ~ 75-5591 Palani Road, Kailua-Kona; 808-326-2695.

Another cartilaginous creature you might see in shallow water near the shoreline is the manta ray, a "winged" plankton feeder with two appendages on either side of its head that work to direct food into its mouth. The eagle ray, a bottom dweller featuring "wings" and a tail longer than its body, feeds in shallow coastal waters. When it's not feeding, it lies on the ocean floor and covers itself with a light layer of sand. Since some eagle rays have stingers, take precautions by shuffling the sand as you walk. Not only will you not be impaled, you will also be less likely to squash smaller, unsuspecting sea creatures.

While on the Big Island, you'll inevitably see fish out of water as well—on your plate. The purple-blue-green-hued mahimahi, or dolphin fish, can reach six feet and 70 pounds. The *opakapaka* is another common dish and resides in the deeper, offshore waters beyond the reef. This small-scaled snapper is a reddish-olive color and can grow up to four feet long. Elongated with a sharply pointed head, the *ono* (also known as the wahoo) is a carnivorous, savage striped fish with dark blue and silver coloring. Perhaps the most ubiquitous fish is the ahi, or tuna, often used for sashimi.

**BIRDS**  The island is also home to many rare and endangered birds. Like the flora, the birds in the Hawaiian Islands are highly specialized. The state bird, the nene, or Hawaiian goose, is a cousin to the Canadian goose and mates for life.

Known in Hawaiian mythology for its protective powers, the *pueo*, or Hawaiian owl, a brown-and-white-feathered bird, resides on the Big Island, Kauai, and in Haleakala crater on Maui.

Endemic to the island, the *puaiohi* (small Kauai thrush) is a dark-brown forest bird that nests in fern-choked cliffs. The tiny bright-yellow *anianiau* is the smallest of the native Hawaiian honeycreepers.

There *are* a few birds native to Hawaii that have thus far avoided the endangered species list. Two of the most common birds are the yellow-green *amakihi* and the red *iiwi*.

The *koae kea*, or "tropic bird," lives in the Big Island's Kilauea Crater, Kauai's Waimea Canyon and on Maui's Haleakala. Resembling a seagull in size, it has a long, thin white tail and a striking striping pattern on the back of the wings.

Another common bird is the *iwa*, or frigate, a very large creature measuring three to four feet in length, with a wing span averaging seven feet. The males are solid black, while the females have a large white patch on their chest and tail. A predatory bird, they're easy to spot raiding the nesting colonies of other birds along the offshore rocks. If you see one, be careful not to point at it; legend has it that it's bad luck. Other birds that make the islands their home are the Hawaiian stilt and the Hawaiian coot—both water birds—along with the black noddy, American plover, wedge-tailed shearwater.

▼▼▼▼▼▼▼▼▼▼▼▼▼

# Outdoor Adventures

## CAMPING

There are few activities on the Big Island more pleasurable than camping. Beautiful state and county parks dot the island, while enticing hiking trails lead to remote mountain and coastal areas.

No matter what you plan to do on the island, keep in mind that the Kona side is generally dry, while the Hilo side receives considerable rain. Also remember that the mountains can be quite cold and usually call for extra clothing and gear.

Camping at **county parks** requires a permit. These cost $5 per person per day ($2 for ages 13 through 17, $1 for children). Although RV camping is allowed in many county parks, no special parking or electrical hookups are provided. Pick up permits from the County Department of Parks and Recreation. ~ 101 Pauahi Street, Suite 6, Hilo, HI 96720; 808-961-8311. Permits are also available at the South Kona Recreation Office. ~ P.O. Box 314, Captain Cook, HI 96740; 808-323-3060. The main county parks and recreation office for the west side of the island is the Hale

Hawawai office in Kailua-Kona. ~ 808-327-3560. County permits are issued for both tent and trailer camping, and can be obtained for up to two weeks at each park (one week during the summer).

Free **state parks** permits can be obtained through the State Department of Land and Natural Resources, Division of State Parks. ~ 75 Aupuni Street, Hilo, HI 96720; 808-974-6200. Maximum stay at each park is five days. For information on cabin rentals and camping in Volcanoes National Park, see the individual listings in the "Beaches & Parks" sections in this chapter.

**Hilo Hawaii Sales and Surplus** sells sleeping bags, backpacks, tents, stoves and the like. Closed Sunday. ~ 148 Mamo Street, Hilo; 808-935-6398. **Pacific Rent-All** rents family-size tents, sleeping bags, stoves, coolers and other camping equipment. ~ 1080 Kilauea Avenue, Hilo; 808-935-2974.

**FISHING**    The waters off the Kona Coast are among the Pacific's finest fishing grounds, particularly for marlin. Many charter boats operate out of Kailua; check the phone book for names or simply walk along the pier and inquire.

**Kona Charter Skippers Association** represents one of the larger outfits. They sponsor daily charters for marlin, yellowfin tuna, *ono*, mahimahi and other gamefish. Using boats 26 to 54 feet in length, they take out up to six passengers per boat for half- and full-day trips. Private charters are also available. ~ 74-857 Iwalani Place, Kailua-Kona; 808-329-3600, 800-762-7546; www.konabiggamefishing.com.

The **Sea Wife**, with Captain Jim Cox at the helm, sets out Monday through Saturday from Honokohau Harbor in pursuit of marlin, mahimahi or whatever else is running. ~ P.O. Box 2645, Kailua-Kona, HI 96745; 808-329-1806.

Head up to the tuna tower to survey the fishing scene aboard **Pamela**, a 38-foot Bertram that focuses on marlin, short-nosed spearfish, mahimahi, yellowfin and wahoo. ~ Honokohau Harbor, Kailua-Kona; 808-329-3600.

Another company offering similar service is the charter desk in the **Kona Fuel and Marine** building. ~ Honokohau Harbor, Kailua-Kona; 808-329-5735.

**TORCHFISHING & SPEARFISHING**    The old Hawaiians also fished at night by torchlight. They fashioned torches by inserting

# Big Island Campsites

## HAWAII COUNTY CAMPSITES

Please note that availability of county campsites are based on head counts rather than the number of sites. Across the board, adults pay $5 per night and prices range from $1 to $2 for children.

| | |
|---|---|
| Hookena Beach Park, Hookena | 22 head count |
| Isaac Hale Beach Park, MacKenzie State Recreation Area | 22 head count |
| Kapaa Beach Park, Kawaihae | 22 head count |
| Kolekole Beach Park, Hilo | 45 head count |
| Laupahoehoe Beach Park, Honokaa | 45 head count |
| Mahukona Beach Park, Kawaihae | 22 head count |
| Milolii Beach Park, Kailua | 22 head count |
| Punaluu Beach Park, Punaluu | 22 head count |
| Spencer Beach Park, Kawaihae | 68 head count |
| Whittington Beach Park, Naalehu | 22 head count |

*For more information call 808-961-8311*

## STATE OF HAWAII CAMPSITES

| | |
|---|---|
| Hapuna Beach State Park, Kawaihae | 6 A-frame cottages |
| Kalopa State Recreation Area, Kaimu | 2 group cabins for 1–8 people |
| Mackenzie State Recreation Area, Kaimu | 4 sites |
| Manuka State Wayside, Naalehu | 1 group site for 1–12 people |

*For more information call 808-974-6200*

## HAWAII VOLCANOES NATIONAL PARK CAMPSITES

| | |
|---|---|
| Namakani Paio | 10 cabins, 12 sites |
| Kulanaokuaiki | 3 sites |

*For more information call 808-985-6000*

# Sportfishing
## Calendar of Events

These do not include tournaments held by the Hawaii Big Game Fishing Club for members only.

**Late June**   Anglers gather to try for the jackpot awarded for the largest marlin in the annual **Kona Classic Tournament**.

**Early July**   Kailua-Kona celebrates Independence Day with a sportfishing competition in the **Firecracker Open** tournament.

**Mid-July**   Watch as competitive deep-sea anglers weigh in their catch at each day's end in the three-day **Skins Marlin Derby**.

**Late July**   Sportfishing enthusiasts' entry fees go to benefit West Hawaii Family Support Services in Kailua-Kona's Huggo's **Na Pua O'Ke Kai Wahine Tournament**.

**Early August**   Deep-sea fishing, food and entertainment are featured at the **Pro-Am Billfish Tournament**, a warm-up for Kona's oldest and most prestigious fishing event, the **Hawaiian International Billfish Tournament**.

nuts from the *kukui* tree into the hollow end of a bamboo pole, then lighting the flammable nuts. When fish swam like moths to the flame, the Hawaiians speared, clubbed or netted them.

Today, it's easier to use a lantern and spear. (In fact, it's all *too* easy and tempting to take advantage of this willing prey: Take only edible fish and only what you will eat.) It's also handy to bring a facemask or a glass-bottomed box to aid in seeing underwater. The best time for torchfishing is a dark night when the sea is calm and the tide low.

During daylight hours, the best place to spearfish is along coral reefs and in areas where the bottom is a mixture of sand and rock. Equipped with speargun, mask, fins and snorkel, you can explore underwater grottoes and spectacular coral formations while seeking your evening meal. Spearguns can be purchased inexpensively throughout the islands.

**CRABBING**

For the hungry adventurer, there are several crab species in Hawaii. The most sought after are the Kona and Samoan varieties. Kona crabs are found in relatively deep water, and can usually be caught only from a boat. Samoan crabs inhabit sandy and muddy areas in bays and near river mouths. All you need to catch them are a boat and a net fastened to a round wire hoop secured by a string. The net is lowered to the bottom; then, after a crab has gone for the bait, the entire contraption is raised to the surface.

**SQUIDDING**

Between June and December, squidding is another popular sport. Actually, the term is a misnomer: squid inhabit deep water and are not usually hunted. What you'll really be after are octopuses. There are two varieties in Hawaii, both of which are commonly found in water three or four feet deep: the *hee*, a greyish-brown animal that changes color like a chameleon, and the *puloa*, a red-colored mollusk with white stripes on its head.

Both are nocturnal and live in holes along coral reefs. At night by torchlight you can spot them sitting exposed on the bottom. During the day, they crawl inside the holes, covering the entrances with shells and loose coral.

The Hawaiians used to pick the octopus up, letting it cling to their chest and shoulders. When they were ready to bag their prize, they'd dispatch the creature by biting it between the eyes. You'll probably feel more comfortable spearing the beast.

**SHELLFISH GATHERING**

Other excellent food sources are the shellfish that inhabit coastal waters. The ancient Hawaiians used pearl shells to attract the fish, and hooks, some made from human bones, to snare them. Your friends will probably be quite content to see you angling with store-bought artificial lures. Oysters and clams, which use their muscular feet to burrow into sand and soft mud, can be collected along the bottom of Hawaii's bays. Spiny lobsters, rarely found in Hawaii waters, are illegal to spear, but can be taken with short poles to which cable leaders and baited hooks are attached. You can also just grab them with a gloved hand but be careful—spiny lobsters live up to their name! You can also gather limpets, though I don't recommend it. These tiny black shellfish, locally known as *opihi*, cling tenaciously to rocks in the tidal zone. In areas of very rough surf, the Hawaiians gather them by leaping into the water after one set of waves breaks, then jumping out before the next set arrives. Being a coward myself, I simply order them in Hawaiian restaurants.

**SEAWEED GATHERING**  There are still some people who don't think of seaweed as food, but it's very popular among Japanese, and it once served as an integral part of the Hawaiian diet. It's extremely nutritious, easy to gather and very plentiful.

Rocky shores are the best places to find the edible species of seaweed. Some of them float in to shore and can be picked up; other species cling stubbornly to rocks and must be freed with a knife; still others grow in sand or mud. Low tide is the best time to collect seaweed: more plants are exposed, and some can be taken without even getting wet.diving

**DIVING**  Diving in Hawaii means exploring a variety of oceanic realms. The top diving spots on the Big Island offer distinct attractions— and no matter where you end up, you're sure to see something you've never encountered outside this Pacific wonderland. For explorers there's **Suck-em-up** and **Harlequins** with their sea caves and lava tubes. For the ichthyologists out there, **Casa Caves** brings you up close and personal with reef sharks, while **Turtle Pinnacles** is famous for its green sea turtles and **Thunder Reef** is known for its deep-water creatures. Snorkelers will be attracted to beautiful **Kealakekua Bay**, where Captain Cook met his maker.

**KAILUA–KONA AREA**    **Sandwich Isle Divers** is a full-service dive shop that offers repairs and instruction, and has two boats for dive trips. Trip destinations include Turtle Pinnacles, Pine Trees, Golden Arches, Kaiwi Point and Kaloko Arches and more locations along the Kona Coast and beyond. They also conduct a night manta ray dive. ~ Kona Marketplace, Kailua-Kona; 808-329-9188, 888-743-3483; www.sandwichisledivers.com.

**Sea Paradise Scuba** leads trips to lava tubes, caverns, caves and other fascinating formations at 40 locations south of Kailua. ~ 71-7128 Kaleopapa Street, Keauhou; 808-322-2500, 800-322-5662; www.seaparadise.com. **Big Island Dives** offers daytime and night dives along the Kona Coast. ~ Kaahumanu Plaza, 75-5467 Kaiwi Street, Kailua-Kona; 808-329-6068.

# Ocean Safety

**M**any water lovers never realize how awesome the sea can be. Particularly in Hawaii, where waves can reach 30-foot heights and currents flow unobstructed for thousands of miles, the ocean is sometimes as treacherous as it is spectacular. Dozens of people drown every year in Hawaii, many others are dragged from the crushing surf with broken backs, and countless numbers sustain minor cuts and bruises.

These accidents can be entirely avoided if you approach the ocean with a respect for its power as well as an appreciation of its beauty. All you have to do is heed a few simple guidelines. First, never turn your back on the sea. Waves come in sets: one group may be small and quite harmless, but the next set could be large enough to sweep you out to sea. Never swim alone.

Don't try to surf, or even bodysurf, until you're familiar with the sports' techniques and precautionary measures. Be extremely careful when the surf is high.

If you get caught in a rip current, don't swim *against* it: swim *across* it, parallel to the shore. These currents, running from the shore out to sea, can often be spotted by their ragged-looking surface water and foamy edges.

Around coral reefs, wear something to protect your feet against coral cuts. Particularly good are the inexpensive Japanese *tabis*, or reef slippers. If you do sustain a coral cut, clean it with hydrogen peroxide, then apply an antiseptic or antibiotic substance. This is also a good procedure for octopus bites.

When stung by a Portuguese man-of-war or box jellyfish, remove any tentacles and rinse with water (do not use your bare hands to extract tentacles). Vinegar, isopropyl alcohol and human urine, once considered effective remedies for Portuguese man-of-war, are no longer recommended treatments. Applying vinegar to a box jellyfish sting, however, will help prevent additional stings. If you are in pain, ice the affected area.

If you step on the sharp, painful spines of a sea urchin, soak the affected area in very hot water for 15 to 90 minutes. Another remedy calls for applying urine or undiluted vinegar. If the pain persists for more than a day, or you notice swelling or other signs of infection, consult a doctor.

Oh, one last thing. The chances of encountering a shark are about as likely as sighting a UFO. But should you meet one of these ominous creatures, stay calm. He'll be no happier to see you than you are to confront him. Simply swim quietly to shore. By the time you make it back to terra firma, you'll have a hell of a story to tell.

At **Eco Adventures**, scuba-diving classes range from beginning through advanced, while excursions run the gamut from snorkeling to half-day reef and cavern dives. ~ P.O. Box 2639, Kailua-Kona, HI 96745; 74-5590 Luhia Street, Suite 213-A, Kailua-Kona; 808-329-7116, fax 808-329-7091; www.eco-adventure.com, e-mail info@ecodive.com.

Evening snorkel-and-scuba excursions in search of manta rays are the specialty at **Manta Ray Dives of Hawaii**. They also offer multi-dive packages and certification dives. ~ P.O. Box 5554, Kailua-Kona, HI 96745; 808-325-1687, 800-982-6747, fax 808-325-2037; www.mantaraydiveshawaii.com, e-mail mantaray@mantaraydiveshawaii.com.

**Fair Wind Snorkel & Dive** specializes in cruises, snorkeling trips and dives in Kealakekua Bay, a marine sanctuary. ~ 78-7130 Kaleiopapa Street, Kailua-Kona; 808-322-2788, 800-677-9461; www.fair-wind.com, e-mail snorkel@fair-wind.com.

**Jack's Diving Locker** has detailed information and equipment rentals. They also have three dive boats and offer guided trips for snorkelers and scuba divers to offshore reefs. ~ Coconut Grove Market Place, 75-5819 Alii Drive, Kailua-Kona; 808-329-7585, 800-345-4807; www.jacksdivinglocker.com.

**KONA-KAU DISTRICT** Fair Wind offers guided snorkeling, snuba and scuba trips and supplies you with equipment. The doubledecker *Fair Wind II* picks up excursionists at Keauhou Bay and goes to Kealakekua Bay. ~ 78-7130 Kaleopapa Road, Keauhou Bay; 808-322-2788; www.fair-wind.com.

**KOHALA COAST** Kohala Divers is a full-service diving center providing scuba and snorkeling lessons as well as gear rental. There is a two-tank boat dive available, or go out on their 42-foot custom dive boat. ~ Kawaihae Shopping Center, Kawaihae; 808-882-7774; www.kohaladivers.com.

**HILO** Nautilus Dive Center operates one- and two-tank shore dives off the Hilo Coast. You'll see a variety of marine life, including sea turtles, as well as coral formations and caves. Closed Sunday. ~ 382 Kamehameha Avenue, Hilo; 808-935-6939.

**SURFING & WIND-SURFING**

Surfing the Big Island is one adventure you don't want to miss. Several spots on the island are known to locals, and outfitters will give you directions and, for those who need them, lessons.

Some of the better-known spots on the Kona Coast, not advisable for the novice, include Honis, Kon Tiki, Lyman's, Pine Trees and Banyans. On the Hilo side check out Honolii near Hilo, Pohiki and the nearby Isaac Hale Beach Park in the Puna district and Kolekole Beach Park on the Hamakua Coast. Winter is peak season for surfing popular Kona spots such as Lyman's and Banyans. If you're a beginner, or even if you're not, you should chat up the locals or a surf shop to check out conditions at any of these places.

Windsurfing is good year-round. Try Anaehoomalu Beach on the Kona Coast or the South Point area.

Specializing in beginner surfers, **Ocean Eco Tours** has taught thousands of people to catch a wave. They offer group or private lessons, all taught by CPR- and first-aid trained lifeguard instructors. They guarantee you'll be surfing before the class is over! ~ Honokohau Harbor, 74-425 Kealakehe Parkway, Suite 15, Kailua-Kona; 808-324-7873, fax 808-331-1936; www.ocean ecotours.com, e-mail ecoinfo@oceanecotours.com.

**Ocean Sports Hawaii** rents sailboards and offers lessons. ~ Outrigger Waikoloa Resort, Waikoloa; 808-886-6666 ext. 1, 888-724-5234; www.hawaiioceansports.com.

At the Kona Inn Shopping Village, **Honolua Surf Company** sells surfboards and boogieboards and recommends the best locations. ~ 75-5744 Alii Drive, Kailua-Kona; 808-329-1001.

---

#### "MAKE A WAVE"

So you want to be a surfer dude...or *wahine*. One of the first things you need to know is surfer etiquette. Beginners should understand this before setting off: Avoid conflicts with other surfers. A surfer who stands up first on a wave *owns* that wave. If a wave is already breaking, the person closest to the white-water owns that wave. Surfing into either of these situations is a *no no*! Besides, it's extremely dangerous. Remember: always surf at a spot that matches your skill level—check with the experts before you go. You might want to pick up on some lingo, too, or *bag* (leave) the scene. If you're on a wave that's closing out or is too big, *bail* (jump off your board) or you'll get *stuffed* (driven under the water by the wave coming down on you). Avoid the *scabs* (reefs or rocks), *spongers* (bodyboarders) and *bodybashers* (bodysurfers). Don't surf where the *mokes* (local tough guys) surf, and I wish for you *da kine* (the best) waves!

**Pacific Vibrations** will outfit you for a day of surfing and the friendly staff is a great resource for info about local outdoor activities. ~ 75-5702 Alii Drive, Kailua-Kona; 808-329-4140.

**SAILING & PARA-SAILING**

One of the authentic pleasures of a Big Island visit is a sail along the Kona or Kohala coast. Choose from a pleasure sail or take an adventure trip that includes a snorkeling excursion.

Among the popular operators is **Honu Sailing**, which offers half-day, full-day and sunset trips with snorkeling along the Kona coast. ~ Honokohau Harbor, Kailua; 808-896-4668; www.sailkona.com. The **Maile Gulf Star** is a 50-foot sailboat available for a variety of trips around the Big Island. ~ Kawaihae Harbor; 808-326-5174; www.adventuresailing.com.

Another popular sport in Hawaii is parasailing, in which you are strapped to a parachute that is towed aloft by a motorboat. For information, contact UFO **Parasail**. ~ Kailua-Kona; 808-325-5836; www.ufoparasail.net.

**KAYAKING**

Paddlers who come to the Big Island will be fortunate to observe seasonal humpback whales, dancing spinner dolphins and an endless variety of native marine life and coral reefs. Kealakekua Bay is a favorite launch site on the Kona side while Richardson Ocean Park and the Hilo Bayfront Beach Park are Hilo venues. You can rent your own boat or take a kayak tour with the following outfitters.

**Ocean Eco Tours** has a professional aquatic staff that claims it will take you on a "tour of a lifetime" along the Kona Coast. For paddlers of any skill (beginners to ocean voyagers), they'll find the perfect location for you to view Hawaii's marine world. Or if you're into the do-it-yourself thing, they rent kayaks as well. ~ Honokohau Harbor, 74-425 Kealakehe Parkway, Suite 15, Kailua-Kona; 808-324-7873, fax 808-331-1936; www.oceanecotours.com; e-mail ecoinfo@oceanecotours.com.

**Kona Boy** offers guided tours on the island's west side. Rentals of dive, surf, racing or touring kayaks are also available. Kona Boy is a resource for maps, information and advice on sea kayaking. ~ Mamalahoa Highway near Mile marker 113; 808-322-3600.

The Big Island's only Hawaiian-owned and -operated kayak company is **Aloha Kayak Co.** These knowledgeable folks will rent you equipment and take you on exciting tours that include cliff-jumping, snorkeling and even swimming through lava tubes. ~ 79-7428 Kealakekua Highway, Honalo; 808-322-2868; www. alohakayak.com.

**Flumin' Da Ditch** is a unique kayak adventure covering three miles in the century-old flume built to carry water from the Kohala Mountains to hungry sugar plantations. The plantations are gone, but portions of the ditch, as this massive irrigation system was called, remain functional. The ride is tame, accessing the rainforest in a unique and enjoyable way. Reservations are required. ~ 808-889-6922, 877-449-6922, fax 808-889-6944; www. flumindaditch.com, e-mail kmkc@aloha.net.

Between November and May, when about 600 humpback whales inhabit Hawaiian waters, a popular spectator sport is spotting these behemoths in the channels around the islands. The rest of the year, outfitters seek out the lesser-known whales—see page 35—and other marinelife attractions.

**WHALE WATCHING & BOAT TOURS**

**Captain Zodiac** leads four-hour trips twice daily along the Kona Coast. You may see whales, dolphins, sea turtles and other marine life as you journey along the coast and visit sea caves and lava tubes. There's a stop at Kealakekua Bay for snorkeling. Closed Sunday. ~ Honokohau Harbor; 808-329-3199.

Did you know that Mauna Loa is the largest volcano on our planet and covers half of the Big Island? In fact, Mauna Loa's land mass amounts to close to 85 percent of all the other Hawaiian Islands combined.

**Captain Dan McSweeney's Whale Watching Adventures** operates three-hour cruises. If you don't see whales, the company will give you another trip at no charge. ~ Honokohau Harbor, Kailua-Kona; 808-322-0028.

The catamarans maintained by **Ocean Sports** head out several times daily between December and April in search of humpback whales, which breed and calve just off the coast. Naturalists provide educational information and hydrophones allow passengers to listen to the whales underwater. ~ 69-275 Waikoloa Beach Drive, Waikoloa Beach Resort, Waikoloa; 808-886-6666, ext. 1, 888-724-5234; www.hawaiioceansports.com.

Some of the best golfing in the country is found on the Big Island. From stunning links on the Kohala Coast to community courses in the Hilo area, this island has everything you need for a golf-oriented vacation. Sunny conditions on the Kona side mean you

**GOLF**

*Text continued on page 52.*

# Snorkeling & Scuba Diving the Gold Coast

Simply stated, Hawaii's Kona Coast offers some of the world's most spectacular diving. All along this western shoreline lie magnificent submerged caves, lava flows, cliffs and colorful coral reefs.

Protected from prevailing trade winds by Mauna Kea and Mauna Loa, Kona enjoys the gentlest conditions. Usually the weather is sunny, the surf mild and the water clear (visibility is usually in the 100-foot range). Locals claim they get about 345 ideal diving days a year. It's small wonder, then, that adventurers travel from all over the world to explore Kona's underwater world.

What will you see if you join them? The Kona Coast has over 650 species of reef fish including the brightly colored yellow tang, the aptly named raccoon butterflyfish, the trumpetfish, the coronetfish, the cow-eyed porcupine pufferfish, and the black, yellow and white moorish idol. Large marine animals abound as well, including green sea turtles, hawksbill turtles, manta rays, spotted eagle rays, pilot whales, pygmy killer whales and humpback whales.

When looking for marine life, swim over the coral, looking in, under and around all the corners, caves and crevices. Many spectacular sea creatures await discovery in these hiding spots. Keep in mind that while coral looks like rock, it is a living creature that can be easily killed. Standing on it, touching it, kicking it with your fin or even kicking sand onto it from the ocean floor can damage the coral. So gently drift over the reef and you will be rewarded with new discoveries and close encounters with beautiful tropical fish.

Following are brief descriptions of the best snorkeling and diving spots, as well as shops that provide equipment and tours. For specific information on a particular dive sight, drop by one of these shops. I also recommend you buy waterproof fish identification cards. You can take them into the water and use them to identify these magnificently colored creatures.

**KOHALA COAST SPOTS** Anaehoomalu Beach is good for beginners, but it lacks the scenic diversity of other areas. There's good diving at the end of the road leading to Puako, but it's rocky. "69" Beach (or Waialea Bay) features good underwater opportunities when the surf is mild.

Hapuna Beach State Park has an area that abounds in coral and fish near the rocks and cliffs at the end of the beach. Spencer Beach Park is filled with coral and suits beginners and experts alike.

**Mahukona Beach Park** is an old shipping area littered with underwater refuse that makes for great exploring. **Kapaa Beach Park** offers good diving, but it has a rocky entrance and tricky currents. **Keokea Beach Park**, an excellent spearfishing area, is often plagued by wind and high surf.

**KAILUA-KONA AREA SPOTS** Kamakahonu Beach, the sand patch next to Kailua's King Kamehameha Kona Beach Hotel, is a crowded but convenient snorkel site. There are corals and many species of fish here, but watch out for heavy boat traffic along the wharf. On the south side of the pier, at the small beach where the Ironman Triathlon swim begins, is good snorkeling.

**Old Kona Airport State Recreation Area**, just a stone's skip north of town, affords excellent diving on either side. The entry is rocky, but once in, you'll find the waters spectacular. Some glass-bottom boats tour this area.

**Honokohau Beach** has some good spots south of the small-boat harbor. **Kaloko-Honokohau National Historic Park**, north of Honokohau Harbor, has a trail that leads to an excellent beach and snorkeling site. Sometimes nudists are on the beach.

**Kahaluu Beach Park**, with its easy entry to the water and complete beach services including restrooms, lifeguard, picnic tables and showers, is the best spot for beginners. The waters here are too shallow for great scuba diving, which means they're all the better for snorkeling.

**SOUTH KONA SPOTS** Across from Napoopoo Beach Park, at the Captain Cook Monument, is an excellent diving spot—so good, in fact, that it draws diving tours and glass-bottom boats. The best diving is across Kealakekua Bay near the Captain Cook Monument.

**Keei Beach** features a lot of coral and, reportedly, a sea grotto. At **Puuhonua o Honaunau National Historical Park**, also known as the Place of Refuge, there are two natural steps carved into the rocky shoreline that allow for easy entry directly into swarms of reef fish. Because of the abundance of colorful marine life, the accessible location, the easy entry and the variety of depths, this is one of the coast's best spots for snorkelers and scuba divers alike. **Hookena Beach Park** offers good dive spots near the cliffs south of the beach. **Milolii** has excellent diving areas as well as fascinating tidepools.

generally don't need to worry about taking a rain check. Throw in views of the lava landscape, verdant shorelines and swaying palm trees, and you've created a duffer's view of paradise.

**HILO**    Naniloa Country Club is a nine-hole, par-35 course overlooking Hilo Bay. This narrow course may look easy but don't be deceived: Water hazards and trees along the fairways create plenty of challenges. ~ 120 Banyan Drive, Hilo; 808-935-3000.

Hilo Municipal Golf Course is one of the best bargains on the islands. This 18-hole course has great views of the water and the mountains. Be sure to reserve tee times on the weekends. You can sharpen your skills on the driving range and practice greens. ~ 340 Haihai Street, Hilo; 808-959-7711.

**HAMAKUA COAST**    Hamakua Country Club is another inexpensive choice. Located on the north shore about 40 miles from Hilo, this nine-hole course bans power carts. While it lacks the amenities of the resort links, Hamakua has a nice neighborhood feel. ~ Honokaa; 808-775-7244.

**KOHALA COAST**    The Kohala Coast is where the monied set swings their clubs. So if you're going to play golf at these five-star luxury resorts, bring a fat wallet. Creating a great golf course is easy if you just dip into Laurence Rockefeller's deep pockets, hire Robert Trent Jones, Sr., and buy some lava-strewn oceanfront terrain. What you'll end up with is the 18-hole **Mauna Kea Beach Golf Course**. ~ Kawaihae; 808-882-7222. Quite a challenge, the original links have been complemented by the 18-hole **Hapuna Golf Course** created by Arnold Palmer. ~ 808-880-3000.

Waikoloa Village Golf Course is an 18-hole, par-72 layout that also includes a driving range and practice greens. This windy

### A WINDOW IN THE SKY

The air is so rarefied atop Mauna Kea's 13,796-foot peak—located above 40 percent of the earth's atmosphere—that views from the 13 telescopes there are an astronomer's dream. Here the world's most powerful astronomical observatory—the combined light-gathering power of the telescopes is 60 times greater than that of the Hubble Telescope—is managed by 11 different countries. Because the Big Island is so remote from the earth's population centers the night sky is perfectly illuminated, drawing the most curious star gazers from around the world.

course, designed by Robert Trent Jones, Jr., has great views of Mauna Kea and Mauna Loa. ~ Waikoloa; 808-883-9621. Nearby the **Waikoloa Beach Resort Golf Course** was also designed by Robert Trent Jones, Jr. ~ Waikoloa; 808-886-7888. The adjacent **Waikoloa Kings' Golf Course** has another popular course. ~ Waikoloa; 808-886-7888. Convenient to the Hyatt Regency Waikoloa and the Royal Waikoloan, each course has unique features. The beach course heads through petroglyph fields while the Kings' Golf Course also has beautiful lava hazards.

**Mauna Lani Golf Course** has two 18-hole links built across rugged lava beds. If you miss the fairway, don't expect to find your ball out there in the volcanic landscape. There's also a driving range and practice greens. ~ Kohala Coast; 808-885-6655.

**KAILUA-KONA AREA** Located on the slopes of Hualalai, about eight miles north of Kailua-Kona, **Makalei Hawaii Country Club** offers cool Upcountry play between 2000 and 3000 feet above sea level. Play is hilly with narrow fairways that favor accuracy. The views are rewarding. ~ 72-3890 Hawaii Belt Road (Route 190), Kalaoa; 808-325-6625.

At the **Kona Country Club**, a pair of 18-hole golf courses are ideal for those who want to bunker down. Bring along your camera to capture memorable views of the ocean course. Or head uphill to fully enjoy the challenging Mauka course. If you're looking for over-water holes and hidden hazards, you've come to the right place. ~ 78-7000 Alii Drive, Kailua-Kona; 808-322-2595.

**KONA/KAU DISTRICT** Sea Mountain Golf Course is a popular 18-hole course located south of Kilauea volcano. It's beautifully landscaped with coconut and banyan trees. ~ Route 11, Punaluu; 808-928-6222.

**HAWAII VOLCANOES NATIONAL PARK** Volcano Golf and Country Club is the only course I know located in the vicinity of an erupting volcano. The high elevation (4200 feet) will give your ball an extra lift on this 18-hole course. ~ Volcanoes National Park; 808-967-7331.

Though many riding stables are going the way of the wild horse because of insurance liabilities, there are still a number of opportunities to ride the range on the Big Island. The Waimea area is *the* prime location to saddle up your pony and pretend to be

**RIDING STABLES**

a *paniolo*, but other parts of the island are just as enticing to horseback-riding fans.

With **Naalapa Stables,** you can explore a 12,000-acre working cattle and sheep ranch complete with cinder cones, ancient Hawaiian ruins and lush pastures, or head for the waterfalls and jungles of the Waipio Valley. Open-range riding is catered to your own riding ability—experienced riders can canter through the ranchland, while beginners go at a slower pace. Reservations are a must. ~ P.O. Box 437185, Kamuela, HI 96743; 808-889-0022, fax 808-775-9318; www.naalapastables.com.

**Hawaii Forest & Trail** offers mule trips through the Kohala Mountains, where sweeping views of the coastline, Pololu Valley and Haleakala are the attraction. The guides are friendly and informative. ~ 74-5035B Kaahumanu Highway, Kailua-Kona; 808-331-8505, 800-464-1993; www.hawaii-forest.com.

**Kings' Trail Rides O' Kona** offers a riding/snorkeling combo. Riders descend the Kaawaloa Trail to Kealakekua Bay. Lunch is included, and children over seven with riding experience can participate. ~ Kealakekua; 808-323-2388; www.konacowboy.com, e-mail sales@konacowboy.com.

In Waipio Valley, **Naalapa Trail Rides** will take you on a two-hour ride through taro patches and waterfalls and (it goes without saying) past magnificent views. They also offer excursions in the Kohala Mountains. ~ Waipio Valley Artworks, Kukuihaele Village Road, Kukuihaele; 808-775-0419.

**Dahana Ranch** operates a gorgeous spread. Besides offering packages of *paniolo* entertainment and a chance to "brand, rope and pen," they also have rides for the less dedicated. Their one-and-a-half-hour tour takes in views of the working ranch as well as the surrounding valley and mountains. The two-and-a-half-hour option includes participation in an authentic cattle drive. ~ P.O. Box 1293, Kamuela, HI 96743; 808-885-0057, 888-399-0057; www.dahanaranch.com.

**BIKING**

Hawaii offers very good roads and many unpopulated stretches that make it ideal for bikers. Much of the island is mountainous with some fairly steep grades in the interior. Saddle Road, the roads to Waimea, and the road from Hilo up to Volcanoes National Park will all make a heavy breather of you, but the coast roads are generally flat or gently rolling. Most roads have shoulders

# Ski

## Hawaii

During your island tour you'll inevitably pull up behind some joker with a bumper sticker reading "Think Snow." Around you trade winds may be bending the palm trees, sunbronzed crowds will be heading to the beach, and the thermometer will be approaching 80°. Snow will be the furthest thing from your mind.

But up on the 13,796-foot slopes of Mauna Kea, you're liable to see a bikini-clad skier schussing across a mantle of newly fallen snow! Any time from December until April or May, there may be enough dry snow to create ski runs several miles long and fill bowls a half-mile wide and almost a mile long. The slopes range from beginner to expert: Some have a vertical drop of 4500 feet. This is some of the world's highest skiing available.

Situated above the clouds about 80 percent of the time, this snow lover's oasis is baked by a tropical sun many times more powerful than at the beach. So it's easy to tan and easier yet to burn.

Combined with the thin air and winds up to 100 miles per hour, Hawaii's ski slopes are not for the faint-hearted or fair-skinned. But if you're seeking an incredible adventure and want a view of the Hawaiian islands from a 13,000-foot crow's nest, the heights of Mauna Kea await. There are no lifts and no groomed trails; beneath the snow is hard lava rock and cinder. A four-wheel-drive vehicle is required to get you there. It's the same road used to get to the observatories.

**Ski Guides Hawaii** offers all-day downhill skiing and snowboarding tours on Mauna Kea and cross-country skiing on Mauna Loa. The ski season lasts from December until April or May. This is not an inexpensive trip—but then again, skiing never is. ~ P.O. Box 1954, Kamuela, HI 96743; 808-885-4188; www.skihawaii.com.

and light traffic. Keep in mind that the northeast side of the island receives heavy rainfall, while the Kona side is almost always sunny. But wet side or dry, the scenery is spectacular throughout.

Several local organizations host weekly or monthly bike rides. Be sure to contact the **Big Island Mountain Bike Association** (BIMBA), which supports mountain biking with trail and safety programs. This organization is committed to encouraging environmentally responsible mountain biking. BIMBA provides trail maps and organizes rides and races, including a regular Sunday excursion. ~ P.O. Box 6819, Hilo, HI 96720; 808-961-4452; www.bimbahawaii.net.

**Kona Coast Cycling Tours, Inc.** offers bike tours of the Kona Coast, with half- and full-day adventures for all ages and abilities. (Covered trailers and sets of "third wheels" are available for younger children.) For experienced riders, they also organize a challenging multi-day 250-mile island loop, "Tour Da Volcanoes!" ~ P.O. Box 2627, Kailua-Kona, HI 96745; 808-327-1133, 877-592-2453, fax 808-327-1144; www.cyclekona.com, e-mail bikeinfo@cyclekona.com.

**Backroads** offers a six-day bike trip, "From Coast to Crater," several times a year. Beginning in Kailua-Kona, they ride to the "Place of Refuge," through Kona coffee country and a lava desert. Next comes a gradual 4000-foot climb to Volcanoes National Park, with a volcanologist-guided tour of Kilauea and a bike ride around the rim of the crater. The trip finishes with a ride through Hilo and up the Hamakua and Kohala coasts. Luxury accommodations await riders at the end of each day. ~ 801 Cedar Street, Berkeley, CA 94710; 510-527-1555, 800-462-2848, fax 510-527-1444; www.backroads.com.

**Bike Rentals** **Dave's Bike and Triathlon Shop** rents mountain and cross-training bikes—with shuttles to and from Kailua hotels—and do repairs. If you want, you can ship your bike and Dave's will have it assembled before you arrive. ~ 75-5669 Alii Drive, Kailua-Kona; 808-329-4522. **B & L Bike & Sports** rents mountain bikes, road bikes and hybrids. Closed Sunday. ~ 75-5699 Kopiko Place, Kailua-Kona; 808-329-3309. **Hawaiian Pedals** offers hybrids and basic mountain bikes as well as gear and accessories. Rental times range from 5 hours to all day. ~ 75-5744 Alii Drive, Kailua-Kona; 808-329-2294; www.hawaiianpedals.

com. Hawaiian Pedal's sister company, **HP Bikeworks**, rents front- and full-suspension mountain bikes. ~ 74-5599 Luhia Street, Kailua-Kona; 808-326-2453; www.hpbikeworks.com. There are no bike rentals in Hilo.

**Bike Repairs**    The folks at **Mid-Pacific Wheels** will do repair work or sell you bike accessories. ~ 1133-C Manono Street, Hilo; 808-935-6211. **Hilo Bike Hub** also sells and repairs bikes. ~ 318 East Kawili Street, Hilo; 808-961-4452. **B & L Bike & Sports** does repairs. ~ 75-5699 Kopiko Place, Kailua-Kona; 808-329-3309.

Of all the islands in the chain, Hawaii has the finest hiking trails. The reason? Quite simply, it's the Big Island's size. Larger than all the other islands combined and boasting the highest peaks, Hawaii offers the greatest diversity to explorers.

**HIKING**

Mauna Loa and Mauna Kea, each rising over 13,000 feet, provide rugged mountain climbing. To the north, the Kohala Mountains feature trails through dense tropical terrain and along awesome cliffs. In Volcanoes National Park, hikers can experience the challenge of walking through a lava wasteland and into the belly of an active volcano.

Along much of Hawaii's shoreline lies a network of trails that have been under study by the Department of the Interior. Originally a series of access trails for the Hawaiians, they were paid for by local farmers to tax collectors. In 1823, William Ellis, a missionary, tried to follow them to circumnavigate the island. In

**AUTHOR FAVORITE**

Waipio Valley is ripe for exploring, but if you want to leave civilization completely behind, continue instead along the **Waimanu Valley Trail** (9 miles). This track begins at the base of the cliff that marks Waipio's northwest border. It climbs sharply up the 1200-foot rock face in a series of switchbacks, then continues up and down across numerous gulches, and finally descends into Waimanu Valley. This exotic place, half the size of Waipio Valley, is equally as lush. Here, in addition to wild pigs, mountain apple trees and ancient ruins, you'll find naturally running water (requiring purification) and great spots for beachfront picnics. This is a challenging one-day hike, so you may want to camp. You may never want to leave.

more recent times, a group of journalists recreated—to the best of their ability—his route.

The plantations in the northeast destroyed any trails in that corner of the island. The sections that remain on the rest of Hawaii contain archaeological sites that should be left unmolested. Some people have proposed National Trail status for the network, but until then you'll need a topographic map, respect for private property and archaeology, and a yen for adventure to tackle the trails that the Hawaiians once tread.

Hawaii's official hiking trails run through three areas: Volcanoes National Park, Kau Desert and the Kohala Mountains. These are popular and well-defined trails, many of which are described below. Permits are required for any overnight backcountry camping within the boundaries of Hawaii Volcanoes National Park, which includes the Kau Desert. Apply the morning of your trip at the Kilauea Visitor Center. Permits are free, but first-come, first-served. All distances listed for hiking trails are one way unless otherwise noted.

**HAMAKUA COAST**   **Waipio Valley Trail** begins from Waipio Valley lookout at the end of Route 24. Waipio is a broad, lush, awesomely beautiful valley ribboned with waterfalls and rich in history. From the trailhead, a jeep trail drops steeply for one mile to the valley floor. Here the trail joins one road leading up into the valley and another heading to the beach. The high road goes toward 1200-foot Hiilawe Falls and to an abandoned Peace Corps training camp.

**KOHALA COAST**   Stretching along Kohala peninsula's northeast coast is a series of sheer cliffs and wide valleys rivaling Kauai's Na Pali Coast in beauty. At either end of this rainswept *pali* are lush, still valleys that can only be reached by hiking trails. To camp legally in this area can be a challenge, since you need a permit or permission wherever you go, and the land could be State, corporate or owned by one of the dozens of property holders. If you want to camp, start by asking questions at the State Department of Land and Natural Resources; 808-974-4221.

**Pololu Valley Trail** (0.5 mile) descends from the Pololu Valley Lookout at the end of Akoni Pule Highway to the valley floor 400 feet below. There you'll find a secluded beach (beware of the riptides) and a series of trails that lead up through the Kohala Mountains.

# The New Travel

Travel has become a personal art form. A destination no longer serves as just a place to relax: It's also a point of encounter. To many, this new wave in travel customs is labeled "adventure travel" and involves trekking glaciers or dusting the cliffs in a hang glider; to others, it connotes nothing more daring than a restful spell in a secluded resort. Actually, it's a state of mind, a willingness not only to accept but seek out the uncommon and unique.

Few places in the world are more conducive to this imaginative travel than Hawaii. Several organizations in the islands cater specifically to people who want to add local customs and unusual adventures to their vacation itineraries.

**Hawaiian Adventure Tours** features a ten-day, multi-island tour. The trip begins on Kauai, moves to Maui and wraps up on the Big Island, where over four days you'll visit Volcanoes National Park, kayak and snorkel the Kohala coast, and shop in Kailua-Kona. For a shorter adventure, opt for the half-day kayak package that includes snorkeling. ~ P.O. Box 1269, Kapaau, HI 96755; 808-889-0227, 800-659-3544; www.hawaiianadventuretours.com.

The **Sierra Club** sponsors hikes on the Big Island, as well as trail building and other projects aimed at helping to preserve the island's natural heritage. There is a small fee ($3) for non-members who want to participate in the outings. ~ P.O. Box 1137, Hilo, HI 96721; 808-965-9695; www.hi.sierraclub.org.

When you're ready to take up the challenge of this style of free-wheeling travel, check with these outfits. Or plan your own trip. To traditional tourists, Hawaii means souvenir shops and fast-food restaurants. But for those with spirit and imagination, it's a land of untracked beaches and ancient volcanos waiting to be explored.

**KONA/KAU AREA**    From Volcanoes National Park's southern section several trails lead into the hot, arid Kau Desert. All are long, dusty trails offering solitude to the adventurous hiker.

**Kau Desert Trail** (3.5 miles) branches off Crater Rim Trail and drops 2000 feet en route to the lookout at the end of Hilina Pali Road. The shelter along the way, at Kipuka Pepeiau, provides a welcome resting place on this lengthy trek.

**Mauna Iki Trail** (3.6 miles) leads from Mamalahoa Highway (Route 11) to Hilina Pali Road. The trail passes near Footprints Trail, where a sudden volcanic eruption in 1790 engulfed a Hawaiian army at war with Kamehameha.

**HAWAII VOLCANOES NATIONAL PARK**    The most interesting and easily accessible trails lead through the **Kilauea Caldera** area. The caldera, three miles long and 4000 feet above sea level, can be explored either by hiking along one extended trail or over several shorter connecting trails.

**Crater Rim Trail** (11.6-mile loop) begins near the park headquarters and encircles Kilauea Caldera. An excellent introduction to the volcanoes, this lengthy loop trail passes steam vents, the Kau Desert, the fractured Southwest Rift area and a fascinating fern forest. The views from along the rim are spectacular.

That gray substance that sometimes hangs over the island is called "vog," a combination of volcanic smoke and fog.

**Sulphur Banks Trail** (0.3 mile) begins at park headquarters and parallels Crater Rim Drive past steam vents and sulphur deposits.

**Halemaumau Trail** (3.5 miles) starts near Volcano House, then descends into Kilauea Caldera. The trail crosses the crater floor and affords astonishing views down into steaming Halemaumau crater, then climbs back up to join Crater Rim Trail. This has got to be one of the park's finest hikes.

**Kilauea Iki Trail** (5 miles) loops from the Thurston Lava Tube parking lot down into Kilauea Iki crater and returns via Crater Rim Trail. Crossing the crater floor, the trail passes over a lava crust beneath which lies a pool of hot rock. Rainwater percolates through the crust, reaches the hot rock, and emerges as steam. Step lightly.

**Sandalwood Trail** (1.5-mile loop) loops from near the Volcano House past sandalwood and *ohia* trees and then along the side of Kilauea Caldera.

**Byron Ledge Trail** (4 miles) branches off Halemaumau Trail, crosses the Kilauea caldera floor, and then climbs along Byron Ledge before rejoining Halemaumau. This makes an excellent connecting trail.

Starting within the Kapapala Forest Reserve at 5650 feet, the **Ainapo Trail** (3.5 miles) takes hikers on a moderately challenging trek past mesic *koa* and *ohia* trees. On the way up to the Ainapo Trail Shelter at Halewai, you'll catch sight of mountain goats and sheep. More experienced hikers can climb the rest of the fog-covered trail (7.5 miles) and will be rewarded with views from the rim of the Mokuaweoweo Caldera in Hawaii Volcanoes National Park. The trailhead begins at the cattleguard between the 40- and 41-mile markers on the Mamalahoa Highway between Volcano and Pahala. This hike requires permits from the National Park *and* the Division of Forestry and Wildlife in Hilo (808-974-4221). Reservations for the shelter can be made up to 30 days in advance.

Volcanoes National Park's premier hike is along **Mauna Loa Trail**. This tough 18-mile trek, requiring at least three days, leads to the top of the world's largest shield volcano. Cold-weather equipment and a sturdy constitution are absolute necessities for this challenging adventure. Permits are required for this hike.

Climbers usually hike seven miles the first day from the trailhead at the end of Mauna Loa Strip Road up to Red Hill (Pu'u 'Ula'ula). At this 10,035-foot way station, there is a rudimentary cabin with eight bunks with mattresses, but no provisions. A hearty 11-mile trek the second day leads to the rim of Mauna Loa's summit caldera, and to the Mokuaweoweo cabin (located on the rim). The return trip takes one or two days, depending on how fast you want to come down.

Beware of altitude sickness and hypothermia, and be sure to register for a permit at park headquarters before and after hiking. Purification tablets for the water and white gas for the stoves are also essential. Don't treat this as a casual jaunt; it's a real trek. Good planning will ensure your safety and enjoyment.

A single-lane paved road climbs from Saddle Road to an area near Mauna Loa summit. This alternative hiking route lacks the adventure but reduces the time needed to ascend Mauna Loa. This road is not open to rental cars.

# THREE

# History and Culture

**POLYNESIAN ARRIVAL** The island of Big Island was the last land mass created in the ongoing dramatic geologic upheaval that formed the Hawaiian islands. And, according to some historians. Perhaps as early as the third century, Polynesians sailing from the Marquesas Islands, and then later from Tahiti, landed in Hawaii. In Europe, mariners were rarely venturing outside the Mediterranean Sea, and it would be centuries before Columbus happened upon the New World. Yet in the Pacific, entire families were crossing 2500 miles of untracked ocean in hand-carved canoes with sails woven from coconut fibers. The boats were formidable structures, catamaran-like vessels with a cabin built on the platform between the wooden hulls and sails woven from *hala* (pandanus) leaves. Some of the vessels were 100 feet long and could do 20 knots, making the trip to Hawaii in a month.

The Polynesians had originally come from the coast of Asia about 3000 years before. They had migrated through Indonesia, then pressed inexorably eastward, leapfrogging across archipelagoes until they finally reached the last chain, the most remote—Hawaii.

These Pacific migrants were undoubtedly the greatest sailors of their day, and stand among the finest in history. When close to land they could smell it, taste it in the seawater, see it in a lagoon's turquoise reflection on the clouds above an island. They knew 150 stars. From the color of the water they determined ocean depths and current directions. They had no charts, no compasses, no sextants; sailing directions were simply recorded in legends and chants. Yet Polynesians discovered the Pacific, from Indonesia to Easter Island, from New Zealand to Hawaii. They made the Vikings and Phoenicians look like landlubbers.

**CAPTAIN COOK** They were high islands, rising in the northeast as the sun broke across the Pacific. First one, then a second and, finally, as the tall-masted ships drifted west, a third island loomed before them. Landfall! The British crew was ecstatic. It meant fresh water, tropical fruits, solid ground on which to set their boots and a chance to carouse with the native women. For their captain, James Cook, it was another in an amazing career of discoveries. The man whom many call history's greatest explorer was about to land in one of the last spots on earth to be discovered by the West.

He would name the place for his patron, the British earl who became famous by pressing a meal between two crusts of bread. The Sandwich Islands. Later they would be called Owhyhee, and eventually, as the Western tongue glided around the uncharted edges of a foreign language, Hawaii.

It was January 1778, a time when the British Empire was still basking in a sun that never set. The Pacific had been opened to Western powers over two centuries before, when a Portuguese sailor named Magellan crossed it. Since that time, the British, French, Dutch and Spanish had tracked through in search of future colonies.

They happened upon Samoa, Fiji, Tahiti and the other islands that spread across this third of the globe, but somehow they had never sighted Hawaii. Even when Cook finally spied it, he little realized how important a find he had made. Hawaii, quite literally, was a jewel in the ocean, rich in fragrant sandalwood, ripe for agricultural exploitation and crowded with sea life. But it was the archipelago's isolation that would prove to be its greatest resource. Strategically situated between Asia and North America, it was the only place for thousands of miles to which whalers, merchants and bluejackets could repair for provisions and rest.

Cook was 49 years old when he shattered Hawaii's quiescence. The Englishman hadn't expected to find islands north of Tahiti. Quite frankly, he wasn't even trying. It was his third Pacific voyage and Cook was hunting bigger game, the fabled Northwest Passage that would link this ocean with the Atlantic.

But these mountainous islands were still an interesting find. He could see by the canoes venturing out to meet his ships that the lands were inhabited; when he finally put ashore in Waimea on Kauai, Cook discovered a Polynesian society. He saw irrigated fields, domestic animals and high-towered temples. The women were bare-breasted, the men wore loincloths. As his crew bartered for pigs, fowls and bananas, he learned that the natives knew about metal and coveted iron like gold.

If iron was gold to these "Indians," then Cook was a god. He soon realized that his arrival had somehow been miraculously timed, coinciding with the Makahiki festival, a months-long celebration highlighted by sporting competitions, feasting, hula and exaltation of the ruling chiefs. Even war ceased during this gala affair. Makahiki honored the roving deity Lono, whose return to Hawaii on "trees that would move over seas" was foretold in ancient legend. Cook was a strange white man sailing tall-masted ships—obviously he was Lono. The Hawaiians gave him gifts, fell in his path and rose only at his insistence.

But even among religious crowds, fame is often fickle. After leaving Hawaii, Cook sailed north to the Arctic Sea, where he failed to discover the Northwest Passage. He returned the next year to Kealakekua Bay, arriving at the tail end of another exhausting Makahiki festival. By then the Hawaiians had tired of his constant demands for provisions and were suffering from a new disease that was obviously carried by Lono's archangelic crew—syphilis. This Lono was proving something of a freeloader.

Tensions ran high. The Hawaiians stole a boat. Cook retaliated with gunfire. A scuffle broke out on the beach and in a sudden violent outburst, which surprised the islanders as much as the interlopers, the Hawaiians discovered that their god could bleed. The world's finest mariner lay face down in foot-deep water, stabbed and bludgeoned to death.

Cook's end marked the beginning of an era. He had put the Pacific on the map, his map, probing its expanses and defining its fringes. In Hawaii he ended a thousand years of solitude. The archipelago's geographic isolation, which has always played a crucial role in Hawaii's development, had finally failed to protect it, and a second theme had come into play—the islands' vulnerability. Together with the region's "backwardness," these conditions would now mold Hawaii's history. All in turn would be shaped by another factor, one which James Cook had added to Hawaii's historic equation: the West.

**KAMEHAMEHA AND KAAHUMANU**   The next man whose star would rise above Hawaii was present at Cook's death. Some say he struck the Englishman, others that he took a lock of the great leader's hair and used its residual power, its *mana*, to become king of all Hawaii.

Kamehameha was a tall, muscular man with a furrowed face, a lesser chief on the powerful island of Hawaii. When he began his career of conquest a few years after Cook's death, he was a mere upstart, an ambitious, arrogant young chief. But he fought with a general's skill and a warrior's cunning, often plunging into the midst of a melee. He had an astute sense of technology, an intuition that these new Western metals and firearms could make him a king.

In Kamehameha's early years, the Hawaiian islands were composed of many fiefdoms. Several kings or great chiefs, continually warring among themselves, ruled individual islands. At times, a few kings would carve up one island or a lone king might seize several. Never had one monarch controlled all the islands.

But fresh players had entered the field: Westerners with ample firepower and awesome ships. During the decade following Cook, only a handful had arrived, mostly Englishmen and Americans, and they had not yet won the influence they soon would wield. However, even a few foreigners were enough to upset the balance of power. They sold weapons and hardware to the great chiefs, making several of them more powerful than any of the others had ever been. War was imminent.

### LITTLE BITS OF BIG ISLAND HISTORY

- Legend has it that the Big Island was discovered by a Polynesian fisherman named Hawaii-loa, and some believe that's where the name of the islands originated. (There are lots of other theories as well.)
- Polynesians began to populate the island around the fifth century and by A.D. 1000 coastal areas were fairly well established.
- Waipio Valley was once the capital of the island.
- A shipwreck off the south Kona coast was thought to be the first Big Island contact Hawaiians had with Westerners. Survivors of a Spanish vessel included the ship's captain and his sister who, it's purported, later married Hawaiians and founded a line of chiefs.

Kamehameha stood in the center of the hurricane. Like any leader suddenly caught up in the terrible momentum of history, he never quite realized where he was going or how fast he was moving. And he cared little that he was being carried in part by Westerners who would eventually want something for the ride. Kamehameha was no fool. If political expedience meant Western intrusion, then so be it. He had enemies among chiefs on the other islands; he needed the guns.

The most isolated population center on earth, Hawaii is 2390 miles from the mainland United States and 4900 miles from China.

When two white men came into his camp in 1790, he had the military advisers to complement a fast-expanding arsenal. Within months he cannoned Maui. In 1792, Kamehameha seized the Big Island by inviting his main rival to a peaceful parley, then slaying the hapless chief. By 1795, he had consolidated his control of Maui, grasped Molokai and Lanai, and begun reaching greedily toward Oahu. He struck rapidly, landing near Waikiki and sweeping inland, forcing his enemies to their deaths over the precipitous cliffs of the Nuuanu Pali.

The warrior had become a conqueror, controlling all the islands except Kauai, which he finally gained in 1810 by peaceful negotiation with King Kaumualii. Kamehameha proved to be as able a bureaucrat as he had been a general. He became a benevolent despot who, with the aid of an ever-increasing number of Western advisers, expanded Hawaii's commerce, brought peace to the islands and moved his people inexorably toward the modern age.

He came to be called Kamehameha the Great, and history first cast him as the George Washington of Hawaii, a wise and resolute leader who gathered a wartorn archipelago into a kingdom. Kamehameha I. But with the revisionist history of the 1960s and 1970s, as Third World people questioned both the Western version of events and the virtues of progress, Kamehameha began to resemble Benedict Arnold. He was seen as an opportunist, a megalomaniac who permitted the Western powers their initial foothold in Hawaii. He used their technology and then, in the manner of great men who depend on stronger allies, was eventually used by them.

As long a shadow as Kamehameha cast across the islands, the event that most dramatically transformed Hawaiian society occurred after his death in 1819. The kingdom had passed to Kamehameha's son Liholiho, but Kamehameha's favorite wife, Kaahumanu, usurped the power. Liholiho was a prodigal son, dissolute, lacking self-certainty, a drunk. Kaahumanu was a woman for all seasons, a canny politician who combined brilliance with boldness, the feminist of her day. She had infuriated Kamehameha by eating forbidden foods and sleeping with other chiefs, even when he placed a taboo on her body and executed her lovers. She drank liquor, ran away, proved completely uncontrollable and won Kamehameha's love.

It was only natural that when he died, she would take his *mana*, or so she reckoned. Kaahumanu gravitated toward power with the drive of someone whom fate has unwisely denied. She carved her own destiny, announcing that Kamehameha's wish had been to give her a governmental voice. There would be a new post and she would fill it, becoming in a sense Hawaii's first prime minister.

And if the power, then the motion. Kaahumanu immediately marched against Hawaii's belief system, trying to topple the old idols. For years she had bristled under a polytheistic religion regulated by taboos, or *kapus*, which severely restricted women's rights. Now Kaahumanu urged the new king, Liholiho, to break a very strict *kapu* by sharing a meal with women.

Since the act might help consolidate Liholiho's position, it had a certain appeal to the king. Anyway, the *kapus* were weakening: these white men, coming now in ever greater numbers, defied them with impunity. Liholiho vacillated, went on a two-day drunk before gaining courage, then finally sat down to eat. It was a last supper, shattering an ancient creed and opening the way for a radically new divinity. As Kaahumanu had willed, the old order collapsed, taking away a vital part of island life and leaving the Hawaiians more exposed than ever to foreign influence.

Already Western practices were gaining hold. Commerce from Honolulu, Lahaina and other ports was booming. There was a fortune to be made dealing sandalwood to China-bound merchants, and the chiefs were forcing the common people to strip Hawaii's forests. The grueling labor might make the chiefs rich, but it gained the commoners little more than a barren landscape. Western diseases struck virulently. The Polynesians in Hawaii, who numbered 300,000 in Cook's time, were extremely susceptible. By 1866, their population had dwindled to less than 60,000. It was a difficult time for the Hawaiian people.

**MISSIONARIES AND MERCHANTS**    Hawaii was not long without religion. The same year that Kaahumanu shattered tradition, a group of New England missionaries boarded the brig *Thaddeus* for a voyage around Cape Horn. It was a young company—many were in their twenties or thirties—and included a doctor, a printer and several teachers. They were all strict Calvinists, fearful that the second coming was at hand and possessed of a mission. They were bound for a strange land called Hawaii, 18,000 miles away.

Hawaii, of course, was a lost paradise, a hellhole of sin and savagery where men slept with several wives and women neglected to wear dresses. To the missionaries, it mattered little that the Hawaiians had lived this way for centuries. The churchmen would save these heathens from hell's everlasting fire whether they liked it or not.

The delegation arrived in Kailua on the Big Island in 1820 and then spread out, establishing important missions in Honolulu and Lahaina. Soon they were building schools and churches, conducting services in Hawaiian and converting the natives to Christianity.

The missionaries rapidly became an integral part of Hawaii, despite the fact that they were a walking contradiction to everything Hawaiian. They were a contentious, self-righteous, fanatical people whose arrogance toward the Hawaiians blinded them to the beauty and wisdom of island lifestyles. Where the natives lived in thatch homes open to the soothing trade winds, the missionaries built airless clapboard houses with New England–style fireplaces. While the Polynesians swam and surfed frequently, the new arrivals, living near the world's finest beaches, stank from not bathing. In a region where the thermometer rarely drops much below 70°, they wore long-sleeved woolens, ankle-length dresses and claw-hammer coats. At dinner they preferred salt pork to fresh beef, dried meat to fresh fish. They considered coconuts an abomination and were loath to eat bananas.

And yet the missionaries were a brave people, selfless and God-fearing. Their dangerous voyage from the Atlantic had brought them into a very alien land. Many would die from disease and overwork; most would never see their homeland again. Bigoted though they were, the Calvinists committed their lives to the Hawaiian people. They developed the Hawaiian alphabet, rendered Hawaiian into a written language and, of course, translated the Bible. Theirs was the first printing press west of the Rockies. They introduced Western medicine throughout the islands and created such an effective school system that, by the mid-19th century, 80 percent of the Hawaiian population was literate. Unlike almost all the other white people who came to Hawaii, they not only took from the islanders, they also gave.

But to these missionaries, *giving* meant ripping away everything repugnant to God and substituting it with Christianity. They would have to destroy Hawaiian culture in order to save it. Though instructed by their church elders not to meddle in island politics, the missionaries soon realized that heavenly wars had to be fought on earthly battlefields. Politics it would be. After all, wasn't government just another expression of God's bounty?

They allied with Kaahumanu and found it increasingly difficult to separate church from state. Kaahumanu converted to Christianity, while the missionaries became government advisers and helped pass laws protecting the sanctity of the Sabbath. Disgusting practices such as hula dancing were prohibited.

Samuel Ruggles, an island missionary originally from Connecticut, planted the first coffee plants on the Big Island in 1828.

Politics can be a dangerous world for a man of the cloth. The missionaries were soon pitted against other foreigners who were quite willing to let the clerics sing hymns, but were damned opposed to permitting them a voice in government. Hawaii in the 1820s had become a favorite way station for the whaling fleet. As the sandalwood forests were decimated, the island merchants began looking for other industries. By the 1840s, when over 500 ships a year anchored in Hawaiian ports, whaling had become the islands' economic lifeblood.

Like the missionaries, the whalers were Yankees, shipping out from bustling New England ports. But they were a hell of a different cut of Yankee. These were rough, crude, boisterous men who loved rum and music, and thought a lot more of fornicating with island women than saving them. After the churchmen forced the passage of laws prohibiting prostitution, the sailors rioted along the waterfront and fired cannons at the mission homes. When the smoke cleared, the whalers still had their women.

Religion simply could not compete with commerce, and other Westerners were continuously stimulating more business in the islands. By the 1840s, as Hawaii adopted a parliamentary form of government, American and British fortune hunters were replacing missionaries as government advisers. It was a time when anyone, regardless of ability or morality, could travel to the islands and become a political powerhouse literally overnight. A consumptive American, fleeing the mainland for reasons of health, became chief justice of the Hawaiian Supreme Court while still in his twenties. Another lawyer, shadowed from the East Coast by a checkered past, became attorney general two weeks after arriving.

The situation was no different internationally. Hawaii was subject to the whims and terrors of gunboat diplomacy. The archipelago was solitary and exposed, and Western powers were beginning to eye it covetously. In 1843, a maverick British naval officer actually annexed Hawaii to the Crown, but the London government later countermanded his actions. Then, in the early 1850s, the threat of American annexation arose. Restless Californians, fresh from the gold fields and hungry for revolution, plotted unsuccessfully in Honolulu. Even the French periodically sent gunboats in to protect their small Catholic minority.

Finally, the three powers officially stated that they wanted to maintain Hawaii's national integrity. But independence seemed increasingly unlikely. European countries had already begun claiming other Pacific islands, and with the influx of Yankee missionaries and whalers, Hawaii was being steadily drawn into the American orbit.

**THE SUGAR PLANTERS**    There is an old Hawaiian saying that describes the 19th century: The missionaries came to do good, and they did very well. Actually the early evangelists, few of whom profited from their work, lived out only half the maxim. Their sons would give the saying its full meaning.

This second generation, quite willing to sacrifice glory for gain, fit neatly into the commercial society that had rendered their fathers irrelevant. They were shrewd, farsighted young Christians who had grown up in Hawaii and knew both the islands' pitfalls and potentials. They realized that the missionaries had never quite found Hawaii's pulse, and they watched uneasily as whaling became the lifeblood of the islands. Certainly it brought wealth, but whaling was too tenuous—there was always a threat that it might dry up entirely. A one-industry economy would never do; the mission boys wanted more. Agriculture was the obvious answer, and eventually they determined to bind their providence to a plant that grew wild in the islands—sugar cane.

The first sugar plantation, the Koloa Sugar Company, was started on Kauai in 1835, but not until the 1870s did the new industry blossom. By then, the Civil War had wreaked havoc with the whaling fleet, and a devastating winter in the Arctic whaling grounds practically destroyed it. The mission boys, who had prophesied the storm, weathered it quite comfortably. They had already begun fomenting an agricultural revolution.

**THE GREAT MAHELE**   Agriculture, of course, means land, and until the 19th century all Hawaii's acreage was held by chiefs. So in 1848, the mission sons, together with other white entrepreneurs, pushed through the Great Mahele, one of the slickest real estate laws in history. Rationalizing that it would grant chiefs the liberty to sell land to Hawaiian commoners and white men, the mission sons established a Western system of private property.

The Hawaiians, who had shared their chiefs' lands communally for centuries, had absolutely no concept of deeds and leases. What resulted was the old $24-worth-of-beads story. The benevolent Westerners wound up with the land, while the lucky Hawaiians got practically nothing. Large tracts were purchased for cases of whiskey; others went for the cost of a hollow promise. The entire island of Niihau, which is still owned by the same family, sold for $10,000. It was a bloodless coup, staged more than 40 years before the revolution that would topple Hawaii's monarchy. In a sense it made the 1893 uprising anticlimactic. By then

## A LAND GRAB

In the Great Mahele it was decreed that the king, who had formerly owned all the land in Hawaii, surrender most of it. In turn, island chiefs could buy back some of the lands they had once owned as fiefdoms. The rest of the land would be divided into *kuleana*, three-acre plots for farming, to be attainable by *all* Hawaiians. What looked like a more equitable land distribution turned into a disaster for most islanders. Because the concept of land ownership was so foreign to them, few Hawaiians completed the necessary paperwork to receive their *kuleana*. On the other hand, the Great Mahele made possible the purchase of land by foreigners. Westerners, well-schooled in the ways of land ownership, took advantage of the opportunity and seized most privately held land. Within a few decades Westerners owned 80 percent of that land.

Hawaii's future would already be determined: white interlopers would own four times as much land as Hawaiian commoners.

Following the Great Mahele, the mission boys, along with other businessmen, were ready to become sugar planters. The *mana* once again was passing into new hands. Obviously, there was money to be made in cane, a lot of it, and now that they had land, all they needed was labor. The Hawaiians would never do. Cook might have recognized them as industrious, hardworking people, but the sugar planters considered them shiftless. Disease was killing them off anyway, and the Hawaiians who survived seemed to lose the will to live. Many made appointments with death, stating that in a week they would die; seven days later they were dead.

Foreign labor was the only answer. In 1850, the Masters and Servants Act was passed, establishing an immigration board to import plantation workers. Cheap Asian labor would be brought over. It was a crucial decision, one that would ramify forever through Hawaiian history and change the very substance of island society. Eventually these Asian workers transformed Hawaii from a chain of Polynesian islands into one of the world's most varied and dynamic locales, a meeting place of East and West.

Hawaii is the only state in the Union to have been ruled by a monarchy—from Kamehameha the Great in 1758 until Liliuokalani's overthrow in 1893. In all, eight monarchs reigned over the kingdom.

The Chinese were the first to come, arriving in 1852 and soon outnumbering the white population. Initially, with their long pigtails and uncommon habits, the Chinese were a joke around the islands. They were poor people from southern China whose lives were directed by clan loyalty. They built schools and worked hard so that one day they could return to their native villages in glory. They were ambitious, industrious and—ultimately—successful.

*Too* successful, according to the sugar planters, who found it almost impossible to keep the coolies down on the farm. The Chinese came to Hawaii under labor contracts, which forced them to work for five years. After their indentureship, rather than reenlisting as the sugar bosses had planned, the Chinese moved to the city and became merchants. Worse yet, they married Hawaiian women and were assimilated into the society.

These coolies, the planters decided, were too uppity, too ready to fill social roles that were really the business of white men. So in the 1880s, they began importing Portuguese. But the Portuguese thought they already *were* white men, while any self-respecting American or Englishman of the time knew they weren't.

The Portuguese spelled trouble, and in 1886 the sugar planters turned to Japan, with its restricted land mass and burgeoning population. The new immigrants were peasants from Japan's southern islands, raised in an authoritarian, hierarchical culture in which the father was a family dictator and the family was strictly defined by its social status. Like the Chinese, they built schools to protect their heritage and dreamed of returning home someday; but unlike their Asian neighbors, they only married other Japanese. They sent home for "picture brides," worshipped their ancestors and Emperor and paid ultimate loyalty to Japan, not Hawaii.

The Japanese, it soon became evident, were too proud to work long hours for low pay. Plantation conditions were atrocious; workers were housed in hovels and frequently beaten. The Japanese simply did not adapt. Worst of all, they not only bitched, they organized, striking in 1909.

So in 1910, the sugar planters turned to the Philippines for labor. For two decades the Filipinos arrived, seeking their fortunes and leaving their wives behind. They worked not only with sugar cane but also with pineapples, which were becoming a big business in the 20th century. They were a boisterous, fun-loving people, hated by the immigrants who preceded them and used by the whites who hired them. The Filipinos were given the most menial jobs, the worst working conditions and the shoddiest housing. In time, another side of their character began to show—a despondency, a hopeless sense of their own plight, their inability to raise passage money back home. They became the untouchables of Hawaii. (Between 1850 and 1930, 180,000 Japanese, 125,000 Filipinos, 50,000 Chinese and 20,000 Portuguese immigrated to Hawaii.)

**REVOLUTIONARIES AND ROYALISTS** Sugar, by the late 19th century, was king. It had become the center of island economy, the principal fact of life for most islanders. Like the earlier whaling industry, it was drawing Hawaii ever closer to the American sphere. The sugar planters were selling the bulk of their crops in California; having already signed several tariff treaties to protect their American market, they were eager to further strengthen mainland ties. Besides, many sugar planters were second-, third- and fourth-generation descendants of the New England missionaries; they had a natural affinity for the United States.

There was, however, one group that shared neither their love for sugar nor their ties to America. To the Hawaiian people, David Kalakaua was king, and America was the nemesis that had long threatened their independence. The whites might own the land, but the Hawaiians, through their monarch, still held substantial political power. During Kalakaua's rule in the 1870s and 1880s, anticolonialism was rampant.

The sugar planters were growing impatient. Kalakaua was proving very antagonistic; his nationalist drumbeating was becoming louder in their ears. How could the sugar merchants convince the United States to annex Hawaii when all these silly Hawaiian royalists were running around pretending to be the Pacific's answer to the British Isles? They had tolerated this long enough. The Hawaiians were obviously unfit to rule, and the planters soon joined with other businessmen to form a secret revolutionary organization. Backed by a force of well-armed followers, they pushed through the "Bayonet Constitution" of 1887, a self-serving document that weakened the king and strengthened the white landowners. If Hawaii was to remain a monarchy, it would have a Magna Carta.

But Hawaii would not be a monarchy long. Once revolution is in the air, it's often difficult to clear the smoke. By 1893, Kalakaua was dead and his sister, Liliuokalani, had succeeded to the throne. She was an audacious leader, proud of her heritage, quick to defend it and prone to let immediate passions carry her onto dangerous ground. At a time when she should have hung fire, she charged, proclaiming publicly that she would abrogate the new constitution and reestablish a strong monarchy. The revolutionaries had the excuse they needed. They struck in January, seized government buildings and, with four boatloads of American marines and the support of the American minister, secured Honolulu. Liliuokalani surrendered.

It was a highly illegal coup; legitimate government had been stolen from the Hawaiian people. But given an island chain as isolated and vulnerable as Hawaii, the revolutionaries reasoned, how much did it really matter? It would be weeks before word reached Washington of what a few Americans had done without official sanction, then several more months before a new American president, Grover Cleveland, denounced the renegade action. By then the revolutionaries would already be forming a republic.

Not even revolution could rock Hawaii into the modern age. For years, an unstable monarchy had reigned; now an oligarchy composed of the revolution's leaders would rule. Officially, Hawaii was a democracy; in truth, the Chinese and Japanese were hindered from voting, and the Hawaiians were encouraged not to bother. Hawaii, reckoned its new leaders, was simply not ready for democracy. Even when the islands were finally annexed by the United States in 1898 and granted territorial status, they remained a colony.

More than ever before, the sugar planters, alias revolutionaries, held sway. By the early 20th century, they had linked their plantations into a cartel, the Big Five. It was a tidy monopoly composed of five companies that owned not only the sugar and pineapple industries, but the docks, shipping companies and many of the stores, as well. Most of these holdings, happily, were the property of a few interlocking, intermarrying mission families— the Doles, Thurstons, Alexanders, Baldwins, Castles, Cookes and others—who had found heaven right here on earth. They golfed together and dined together, sent their daughters to Wellesley and their sons to Yale. All were proud of their roots, and as blindly paternalistic as their forefathers. It was their destiny to control Hawaii, and they made very certain, by refusing to sell land or provide services, that mainland firms did not gain a foothold in their domain.

What was good for the Big Five was good for Hawaii. Competition was obviously not good for Hawaii. Although the Chinese and Japanese were establishing successful businesses in Honolulu and some Chinese were even growing rich, they posed no immediate threat to the Big Five. And the Hawaiians had never been good at capitalism. By the early 20th century, they had become

## TAKE HEED OF THE NIGHT MARCHERS

Don't be surprised if one night you hear drum beats and chanting and see a radiant glow in the distance. These are the **Night Marchers**, spirits of *alii* and gods of the island, protecting their ancestral grounds. They bob along in a group, roaming the entire coastal area. If you do encounter these specters you are advised to pretend you are dead, with your eyes closed. Never look one in the eye. If you do, it's believed you'll be speared to death.

one of the world's most urbanized groups. But rather than competing with white businessmen in Honolulu, unemployed Hawaiians were forced to live in hovels and packing crates, cooking their poi on stoves fashioned from empty oil cans.

Political competition was also unhealthy. Hawaii was ruled by the Big Five, so naturally it should be run by the Republican Party. After all, the mission families were Republicans. Back on the mainland, the Democrats had always been cool to the sugar planters, and it was a Republican president, William McKinley, who eventually annexed Hawaii. The Republicans, quite simply, were good for business.

Don't get confused—that's not the British Union Jack you see flying but the state flag of Hawaii.

The Big Five set out very deliberately to overwhelm any political opposition. When the Hawaiians created a home-rule party around the turn of the 20th century, the Big Five shrewdly co-opted it by running a beloved descendant of Hawaii's royal family as the Republican candidate. On the plantations they pitted one ethnic group against another to prevent the Asian workers from organizing. Then, when labor unions finally formed, the Big Five attacked them savagely. In 1924, police killed 16 strikers on Kauai. Fourteen years later, in an incident known as the "Hilo massacre," the police wounded 50 picketers.

The Big Five crushed the Democratic Party by intimidation. Polling booths were rigged. It was dangerous to vote Democratic—workers could lose their jobs, and if they were plantation workers, that meant losing their houses as well. Conducting Democratic meetings on the plantations was about as easy as holding a hula dance in an old missionary church. The Democrats went underground.

Those were halcyon days for both the Big Five and the Republican Party. In 1900, only five percent of Hawaii's population was white. The rest was composed of races that rarely benefitted from Republican policies. But for the next several decades, even during the Depression, the Big Five kept the Republicans in power.

While the New Deal swept the mainland, Hawaii clung to its colonial heritage. The islands were still a generation behind the rest of the United States—the Big Five enjoyed it that way. There was nothing like the status quo when you were already in power. Other factors that had long shaped Hawaii's history also played into the hands of the Big Five. The islands' vulnerability, which had always favored the rule of a small elite, permitted the Big Five to establish an awesome cartel. Hawaii's isolation, its distance from the mainland, helped protect their monopoly.

**THE JAPANESE AND THE MODERN WORLD**    All that ended on December 7, 1941. On what would afterwards be known as the "Day of Infamy," a flotilla of six aircraft carriers carrying over 400 planes unleashed a devastating assault on Pearl Harbor. Attacking the Pacific Fleet on a Sunday morning, when most of the American ships were unwisely anchored side by side, the Japanese sank or badly damaged six battleships, three destroyers and several other vessels. Over 2400 Americans were killed.

The Japanese bombers that attacked Pearl Harbor sent shock waves through Hawaii that are still rumbling today. World War II changed all the rules of the game, upsetting the conditions that had determined island history for centuries.

Ironically, no group in Hawaii would feel the shift more thoroughly than the Japanese. On the mainland, Japanese Americans were rounded up and herded into relocation camps. But in Hawaii that was impossible; there were simply too many (160,000—fully one-third of the island's population), and they comprised too large a part of the labor force.

Many were second-generation Japanese, *nisei*, who had been educated in American schools and assimilated into Western society. Unlike their immigrant parents, the *issei*, they felt few ties to Japan. Their loyalties lay with America, and when war broke out they determined to prove it. They joined the U.S. armed forces and formed a regiment, the 442nd, which became the most frequently decorated outfit of the war. The Japanese were heroes, and when the war ended many heroes came home to the United States and ran for political office. Men like Daniel Inouye and Spark Matsunaga began winning elections and would eventually become United States senators.

By the time the 442nd returned to the home front, Hawaii was changing dramatically. The Democrats were coming to power. Leftist labor unions won crucial strikes in 1941 and 1946. Jack Burns, an ex-cop who dressed in tattered clothes and drove around Honolulu in a beat-up car, was creating a new Democratic coalition.

Burns, who would eventually become governor, recognized the potential power of Hawaii's ethnic groups. Money was flowing into the islands—first military expenditures and then tourist dollars, and non-whites were rapidly becoming a new middle class. The Filipinos still constituted a large part of the plantation force, and the Hawaiians remained disenchanted, but the Japanese and Chinese were moving up fast. Together they formed a majority of Hawaii's voters.

Burns organized them, creating a multiracial movement and thrusting the Japanese forward as candidates. By 1954, the Democrats controlled the legislature, with the Japanese filling one out of every two seats in the capital. Then, when Hawaii attained statehood five years later, the voters elected the first Japanese ever to serve in Congress. Today one of the state's U.S. senators and a congressman are Japanese. On every level of government, from municipal to federal, the Japanese predominate. They have arrived. The *mana*, that legendary power coveted by the Hawaiian chiefs and then lost to the sugar barons, has passed once again—to a people who came as immigrant farm-workers and stayed to become the leaders of the 50th state.

The Japanese and the Democrats were on the move, but in the period from World War II until the present day, everything was in motion. Hawaii was in upheaval. Jet travel and a population boom shattered the islands' solitude. While in 1939 about 500 people flew to Hawaii, now about seven million visitors land every year. The military population escalated as Oahu became a key base not only during World War II but throughout the Cold War and the Vietnam War, as well. Hawaii's overall population exploded from about a half-million just after World War II to over one million at the present time.

No longer did the islands lag behind the mainland; they rapidly acquired the dubious quality of modernity. Hawaii became America's 50th state in 1959, Honolulu grew into a bustling highrise city, and hotels and condominiums mushroomed along the beaches of Maui, a neighboring island. Outside investors swallowed up two of the Big Five corporations, and several partners in the old monopoly began conducting most of their business outside Hawaii. Everything became too big and moved too fast for Hawaii to be entirely vulnerable to a small interest group. Now, like the rest of the world, it would be prey to multinational corporations.

By the 1980s, it would also be of significant interest to investors from Japan. In a few short years they succeeded in buying

# Hawaiian Sovereignty

**O**ver the past few decades since the advent of Hawaiian Renaissance, there has been a loud call for Hawaiian sovereignty. A bitter feeling of mistrust is held by many Hawaiians against the U.S. government because the monarchy was overthrown by a band of U.S. merchant renegades. Hawaiians have been outspoken in their demand for righting the wrong that was done to them; however, there is confusion among various Hawaiian groups as to what should be done. Some activists see the sovereignty movement as a struggle to elevate the native Hawaiian people to a higher place *within* the structure of the United States of America. Others believe that Hawaii should be moved *out* of the United States—with the monarchy reinstated, giving Hawaii an independent status. Many think something in between should be done. Some activists demand that reparations should be inclusive of all the people of Hawaii, others think it should include only the native Hawaiian people. It is a movement marked with passion and ambiguity.

up a majority of the state's luxury resorts, including every major beachfront hotel in Waikiki, sending real-estate prices into an upward spiral that did not level off until the early 1990s. During the rest of the decade, the economy was stagnant, with real-estate prices dropping, agriculture declining and tourism leveling off at seven million visitors annually; but by the year 2000 Hawaii was beginning to experience yet another boom.

One element that has not plateaued during the last ten years is the Native Hawaiian movement. Nativist sentiments were spurred in January 1993 by the 100th anniversary of the American overthrow of the Hawaiian monarchy. Over 15,000 people turned out to mark the illegal coup. Later that year, President Clinton signed a statement issued by Congress formally apologizing to the Hawaiian people. In 1994, the United States Navy returned the island of Kahoolawe to the state of Hawaii. Long a rallying symbol for the Native Hawaiian movement, the unoccupied island had been used for decades as a naval bombing target. By 1996, efforts to clean away bomb debris and make the island habitable were well under way, although completion of the clean-up is still years off. Then in 1998, the issue of Hawaii's monarchy arose again when demonstrators marched around the entire island of Oahu and staged rallies to protest the 100th anniversary of the United States' annexation of Hawaii.

Today, numerous perspectives remain to be reconciled, with grassroots movements working to secure a degree of autonomy for Hawaii's native people. The most common goal seems to be a status similar to that accorded the American Indians by the federal government, although there are still those who seek a return to an independent Hawaii, either as a restored monarchy or along democratic lines. Also pending resolution is the distribution of land to Native Hawaiians with documented claims, as well as a financial settlement with the state government. It's a complex situation involving the setting right of injustices of a century past.

## Culture

Hawaii, according to Polynesian legend, was discovered by Hawaii-loa, an adventurous sailor who often disappeared on long fishing trips. On one voyage, urged along by his navigator, Hawaii-loa sailed toward the planet Jupiter. He crossed the "many-colored ocean," passed over the "deep-colored sea," and eventually came upon "flaming Hawaii," a mountainous island chain that spewed smoke and lava.

History is less romantic. The Polynesians who found Hawaii were probably driven from their home islands by war or some similar calamity. They traveled in groups, not as lone rangers, and shared their canoes with dogs, pigs and chickens, with which they planned to stock new lands. Agricultural plants such as coconuts, yams, taro, sugar cane, bananas and breadfruit were also stowed on board.

### HEAD TO THE HILLS

If you hear loud sirens blaring, it's probably the tsunami warning system. More than likely, you're just hearing a test—sirens are tested on the first state work day of each month. After the calamitous tsunami of 1946, the Pacific Tsunami Warning System was created to prevent further catastrophes. However, if it's not one of those testing days, head for high ground—away from the surf. Don't dawdle. These amazing forces of nature can travel up to 500 miles per hour. (The telephone book has evacuation instructions—take a look.)

Most important, they transported their culture, an intricate system of beliefs and practices developed in the South Seas. After undergoing the stresses and demands of pioneer life, this traditional lifestyle was transformed into a new and uniquely Hawaiian culture.

It was based on a caste system that placed the *alii*, or chiefs, at the top and the slaves, *kauwas*, on the bottom. Between these two groups were the priests, *kahunas*, and the common people, or *makaainanas*. The chiefs, much like feudal lords, controlled all the land and collected taxes from the commoners who farmed it.

Life centered around the *kapu*, a complex group of regulations that dictated what was sacred or profane. For example, women were not permitted to eat pork or bananas; commoners had to prostrate themselves in the presence of a chief. These strictures were vital to Hawaiian religion; *kapu* breakers were directly violating the will of the gods and could be executed for their actions. And there were a lot of gods to watch out for, many quite vindictive. The four central gods were *Kane*, the creator; *Lono*, the god of agriculture; *Ku*, the war god; and *Kanaloa*, lord of the underworld. They had been born from the sky father and earth mother, and had in turn created many lesser gods and demigods who controlled various aspects of nature.

It was, in the uncompromising terminology of the West, a stone-age civilization. Though the Hawaiians lacked metal tools, the wheel and a writing system, they managed to include within their inventory of cultural goods everything necessary to sustain a large population on a chain of small islands. They fashioned fish nets from native *olona* fiber, made hooks out of bone, shell and ivory, and raised fish in rock-bound ponds. The men used irrigation in their farming. The women made clothing by pounding mulberry bark into a soft cloth called *tapa*, dyeing elaborate patterns into the fabric. They built peak-roofed thatch huts from native *pili* grass and *hala* leaves. The men fought wars with spears, slings, clubs and daggers. The women used mortars and pestles to pound the roots of the taro plant into poi, the islanders' staple food. Bread, fruit, yams and coconut were other menu standards.

The West labeled these early Hawaiians "noble savages." Actually, they often lacked nobility. The Hawaiians were cannibals who practiced human sacrifice during religious ceremonies and often used human bone to fashion fish hooks. They constantly warred among themselves and would mercilessly pursue a retreating army, murdering as many of the vanquished soldiers as possible.

But they weren't savages either. The Hawaiians developed a rich oral tradition of genealogical chants and created beautiful lilting songs to accompany their hula dancing. Their musicians mastered several instruments including the *ukeke* (a single-stringed device resembling a bow), an *ohe hano ihu* or nose flute, rattles and drums made from gourds, coconut shells or logs. Their craftsmen produced the world's finest featherwork, tying thousands of tiny feathers onto netting to produce golden cloaks and ceremonial helmets. The Hawaiians helped develop the sport of surfing. They also swam, boxed, bowled and devised an intriguing game called *konane*, a cross between checkers and the Japanese game of go. They built networks of trails across lava flows, and created an elemental art form in the images—petroglyphs—that they carved into lava rock along the trails.

They also achieved something far more outstanding than their varied arts and crafts, something that the West, with its awesome knowledge and advanced technology, has never duplicated. The Hawaiians created a balance with nature. They practiced conservation, establishing closed seasons on certain fish species and carefully guarding their plant and animal resources. They led a simple life, without the complexities the outside world would eventually thrust upon them. It was a good life: food was plentiful, people were healthy and the population increased. For a thousand years, the Hawaiians lived in delicate harmony with the elements. It wasn't until the West entered the realm, transforming everything, that the fragile balance was destroyed. But that is another story entirely.

**PEOPLE**

Because of its unique history and isolated geography, Hawaii is truly a cultural melting pot. It's one of the few states in the union in which caucasians are a minority group. Whites, or *haoles* as they're called in the islands, comprise only about 22 percent of Hawaii's 1.2 million population. Japanese constitute 18 percent, Filipinos 13 percent, Hawaiians and part-Hawaiians account for 21 percent, Chinese about 3 percent and other racial groups 23 percent. It's a very vital society, with one fifth of the people born of racially mixed parents.

One trait characterizing many of these people is Hawaii's famous spirit of *aloha*, a genuine friendliness, an openness to strangers, a willingness to give freely. Undoubtedly, it is one of the finest qualities any people has ever demonstrated. *Aloha* originated with the Polynesians and played an important role in ancient Hawaiian civilization.

The aloha spirit is alive and well in the islands, although bad attitudes toward *haoles*, the pejorative term used for whites, are not unknown. All parties, however, seem to understand the crucial role tourism has come to play in Hawaii's economy, which means you're not likely to experience unpleasantness from the locals you'll meet.

**CUISINE**

Nowhere is the influence of Hawaii's melting pot population stronger than in the kitchen. While in the islands, you'll probably eat not only with a fork, but with chopsticks and fingers as well. You'll sample a wonderfully varied cuisine. In addition to standard American fare, hundreds of restaurants serve Hawaiian, Japanese, Chinese, Korean, Portuguese and Filipino dishes. There are also fresh fruits aplenty—pineapples, papayas, mangos, bananas and tangerines—plus native fish such as mahimahi, marlin and snapper.

The mainstay of the traditional Hawaiian diet is poi, a purplish paste pounded from baked or steamed taro tubers. It's pretty bland fare, but it does make a good side dish with *imu*-cooked pork or tripe stew. Poi was considered such a sacred a part of daily Hawaiian life that whenever a bowl of poi was uncovered at a family gathering, it was believed that the spirit of Haloa, the ancestor of the Hawaiian people, was present. That meant that all conflict among family members had to stop.

### SOUNDS FISHY

What are all those strange-sounding fish dishes on the menu? A quick translation will help you when choosing a seafood platter from Hawaiian waters. Firm-textured with a light taste, the most popular fish is *mahimahi*, or dolphin fish (no, it's not one of those amazing creatures that do fancy tricks on the waves); its English equivalent is dorado. *Ahi* is yellowfin tuna and is especially delicious as sashimi (raw) or blackened. *Opakapaka* is pink snapper and is a staple of Pacific Rim cuisine. Other snappers include *uku* (gray snapper), *onaga* (ruby snapper) and *ehu* (red snapper). *Ono* (which means delicious in Hawaiian) is king mackerel, or wahoo, a white fish that lives up to its name.

You should also try *laulau*, a combination of fish, pork and taro leaves wrapped in a *ti* leaf and steamed. And don't neglect to taste baked *ulu* (breadfruit) and *opihi* (limpets). Among the other Hawaiian culinary traditions are *kalua* pig, a shredded pork dish baked in an *imu* (underground oven); *lomilomi* salmon, which is salted and mixed with onions and tomatoes; and chicken *luau*, prepared in taro leaves and coconut milk.

A good way to try all these dishes at one sitting is to attend a luau. I've always found the tourist luaus too commercial, but you might watch the newspapers for one of the special luaus sponsored by civic organizations.

Japanese dishes include sushi, sukiyaki, teriyaki and tempura, plus an island favorite—sashimi, or raw fish. On most any menu, including McDonald's, you'll find *saimin*, a noodle soup filled with meat, vegetables and *kamaboko* (fishcake).

You can count on the Koreans for *kim chi*, a spicy salad of pickled cabbage, and *kalbi*, barbecued beef short ribs prepared with soy and sesame oil. The Portuguese serve up some delicious sweets including *malasadas* (donuts minus the holes) and *pao doce*, or sweet bread. For Filipino fare, I recommend *adobo*, a pork or chicken dish spiced with garlic and vinegar, and *pochero*, a meat entrée cooked with bananas and several vegetables. In addition to a host of dinner dishes, the Chinese have contributed treats such as *manapua* (a steamed bun filled with barbecued pork) and oxtail soup. They also introduced crack seed to the islands. Made from dried and preserved fruit, it provides a treat as sweet as candy.

As the Hawaiians say, *"Hele mai ai."* Come and eat!

**LANGUAGE**    The language common to all Hawaii is English, but because of its diverse cultural heritage, the archipelago also supports several other tongues. Foremost among these are Hawaiian and pidgin. Hawaiian, closely related to other Polynesian languages, is one

## A SLICE OF THE PIE

In ancient Hawaii, each island was divided like a pie into wedge-shaped plots, *ahupuaas*, which extended from the ocean to the mountain peaks. In that way, every chief's domain contained fishing spots, village sites, arable land and everything else necessary for the survival of his subjects.

of the most fluid and melodious languages in the world. It's composed of only twelve letters: five vowels—*a, e, i, o, u* and seven consonants—*h, k, l, m, n, p, w.* The glottal stop ('), when used, counts as a thirteenth letter.

At first glance, the language appears formidable: how the hell do you pronounce *humuhumunukunukuapuaa*? But actually it's quite simple. After you've mastered a few rules of pronunciation, you can take on any word in the language.

The first thing to remember is that every syllable ends with a vowel, and the next to last syllable usually receives the accent.

The next rule to keep in mind is that all the letters in Hawaiian are pronounced. Consonants are pronounced the same as in English (except for the *w*, which is pronounced as a *v* when it introduces the last syllable of a word—as in *ewa* or *awa*. Vowels are pronounced the same as in Spanish: *a* as in *among*, *e* as in *they*, *i* as in *machine*, *o* as in *no* and *u* as in *too*. Hawaiian has four vowel combinations or diphthongs: *au*, pronounced *ow*; *ae* and *ai*, which sound like *eye*; and *ei*, pronounced *ay*. As noted above, the glottal stop (') occasionally provides a thirteenth letter.

By now, you're probably wondering what I could possibly have meant when I said Hawaiian was simple. I think the glossary that follows will simplify everything while helping you pronounce common words and place names. Just go through the list, starting with words like aloha and luau that you already know. After you've practiced pronouncing familiar words, the rules will become second nature; you'll no longer be a *malihini*.

Just when you start to speak with a swagger, cocky about having learned a new language, some young Hawaiian will start talking at you in a tongue that breaks all the rules you've so carefully mastered. That's pidgin. It started in the 19th century as a lingua franca among Hawaii's many races. Pidgin speakers mix English and Hawaiian with several other tongues to produce a spicy creole. It's a fascinating language with its own vocabulary, a unique syntax and a rising inflection that's hard to mimic.

Pidgin is definitely the hip way to talk in Hawaii. A lot of young Hawaiians use it among themselves as a private language. At times they may start talking pidgin to you, acting as though they don't speak English; then if they decide you're okay, they'll break into English. When that happens, you be one *da kine brah*.

So *brah*, I take *da kine* pidgin words, put 'em together with Hawaiian, make one big list. Savvy?

*aa* (ah-**ah**)—a type of rough lava

*ae* (eye)—yes

*aikane* (eye-**kah**-nay)—friend, close companion

*akamai* (ah-kah-**my**)—wise

*alii* (ah-**lee**-ee)—chief

*aloha* (ah-**lo**-ha)—hello; greetings; love

*aole* (ah-**oh**-lay)—no

*auwe* (ow-**way**)—ouch!

*brah* (bra)—friend; brother; bro'

*bumby* (**bum**-bye)—after a while; by and by

*da kine* (da kyne)—whatdyacallit; thingamajig; that way

*dah makule guys* (da mah-**kuh**-lay guys)—senior citizens

*duh uddah time* (duh **uh**-duh time)—once before

*hale* (**hah**-lay)—house

*hana hou* (hah nah hou)—encore

*haole* (**how**-lee)—Caucasian; white person

*hapa* (**hah**-pa)—half

*hapa-haole* (**hah**-pa **how**-lee)—half-Caucasian

*heiau* (hey-**yow**)—temple

*hele on* (**hey**-lay own)—let's go

*hoaloha* (ho-ah-**lo**-ha)—friend

*holo holo* (**ho**-low **ho**-low)—to visit

*howzit?* (hows-it)—how you doing? what's happening?

*huhu* (hoo-hoo)—angry

*hukilau* (**who**-key-lau)—community fishing party

*hula* (**who**-la)—Hawaiian dance

*imu* (**ee**-moo)—underground oven

*ipo* (**ee**-po)—sweetheart

*kahuna* (kah-**who**-nah)—priest; specialist or expert
  in any field

*kai* (kye)—ocean

*kaka-roach* (**kah**-kah roach)—ripoff; theft

*kamaaina* (kah-mah-**eye**-nah)—one born and raised
  in Hawaii; a longtime island resident

*kane* (**kah**-nay)—man

*kapu* (**kah**-poo)—taboo; forbidden

*kaukau* (cow-cow)—food

*keiki* (**kay**-key)—child

*kiawe* (key-**ah**-vay)—mesquite tree

*kokua* (ko-**coo**-ah)—help

*kona winds* (**ko**-nah winds)—winds that blow against
  the trades

*lanai* (lah-**nye**)—porch; also island name

*lauhala* (lau-**hah**-lah) or *hala* (**hah**-lah)—a pandanus tree whose leaves are used in weaving

*lei* (lay)—flower garland

*lolo* (low-low)—stupid

*lomilomi* (**low**-me-**low**-me)—massage; also raw salmon

*luau* (**loo**-ow)—feast

*mahalo* (mah-**hah**-low)—thank you

*mahalo nui loa* (mah-**ha**-low **new**-ee **low**-ah)—thank you very much

*mahu* (**mah**-who)—gay; homosexual

*makai* (mah-**kye**)—toward the sea

*malihini* (mah-lee-**hee**-nee)—newcomer; stranger

*mauka* (**mau**-kah)—toward the mountains

*nani* (**nah**-nee)—beautiful

*ohana* (oh-**hah**-nah)—family

*okole* (oh-**ko**-lay)—rear; ass

*okolemaluna* (oh-ko-lay-mah-**loo**-nah)—a toast: bottoms up!

*ono* (**oh**-no)—tastes good

*pahoehoe* (pah-**hoy**-hoy)—smooth or ropy lava

*pakalolo* (pah-kah-**low**-low)—marijuana

*pakiki head* (pah-**key**-key head)—stubborn

*pali* (**pah**-lee)—cliff

*paniolo* (pah-nee-**oh**-low)—cowboy

*pau* (pow)—finished; done

*pilikia* (pee-lee-**key**-ah)—trouble

*puka* (**poo**-kah)—hole

*pupus* (**poo**-poos)—hors d'oeuvres

*shaka* (**shah**-kah)—great; perfect

*swell head*—"big head"; egotistical

*tapa* (**tah**-pah)—also *kapa*; fabric made from the beaten bark of mulberry trees

*wahine* (wah-**hee**-nay)—woman

*wikiwiki* (**wee**-key-**wee**-key)—quickly; in a hurry

*you get stink ear*—you don't listen well

### NO OOMPAH-PAH! MO' BETTAH BRAH!

Strangely enough, a Prussian bandmaster named Henry Berger had a major influence on contemporary Hawaiian music. Brought over in the 19th century by King Kalakaua to lead the Royal Hawaiian Band, Berger helped Hawaiians make the transition to Western instruments.

**MUSIC**

Music has long been an integral part of Hawaiian life. Most families keep musical instruments in their homes, gathering to play at impromptu living room or backyard jam sessions. Hawaiian folk tunes are passed down from generation to generation. In the earliest days, it was the sound of rhythm instruments and chants that filled the air. Drums were fashioned from hollowed-out gourds, coconut shells or hollowed sections of coconut palm trunks, then covered with sharkskin. Gourds and coconuts, adorned with tapa cloth and feathers, were also filled with shells or pebbles to produce a rattling sound. Other instruments included the nose flute, a piece of bamboo similar to a mouth flute, but played by exhaling through the nostril; the bamboo organ; and *puili*, sections of bamboo split into strips, which were struck rhythmically against the body.

Western musical scales and instruments were introduced by explorers and missionaries. As ancient Hawaiian music involved a radically different musical system, Hawaiians had to completely re-adapt. Actually, western music caught on quickly, and the hymns brought by missionaries fostered a popular musical style—the *himeni*, or Hawaiian church music.

Hawaii has been the birthplace of several different musical instruments and styles. The ukulele, modeled on a Portuguese guitar, quickly became the most popular Hawaiian instrument. Its small size made it easy to carry, and with just four strings, it was simple to play. During the early 1900s, the steel guitar was exported to the mainland. Common in country-and-western music today, it was invented by a young man who experimented by sliding a steel bar across guitar strings.

**LOVELY HULA HANDS**

Each year Hilo is host to the premier hula competition, **The Merrie Monarch Festival**, a week-long cultural event. More than 5000 people file into Edith Kanakaole Tennis Stadium to watch the best of the best perform the ancient art of hula. *Halaus* (hula schools) come from all over to dance, to celebrate, and to honor this tradition. The festival was named for the last king of the Hawaiian Islands, David Kalakaua, who at his coronation revived the once-forbidden dance. Festivities start on Easter Sunday and culminate with the hula competition events—Hula Kahiko on Friday and Hula 'Auana on Saturday. Plan ahead: This a festival not to be missed.

The slack-key style of guitar playing also comes from Hawaii, where it's called *ki ho'alu*. When the guitar was first brought to Hawaii in the 1830s by Mexican and Spanish cowboys, the Hawaiians adapted the instrument to their own special breed of music. In tuning, the six (or twelve) strings are loosened so that they sound a chord when strummed and match the vocal range of the singer. Slack-key is played in a variety of ways, from plucking or slapping the strings to sliding along them. A number of different tunings exist, and many have been passed down orally through families for generations.

During the late 19th century, "*hapa*-haole" songs became the rage. The ukulele was instrumental in contributing to this Hawaiian fad. Written primarily in English with pseudo-Hawaiian themes, songs like "Tiny Bubbles" and "Lovely Hula Hands" were later introduced to the world via Hollywood.

The Hawaiian craze continued on the mainland with radio and television shows such as "Hawaii Calls" and "The Harry Owens Show." In the 1950s, little mainland girls donned plastic hula skirts and danced along with Hilo Hattie and Ray Kinney.

It was not until the 1970s that both the hula and music of old Hawaii made a comeback. Groups such as the Sons of Hawaii and the Makaha Sons of Niihau, along with Auntie Genoa Keawe and the late Gabby Pahinui, became popular. Before long, a new form of Hawaiian music was being heard, a combination of ancient chants and contemporary sounds, performed by such islanders as Henry Kapono, Kalapana, Olomana, the Beamer Brothers, the Peter Moon Band and the Brothers Cazimero.

Today many of these groups, along with other notables such as the Kaau Crater Boys, Brother Noland, Willie K., Butch Helemano and Obrien Eselu, bring both innovation to the Hawaiian music scene and contribute to the preservation of an ancient tradition. The trend continues with hybrid infusions of reggae and rock, while performers like Kealii Reichel and groups like Kapena maintain the soft-edged sounds so well-suited to the islands.

Another entire category of music was established in Hawaii: dubbed "Jawaiian," the sound incorporates Jamaican reggae and contemporary Hawaiian music, and is especially popular among the state's younger population. In addition, now-deceased masters of Hawaiian song like Gabby Pahinui and Israel Kamakawiwoole have gained renewed popularity and respect for the links they created between old and contemporary Hawaiian music.

For both classic and contemporary Hawaiian music, tune your radio dial to KONG (93.5 FM), KSRF (95.9 FM), KUAI (720 AM) and KTOH (99.9 FM).

**HULA**

Along with palm trees, the hula—swaying hips, grass skirts, colorful leis—is linked forever in people's minds with the Hawaiian Islands. This Western idea of hula is very different from what the dance has traditionally meant to native Hawaiians.

Hula is an old dance form, its origin shrouded in mystery. The ancient hula, *hula kahiko*, was more concerned with religion and spirituality than entertainment. Originally performed only by men, it was used in rituals to communicate with a deity—a connection to nature and the gods. Accompanied by drums and chants, *hula kahiko* expressed the islands' culture, mythology and history in hand and body movements. It later evolved from a strictly religious rite to a method of communicating stories and legends. Over the years, women were allowed to study the rituals and eventually became the primary dancers.

When Westerners arrived, the *hula kahiko* began another transformation. Explorers and sailors were more interested in its erotic element, ignoring the cultural significance. Missionaries simply found it scandalous and set out to destroy the tradition. They dressed Hawaiians in Western garb and outlawed the *hula kahiko*.

The hula tradition was resurrected by King David Kalakaua. Known by the moniker "Merrie Monarch," Kalakaua loved music and dance. For his coronation in 1883, he called together the kingdom's best dancers to perform the chants and hulas once again. He was also instrumental in the development of the contemporary hula, the *hula auwana*, which added new steps and movements and was accompanied by ukuleles and guitars rather than drums.

By the 1920s, modern hula had been popularized by Hollywood, westernized and introduced as kitschy tropicana. Real grass skirts gave way to cellophane versions, plastic leis replaced fragrant island garlands, and exaggerated gyrations supplanted the hypnotic movements of the traditional dance.

Fortunately, with the resurgence of Hawaiian pride in recent decades, Polynesian culture has been reclaimed and *hula kahiko* and traditional chants have made a welcome comeback.

# FOUR

# Kailua-Kona Area

At the center of the tourist scene on the Kona Coast is the contemporary town of Kailua or Kailua-Kona—a reference to the district in which it's located. Here, extending for eight miles along Alii Drive from the King Kamehameha Hotel to Keauhou Bay, is a string of hotels, restaurants, condominiums and shopping malls.

Like a little Waikiki, Kailua-Kona is the commercial focus for this side of the island. In part, Kailua has been able to maintain an appealing sense of place because residential and commercial expansion has been directed to the periphery of town, where everything from Costco to Home Depot are located. While sprawling suburban communities dot the lower slopes of Hualalai, the 8000-foot volcanic mountain, which backdrops and defines the dry, sunny climate that prevails along the island's west-facing leeward coast, Kailua-Kona still is at the heart of things.

**SIGHTS**

Despite the tinsel and tourist trappings, this old fishing village and former haunt of Hawaiian royalty still retains some of its charm. If you tour **Kailua wharf** around 4 p.m., the fishing boats may be hauling freshly caught marlin onto the docks. Some of the finest marlin grounds in the world lie off this shoreline and the region is renowned for other deep-sea fish. The wharf itself is a departure point not only for fishing charters but for snorkeling tours and glass-bottom boat cruises as well. It's also a favorite place for viewing Kona's fabled sunsets. ~ Alii Drive.

On the grounds of the nearby King Kamehameha's Kona Beach Hotel rests **Ahuena Heiau**, a culturally significant site that has been reconstructed. Ahuena was once part of Kamakahonu ("the eye of the turtle"), Kamehameha's royal compound. It was here that the exalted Kamehameha retired after uniting Hawaii's islands as a single kingdom. Menacing *kii* (sacred wooden figures) stand guard here, while offerings wrapped in *ti* leaves are still left by the faithful. Unfortunately, a hotel luau facility was built immediately next to the site. Tours of the hotel grounds are offered Monday through Friday at 1:30 p.m. ~ 75-5660 Palani Road; 808-329-2911, fax 808-329-4602; www.konabeachhotel. com, e-mail reservations@hthcorp.com.

**Hulihee Palace,** a small but elegant estate built in 1838, sits on Alii Drive in the middle of town. Today it's a museum housing royal Hawaiian relics. This two-story estate was built by the brother-in-law of Kamehameha I and later used by King Kalakaua as a summer palace during the 1880s. Of particular interest are the redwood pillars in the Entry Hall, a souvenir of King Kalakaua's from a trip to California. In the Kuhio Room, a stunning *koa* dining table that belonged to the Kalakaua family dominates. And of interest in the Kuakini Room is a reproduction of a Hawaiian sled, a *papa holua* (see "Extreme Sport of Another Era" below). A pair of *kahili*, Royal Standards, in the Victorian-furnished second-floor Sitting Room adds an eclectic touch, while a cradle and large round container, an *umeke*, made from the trunk of a coconut tree and used as a hat box are attention-getters in Princess Ruth's bedroom. The Kawanakoa Room is dominated by a large *koa* wardrobe commissioned by King Kalakaua. Admission. ~ 75-5718 Alii Drive; 808-329-1877, fax 808-329-1321; www.huliheepalace.org, e-mail hulihee@ilhawaii.net.

**Mokuaikaua Church,** directly across the street, is the oldest church in the islands. The first missionaries anchored offshore in

### EXTREME SPORT OF ANOTHER ERA

Ancient Hawaiians had their own form of Extreme Sports: *holua*, a precursor to the luge. Races were held on tracks consisting of layers of rock, soil and *ti* leaves and grass. *Papas*, or sleds, were constructed of two 17-foot-long runners tapered from about two inches in the front to six inches in the back, with matting affixed on cross bars to provide a platform. Winners were determined by who traveled the farthest, assuming they survived the great speeds! (A reproduction of the sled is found at the Hulihee Palace in the Kuakini Room.)

1820 after sailing over 18,000 miles around Cape Horn from Boston. By 1836, with most of the Hawaiians converted to Protestant Christianity, the missionaries dedicated this imposing lava-and-coral structure. By the way, that churchyard tree with the weird salami-shaped fruit is a sausage tree from West Africa.

Contrasting with these venerable sites is **Atlantis Adventures**, an impressive 80-ton submarine. Diving to depths of 120 feet, this 48-passenger sub explores tropical reefs. During the hour-long voyage, passengers view the underwater world through large viewing ports. Admission. ~ 808-329-6626, 800-548-6262, fax 808-329-1153; www.atlantisadventures.com.

Almost everything in Kailua sits astride Alii Drive, the waterfront street that extends south from town to Keauhou Bay. Several miles from Kailua, this road passes **Disappearing Sands Beach** (or Magic Sands Beach). The lovely white sand here is often washed away by heavy winter surf and then redeposited when the big waves subside.

Farther along, on the rocky shore of Kahaluu Bay, is **St. Peter's Catholic Church**. This stark blue-and-white clapboard chapel, also known as the "Little Blue Church" precariously perched on a lava foundation, is reputedly the world's second-smallest church and was established in 1889.

Located just across the bay are several interesting historical sites: two *heiaus* and the **King's Pool**. You can continue on to Keauhou Bay, where a monument marks the **Birthplace of Kamehameha III**.

The sea's resources are put to potentially constructive use at the **Natural Energy Laboratory of Hawaii**, where several aquaculture and energy-producing projects are underway. Located adjacent to one of the steepest offshore slopes in the islands, it provides a one-of-a-kind technological setting for ocean-related research. Public visits include a view of deep and surface seawater intake sites and an exhibit area. A public exhibit area is open weekdays from 8 a.m. to 4 p.m. Two-hour-long tours of the site, accessed from Route 19 on a road Kailua-side of Kona International Airport, are offered 10 a.m. on Wednesday and Thursday for $3. Reservations are required. ~ 808-329-7341; www.nelha.org.

You can pay your respects to the crew of the space shuttle *Challenger* at the **Astronaut Ellison S. Onizuka Space Center**. Located eight miles north of Kailua at Kona International Airport, this interactive learning center is a tribute to Onizuka, who lived in Hawaii, and the other astronauts who died in the 1986 tragedy. Videos and interactive displays trace the astronauts' lives and the development of the space program. Admission. ~ 808-329-3441, fax 808-326-9751; www.onizukaspacecenter.org.

**LODGING**  **Patey's Place in Paradise,** a hostel in the center of Kailua, is small, clean and—remarkable for this area—conveniently priced. There are dormitory-style accommodations for 20 people as well as two private rooms that sleep two and another two that sleep four. Kitchen facilities, internet access, a television room and airport pickup are provided. ~ 75-195 Ala Ona Ona Street; 808-326-7018, 800-972-7408, fax 808-326-7640; www.hawaiian-hostels.com, e-mail ipatey@gte.net. BUDGET.

**Kona Seaside Hotel,** a sprawling 225-room complex, resides in the heart of Kailua. Located across the street from the ocean, this multi-faceted facility features the Tower Wing; the Garden Wing, where the rooms come with mini-kitchenettes; and the Pool Wing, where the rooms are smaller and less fashionable but are conveniently placed around one of the hotel's two swimming pools. While the more expensive rooms add lanais and wall-to-wall carpeting, all the accommodations are tastefully done. A restaurant is adjacent. ~ 75-5646 Palani Road; 808-329-2455, 800-560-5558, fax 808-329-6157; www.sand-seaside.com. DELUXE.

**Kona Bay Hotel** is part of the old Kona Inn, the rest of which fell to Kailua developers who have perversely transformed it into yet another shopping mall. What remains is a four-story semi-circular structure with a pool, bar, restaurant and lounge in the center. The rooms are large, tastefully furnished and quiet. Some have lava walls that provide a pleasant backdrop plus excellent soundproofing. The staff is friendly, and the atmosphere is very appealing. I once spent a relaxing month here and highly recommend the place. ~ 75-5739 Alii Drive; 808-329-1393, 800-367-5102, fax 808-935-7903; www.unclebilly.com/kb.html, e-mail resv@unclebilly.com. MODERATE.

Overlooking dramatic Kailua Bay is the full-service **Royal Kona Resort.** Easily accessible to Kailua-Kona, this 452-room hotel is set in three open-air buildings on 11 acres, with a majority of the guest rooms sporting ocean views. All guest rooms offer air conditioning, cable television, refrigerator, and private lanai.

There's a sheltered sandy beach and saltwater lagoon ideal for swimming and snorkeling. For those not interested in saltwater, there's a lovely split-level oceanfront pool. Two restaurants are convenient for those who don't want to make the short walk into town. ~ 75-5852 Alii Drive; 800-919-8333, fax 808-329-7230; www.rkona.com, e-mail rkr@dps.net. MODERATE TO DELUXE.

**Kona Tiki Hotel**, a mile down the road, is a quaint hotel neatly situated on the ocean. The rooms are bright and clean. Despite the contrasting decorative themes and the noise from Alii Drive, I recommend this 15-unit establishment for its oceanview lanais, oceanfront pool, barbecue, garden and complimentary

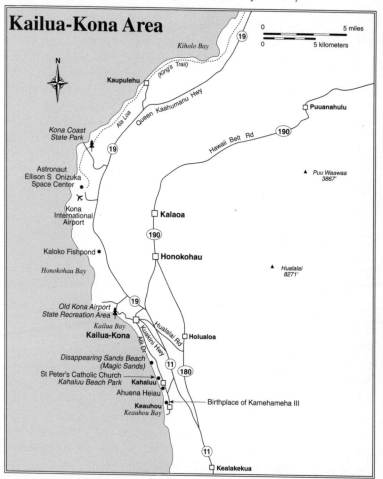

**Kailua-Kona Area**

continental breakfast. Some of the rooms are equipped with mini-kitchenettes (sink, refrigerator and two-burner stove crowded into one unit). ~ 75-5968 Alii Drive; 808-329-1425, fax 808-327-9402. BUDGET TO MODERATE.

**Kona Islander Inn** occupies several three-story buildings spread across a lush swath of land. Set between Alii Drive and Route 11 on Kailua's outskirts, this hotel has a large lobby and an oval pool flanked by MacArthur palms. All rooms have small lanais, cable televisions, microwaves, refrigerators, carpets and air conditioning. Tastefully appointed, but lacking a good ocean view. ~ 75-5776 Kuakini Highway; 808-329-3333, 800-622-5348, fax 808-326-4137; www.konahawaii.com, e-mail kona hawaii@hotmail.com. BUDGET TO MODERATE.

**Kona White Sands Apartment Hotel**, located just across the street from Disappearing Sands Beach (the nicest beach along Alii Drive), is a ten-unit hotel of one-bedroom apartments. Each comes with a kitchenette and ceiling fans. The cinderblock and plasterboard walls are pretty plain, but who needs fancy interior decoration with that knockout ocean view? Rooms are cross-ventilated, and the cooling breeze will probably bring along noise from cars and sun revelers. That's the extra price for living this close to the Kona Coast. Many people are willing to pay it, so you'll have to reserve a room far in advance. ~ 77-6467 Alii Drive. For reservations here and at Kona Islander Inn, contact the Hawaii Resorts Management, 75-5776 Kuakini Highway, Suite 105-C, Kailua-Kona, HI 96740; 808-329-9393, 800-553-5035, fax 808-326-4137; www.konahawaii.com. MODERATE.

Anchoring one end of Kailua Bay is the town's most historic hotel. The **King Kamehameha Kona Beach Hotel** is deserving of note. The lobby alone is worth the price of admission: It's a wood-paneled affair along which you can trace the history of ancient Hawaii. For its guests, the "King Kam" has a pool, tennis courts and jacuzzi, plus a host of other amenities ranging from an activities desk to room service. The rooms themselves are quite spacious, fashionably decorated and equipped with positively everything. You will find plush carpeting, color televisions, air conditioning, refrigerators and lanais with views of the ocean or mountains. ~ 75-5660 Palani Road; 808-329-2911, 800-367-2111, fax 808-329-4602; www.konabeachhotel.com, e-mail hth corp@worldnet.att.net. MODERATE TO DELUXE.

Of course, when money is no object the place to stay is **Kona** ◄ *HIDDEN*
**Village Resort**, a very plush, private colony located 12 miles
north of Kailua. Favored by celebrities seeking escape from auto-
graph hounds and aggressive agents, this regal retreat is set along
a white-sand cove in an ancient Hawaiian fishing village. The individual guest cottages are thatched-roof structures (*hales*), var-
iously designed to represent the traditional houses of Hawaiian,
Tahitian, Fijian, Samoan and other Polynesian groups. There are
no TVs, telephones, radios, clocks or air conditioners in the
rooms, but you will find serenity, solitude and a well-heeled version of hidden Hawaii, not to mention a fitness center, tennis
courts, sailboats, outrigger canoes and glass-bottom excursion
boats. Prices are in the stratosphere and are based on the
American plan. Closed the first week of December. ~ P.O. Box
1299, Kaupulehu-Kona, HI 96745; 808-325-5555, 800-367-

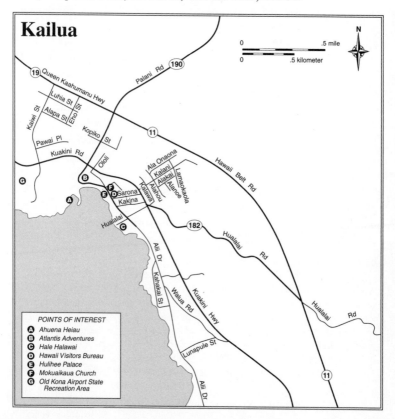

**Kailua**

0 ___ .5 mile
0 ___ .5 kilometer
N

POINTS OF INTEREST
Ⓐ Ahuena Heiau
Ⓑ Atlantis Adventures
Ⓒ Hale Halawai
Ⓓ Hawaii Visitors Bureau
Ⓔ Hulihee Palace
Ⓕ Mokuaikaua Church
Ⓖ Old Kona Airport State
   Recreation Area

5290, fax 808-325-5124; www.konavillage.com, e-mail kvr@
aloha.net. ULTRA-DELUXE.

*Shibui* best describes the **Four Seasons Resort Hualalai at
Historic Kaupulehu**. With 243 understated yet elegant bungalow-
style guest rooms as well as 31 suites (each with a private lanai
and oceanview), this resort offers a bit of heaven here on earth.
Of course, heaven is a bit pricey. But outdoor enthusiasts will be
content with the four oceanfront pools—including a seawater
pool made for snorkelers—the Sports Club and Spa with its lap
pool, eight tennis courts and rock-climbing wall and the PGA
championship golf course designed by Jack Nicklaus. Kids will
like the game room and parents will appreciate the "Kids for all
Seasons Program." (Children under 18 can share their parents'
room at no extra charge.) There are two restaurants for dining.
What will make it a "Hidden Hawaii" experience is a visit to the
Hawaiian cultural center that extends the *Kaupulehu* traditions
of Hawaii to the visitor. They offer such diverse classes as
ukulele, the Hawaiian language, *lauhala* weaving and Hawaiian
navigation. ~ 100 Kaupulehu Drive, Kaupulehu-Kona; 808-325-
8000, fax 808-325-8200; www.fourseasons.com, e-mail huala
lai.reservations@fourseasons.com. ULTRA-DELUXE.

On ten acres of land just five miles from Kailua-Kona is the
comfortable **Silver Oaks Ranch**. Guests can bed down in the
"Ranch House Cottage," the "Ranch View Cottage" and the
"Garden Cottage," or in one of the two rooms in the main house.
Complimentary breakfast is included in the "Garden Cottage"
and for guests staying in the main house. Best of all for families,
children are welcome here—they even provide babysitting if you

**AUTHOR FAVORITE**

**OHANA Keauhou Beach Resort** is a true sleeper. A large, blocky, seven-
story hotel from the outside, it hardly seems like it could possess the
Hawaiian spirit. But the beautifully landscaped grounds include an ancient
*heiau* and other archaeological sites, and the waterfront boasts magnificent
tidepools that extend for acres. The airy Hawaiian-style lobby overlooks
an oceanfront swimming pool, two restaurants and a lounge. Spacious
guest rooms look out over the ocean or gardens. ~ 78-6740 Alii Drive;
808-322-3441, 877-532-8468, fax 808-322-3117; www.ohanahotels.
com, e-mail kbr@ohanahotels.com. MODERATE TO ULTRA-DELUXE.

want some time alone. A pool and hot tub are situated on the property as well. Three-night minimum stay. ~ 73-4570 Mamalahoa Highway; 808-325-2000, 877-325-2300, fax 808-325-2200; www.silveroaksranch.com, e-mail rsvp@silveroaksranch.com. MODERATE TO DELUXE.

Several bed-and-breakfasts in the Kailua area cater to gays. **Puukala Lodge** offers spacious accommodations, including three suites adorned in light and lively Hawaiian decor. Sitting 1500 feet above the coast, coastal views range 180 degrees. The grounds are landscaped with tropical gardens. ~ P.O. Box 2967, Kailua-Kona, HI 96745; 808-325-1729, 888-325-1729; www.puukala-lodge.com, e-mail puukala1@aol.com. MODERATE.

**Hale Kipa 'O Pele** offers two in-house rooms and an adjoining bungalow in a plantation-style home with coastal views. A garden jacuzzi is surrounded by lush vegetation. Each suite has a lanai and is decorated with Hawaiian motifs. A *koi* pond provides this B & B with a distinctive feel. ~ P.O. Box 5252, Kailua-Kona, HI 96740; 808-329-8676, 800-528-2456; www.gaystay hawaii.com, e-mail halekipa@gte.net. MODERATE.

**CONDOS**

Condo complexes come in all sizes, and perhaps the smallest is **Kona Mansions V.** Actually, only one "mansion" is available to rent these days—an individual home in a residential area several blocks up the hill from the shoreline. The single-level, one-bedroom/one-bath unit sleeps four and offers a sweeping ocean view from the patio around the small outdoor pool. Amenities include a full kitchen, an outdoor gas barbecue and laundry facilities—not to mention plenty of privacy. ~ Wailua Road and Kuakini Highway. Book through A1 Vacations, 808-329-2374, 800-854-8843, fax 808-737-8733. MODERATE TO DELUXE.

The **Hale Kona Kai** has 25 rental units in a single three-story, L-shaped building right on the ocean. All are one-bedroom suites, individually furnished, and many are also individually rented by their owners over the internet. Located on a side street with nothing but a V-shaped pool and a seawall between the building and the sea, it's the only truly waterfront condo within walking distance of Kailua-Kona's town center. Though every unit has an ocean view from its large lanai, the corner units are the most spectacular. ~ 75-5870 Kahakai Road; 800-421-3696, fax 808-329-2155; e-mail hkk@kona.net. MODERATE TO DELUXE.

Budget accommodations in Kailua-Kona? Well, almost. Centrally located in town, the **Kona Islander Inn Resort** was one of the first condominium complexes built in the area back in the 1960s, and these days it's probably the most affordable. The 145 refurbished, air-conditioned rooms are studio apartments, each with a single large living/sleeping room, a kitchenette and a lanai. The complex consists of three buildings, each three stories tall, linked by pathways that lead among palm trees and gardens. The complex has a swimming pool and a hot tub, and there's a white-sand beach directly across the highway. ~ 75-5776 Kuakini Highway; 808-329-3333, 800-535-0085, fax 808-326-4137; www.konahawaii.com. MODERATE.

One-bedroom, two-bath apartments at **Kona Alii** run from $119 double (and from $99 during the off-season, April 1 to December 15). This seven-story building is just across the street from the ocean. ~ 75-5782 Alii Drive; book through Hawaii Resorts Management, 75-5776 Kuakini Highway, Suite 105-C, Kailua-Kona; 808-329-9393, 800-553-5035, fax 808-326-4137; www.konahawaii.com.

Another popular condo complex, the 65-unit **Kona Billfisher** has 65 air-conditioned one-bedroom suites with full kitchens. While the decor is individualized within specific guidelines, each guest unit has a king-size bed in the bedroom and a fold-out sofa in the living room. Some have ocean views, while others have lanais looking out toward the volcano that looms over the area. The town center of Kailua-Kona is within walking distance. ~ 75-5841 Alii Drive; 808-329-2401, 800-622-5348, fax 808-329-2401. MODERATE TO DELUXE.

About one mile south of Kailua is the **Sea Village**, which offers one-bedroom garden-view units starting at $110 single or double; two bedrooms, two baths are $165 for one to four people. There's a swimming pool and tennis courts. Oceanfront, but no beach. ~ 75-6002 Alii Drive; book through Sun Quest Vacations, 808-329-6488, 800-367-5168; www.sunquest-hawaii.com, e-mail sqvac@sunquest-hawaii.com.

**Casa de Emdeko Resort** offers air conditioned one- and two-bedroom/two-bath condominium rentals in a three-story, white-washed, red-roofed building. Each individualized guest unit has a queen-size bed in each bedroom, a sofa bed in the living room, and a full kitchen. Private lanais look out over the ocean or attractive gardens and palms surrounding the freshwater swimming pool. There is also a unique saltwater pool on the ocean side, and although there's no beach—the nearest sandy shoreline is Magic Beach, two miles away—a sandy manmade "beach" area surrounds the saltwater pool. The main excitement here happens daily at sunset, when guests convene to watch the staff feed the moray eels that gather in the ocean just beyond the pool area. The resort has a deli-market on the premises. Although there is no minimum stay, rates are significantly lower if you stay three days or longer. ~ 75-6082 Alii Drive; 808-331-8300, 800-845-7559, fax 808-331-3293. MODERATE TO DELUXE.

Representative of many reasonable-rate condominium complexes along this stretch of coast, **Alii Villas** is a group of rather boxy three-story buildings. Many of the 126 units are owned and occupied by full- or part-time residents and are not on the rental market. Others are rented directly by the owners or through various condominium rental agencies. All are one- or two-bedroom suites designed to sleep up to ten people, and all have kitchens and lanais with garden or ocean views. When making reservations, however, be sure to ask to see photos of the individual unit you're considering before you commit. Since the buildings are situated perpendicular to the shoreline, some "ocean views" are sandwiched between them at the far end of the off-street parking area. Amenities include laundry facilities and a circular swimming pool. ~ 75-6016 Alii Drive; 808-329-1288, 800-326-4751. MODERATE TO DELUXE.

**Kona Riviera Villa** is a relatively small condo on a lava-rock beach outside Kailua. It's attractively landscaped, has a pool and rents one-bedroom units for $95 to $115 ($85 to $105 from April 15 to December 14). Three-day minimum. ~ 75-6124 Alii

---

### A WALK ON THE HISTORIC SIDE

The **Kona Historical Society** will give you a taste of historic Kailua-Kona, including an informative visit to Hulihee Palace. The 75-minute tour starts with the reign of King Umi in the 15th century and leads to the present day with plenty of stops in between. This tour is recipient of the Historic Hawaii Foundation's Preservation Award and is offered weekday at 9 a.m. and 11 a.m. Twenty-four-hour advance reservations are required. Fee. ~ 808-323-3222; www.konahistorical.org.

Drive; 808-329-1996. Reserve through Knutson and Associates, 75-6082 Alii Drive, Suite 8, Kailua-Kona; 800-800-6202, fax 808-326-2178; www.konahawaiirentals.com, e-mail knutson@aloha.net.

Located on Banyans Beach in Kona, **Marc Kona Bali Kai** is one of Kailua-Kona's only oceanfront accommodations. Suites are roomy and nicely appointed, and include studios and one- and two-bedroom suites, all with fully equipped kitchens and ceiling fans. Other amenities include laundry facilities, a convenience store, an activities desk, and barbecue areas and limited maid service. There's a courtyard swimming pool and jacuzzi. Rates range from $195 for a mountain studio to $345 for an oceanfront two-bedroom that sleeps 6. ~ 76-6246 Alii Drive; 808-329-9381, fax 808-326-6056; www.marcresorts.com, e-mail kbkai@hawaii.rr.com. DELUXE TO ULTRA-DELUXE.

**Kona Magic Sands** has a studio apartment renting for $75 without air conditioning, $95 with, year-round, single or double. It's located on the ocean, next to Disappearing Sands Beach. ~ 77-6452 Alii Drive. Book through Hawaii Resorts Management, 75-5776 Kuakini Highway, Suite 105-C, Kailua-Kona; 808-329-9393, 800-553-5035, fax 808-326-4137; www. konahawaii.com.

**Aston Kona By The Sea** is a large, trimly landscaped complex on a lava-rock beach. The suites are one- and two-bedroom; all have two baths and a lanai; there's a pool and jacuzzi. Rates start at $235. ~ 75-6106 Alii Drive; 808-327-2300, 800-321-2558, fax 808-327-2333; www.aston-hotels.com.

## CHOCOHOLICS BEWARE

The Big Island is the only place in the United States where cacao beans, the basic ingredient of chocolate, are grown, and the **Original Hawaiian Chocolate Factory** is the only operation on the island that grows, harvests, processes and packages all-Hawaiian chocolate. The husband-and-wife operation above Kaeuhou may be the world's smallest chocolate maker. You'll see their product in stores all over the island; if you want to discover where it comes from, call Bob Cooper and arrange a two-hour tour on which you'll see how the cacao trees grow and bear fruit, how the pods are shucked and the beans are fermented and sun-dried, and how they are transformed into chocolate. The Coopers conduct factory tours about five times a week by reservation only. ~ For reservations and directions, call **808-322-2626**.

Kona Coast Shopping Center houses several inexpensive short-order joints. **Betty's Chinese Kitchen** (808-329-3770) serves tasty, nutritious, inexpensive meals at its cafeteria-style emporium. **Kamuela Deli** (808-334-0017) is a plate-lunch place next door. You can dine on hot and cold sandwiches as well as an array of full meals. Of special interest are *shoyu* chicken and pork with cabbage plates, not to mention the fried rice with Spam. ~ 74-5588 Palani Road. BUDGET.

◄ HIDDEN

A local breakfast favorite, **Buns in the Sun** serves bagels, donuts and pastries accompanied by full-flavored Kona coffee. The little blue-and-white bakery-deli also offers a full line of fresh-made bread, cakes and other baked goods. There's a soup, salad and sandwich lunch menu, and they'll pack you a box lunch for your beach picnic or driving excursion. ~ Lanihau Center, 75-5595 Palani Road; 808-326-2774. BUDGET.

The folks behind the front desk at your hotel are likely to tell you that **Pot Belli Deli** is the best deli on the Big Island. With a full menu of heaping sandwiches on fresh rolls, hot lunch specials that change daily, plus a case filled with picnic fixings and shelves of gourmet delicacies, it just may be. ~ Pawai Place at Kaiwi Street; 808-329-9454. BUDGET.

If this doesn't intrigue you, head downhill to the North Kona Shopping Center. There you'll find the **Sushi Shop**, a take-out window with a patio and tables. Closed Sunday. ~ Kuakini Highway and Kalani Road; 808-987-8490. BUDGET.

In the King Kamehameha Mall, between the King Kamehameha Hotel and the Kona Industrial Area, is **Ocean Seafood Chinese Restaurant**. In traditional Chinese-restaurant style, the menu is divided into 13 sections ("A" through "M"), with about 15 dishes for each category. So I won't even begin to tell you what they have. Suffice it to say that it's all there. ~ 75-5626 Kuakini Highway; 808-329-3055. BUDGET TO MODERATE.

For Mexican food along Alii Drive, you have two choices. At **Tres Hombres Beach Grill** you'll get a good, filling Mexican meal in a comfortable restaurant. ~ Alii Drive and Walua Road; 808-329-2173, fax 808-331-2850. BUDGET. If you're seeking a tropical drink and a tropical sunset over the water, then **Pancho & Lefty's Cantina & Restaurante** is the place. Similar food, different ambience. ~ 75-5719 Alii Drive; 808-326-2171. MODERATE TO DELUXE.

**The Internet Café** is the place to head if you need a high-tech link-up with a quick snack. Open from 9 a.m. to 9:30 p.m. ~ 75-5699 Alii Drive; 808-331-1626. BUDGET.

**Sibu Café** prepares Indonesian and Southeast Asian dishes daily for lunch and dinner. Among the tangy favorites at this outdoor café are beef *saté*, tofu and vegetable stir-fry and Balinese chicken (which is marinated, cooked over an open flame, then served with peanut sauce). ~ Banyan Court, Alii Drive; 808-329-1112, fax 808-328-7308. MODERATE.

The **Oceanview Inn**, a large, informal dining room opposite Kailua Bay, has a voluminous menu. Chinese, American, Hawaiian, fresh fish and meat dishes, served all day, comprise only part of the selection. There's also a complete breakfast menu. This is the place to go to for local color. Closed Monday. ~ Alii Drive; 808-329-9998. BUDGET TO MODERATE.

**Basil's Restaurant**, a hole-in-the-wall bistro punched into a storefront along Alii Drive, has reasonably priced Italian food. The menu is pretty standard as is the red-checkered oilcloth interior, but portions are large and tasty. ~ 75-5707 Alii Drive; 808-326-7836. BUDGET TO MODERATE.

You not only can dine inexpensively at **Aki's Cafe**, you can dine under an umbrella overlooking the water. They may not live up to their motto of "fine Japanese and American food," but the cuisine is passable. They offer hamburgers, fish and chips and spaghetti on the American side of the menu, with sushi, stir-fry and curry dishes on the other. For dinner, there's steak, chicken teriyaki and fish *misoyaki*. ~ 75-5699 Alii Drive; 808-329-0090, fax 808-334-0318. BUDGET.

If you care for Mediterranean, **Cassandra's Greek Tavern** has tables out on the patio as well as in a cozy little dining room. Souvlaki, kebabs, moussaka and dolmas dominate the menu, but they also prepare steak and seafood dishes. ~ 75-5669 Alii Drive; 808-334-1066. MODERATE TO DELUXE.

Look for huge portions at small prices at **Manna Korean BBQ**, the Big Island location of a restaurant chain that has been expanding around the Pacific Rim—from Singapore to Los Angeles—and is well worth discovering. This bright, cheerful buffet-style eatery features heaping plates of thin-sliced beef, *kalbi* ribs, chicken *katsu*, pork or *mandoo* (Korean wonton) with rice and four vegetable side dishes—or skip the main course, opt for a noodle entrée with the side dishes, and you're in vegetarian heaven. ~ Crossroads Shopping Center, 75-1027 Henry Street #104; 808-334-0880. BUDGET.

**Suki's**, in a no-frills setting, features gourmet deli sandwiches on fresh-baked breads, plus a tasty selection of specialty burgers and salads. ~ Alii Sunset Plaza, 75-5799 Alii Drive; 808-329-4661. BUDGET TO MODERATE.

The commemorative sign at the Kona Inn tells the tale of the old inn—how it was built back in the steamship era when Kona was gaining fame as a marlin fishing ground. The bad news is that the original hotel was converted into a shopping mall—of ?which this contemporary namesake is a part. The good news is that the restaurant is quite attractive—an open-air, oceanfront affair with two separate dining facilities. The **Kona Inn Restaurant** serves grilled appetizers and sandwiches in its café/grill. The dining room has a separate menu with several fresh fish dishes daily as well as prime rib and Hawaiian-style chicken. ~ 75-5744 Alii Drive; 808-329-4455, fax 808-327-9358. DELUXE.

Set on a second-story terrace overlooking the ocean, **Lulu's** is one of Kailua's pleasingly windswept addresses. You can lean against the tile bar or sink into a booth, then order from a straightforward sandwiches-salads-and-hamburgers menu. ~ 75-5819 Alii Drive; 808-331-2633, fax 808-329-6766. MODERATE.

**Durty Jake's Café and Bar** serves an "American Continental" menu in an open-air, casual setting, with fresh seafood as well as the usual fare. Open for breakfast, lunch and dinner. ~ 75-5819 Alii Drive; 808-329-7366; www.durtyjakes.com. MODERATE.

**AUTHOR FAVORITE**

Don't let the strip mall setting dissuade you from easing on over to **Oodles of Noodles**. Focus on the fine local art and stellar menu instead. The cuisine varies from Japanese to Thai to Vietnamese to Italian with a single common denominator—everything is prepared with noodles. It's also a showcase for one of Hawaii's finest chefs—Amy Ferguson Ota. If you try the Kona-style tuna casserole, you may be back every day you're on the island. Open for breakfast, lunch and dinner. ~ 75-1027 Henry Street #102; 808-329-9222, fax 808-329-0123; www.oodles kona.com, e-mail info@oodleskona.com. MODERATE TO DELUXE.

While the thought of bubbling cheese and pepperoni may be just the thing to set your tastebuds tingling, you'll find a lot more than pizza at **Rocky's Pizza & BBQ**. Tantalizing barbecued ribs or chicken and overgenerous servings of pasta with salad and garlic bread steal the show. The menu also features several vegetarian options. The indoor dining area is smoke-free; there's also outdoor dining. ~ Keahou Shopping Center, 75-6831 Alii Drive, Keahou, 808-322-3223; second location at Crossroads Shopping Center, 75-1027 Henry Street, 808-329-7444. BUDGET.

At **Taeng-on Thai Café** the focus is said to be northern Thai cuisine, though exactly how northern *pad Thai* differs from regular *pad Thai* is unclear. More striking are the menu selections that offer a Hawaiian spin on Thai food. Can you resist the volcano shrimp with a side order of pineapple fried rice? The atmosphere is peaceful in this second-floor restaurant overlooking the bustling street in the Kona Inn Shopping Village. ~ 75-5744 Alii Drive, North Kona; 808-329-1994. MODERATE.

Don't be deceived by the formica tables and cafeteria atmosphere, or the fact that it's located in an industrial park, four miles north of Kailua. **Sam Choy's Restaurant**, established by one of the islands' premier chefs, is a gourmet ghetto. Stop by for breakfast when they serve fried *poke* omelettes, pork chops and eggs, and Spam with Portuguese sausage. No dinner. ~ 73-5576 Kauhola Street, Kaloko Light Industrial Park, located off Kaahumanu Highway; 808-326-1545, fax 808-334-1230. MODERATE TO DELUXE.

**FARM FRESH**

Kona's two outdoors "farmers markets" go well beyond fresh produce, macadamia nuts, coffee and flowers to include hand-crafted art, resortwear, and Hawaiian-themed souvenirs. **Kailua Village Farmers Market**, where local growers gather under plastic tarps to sell their wares, is a good place to pick up home-grown fruits and vegetables. Open Wednesday, Friday, Saturday and Sunday, 9 a.m. to 5 p.m. ~ Sarona and Alii drives, just south of Hualalai Road. North of town, **Alii Gardens Marketplace** offers a similar range of goods. Open Wednesday through Sunday, 9 a.m. to 5 p.m. ~ Alii Drive and Hualalai Road. There is also a farmers market in Hilo on Wednesday and Saturday. Tie it in to a visit to the volcano if you're headed that way.

Adjacent to the Royal Kona Resort, **Huggo's** offers a relaxing alfresco bayfront setting that attracts locals as well as visitors with good food and friendly service. The catch-of-the-day specials are delicious, as are the hearty sandwiches, burgers, brick oven pizzas and appetizers. ~ 75-5828 Kanaka Road; 808-329-1493. MODERATE.

Set back from the street, the **Outback Steak House** is a spacious restaurant in Kona with large portions of steak and seafood for those in search of the familiar. The theme at this chain restaurant is Australian, with everything from boomerangs to Downunder brochures adorning the walls. ~ 75-5809 Alii Drive; 808-326-2555; www.outback.com. MODERATE TO DELUXE.

The **Martini Yacht Club** strikes an upscale pose with its white linen and ship artworks with well-prepared specialties like rack of lamb, lobster tail and jumbo scallops presented on a roasted cedar plank. The lunch menu offers alternative like gourmet hamburgers and salads. ~ Coconut Grove Marketplace, 75-5815 Alii Drive; 808-329-8200. DELUXE.

The rock-n-roll memorabilia at the Kona branch of the **Hard Rock Café** is fun to browse with a flashy Madonna bustier, Elton John's flashy Uncle Sam outfit, a Leon Russell glitter robe and a gold record for Meet the Beatles. And then there's the food—well, it's the same as all the other Hard Rocks—hamburgers, barbecued baby back ribs and great fajitas—the second story seating offers wide views of Kailua Bay. ~ Coconut Grove Marketplace, 75-5815 Alii Drive; 808-329-8866. MODERATE.

**Jameson's By the Sea** is a lovely waterfront restaurant with an emphasis on fresh local seafood dishes. Tucked unpretentiously into the corner of a large condominium, Jameson's conveys a modest sense of elegance: bentwood furniture, potted palms, a seascape from the lanai or through plate-glass windows and good service. Choose from an enticing menu of fresh local catches, steaks, chicken dishes and other gourmet delights. Lunch and dinner weekdays, dinner only on weekends. ~ 77-6452 Alii Drive near Disappearing Sands Beach; 808-329-3195, fax 808-329-0780. DELUXE TO ULTRA-DELUXE.

For Continental cuisine in a fashionable setting, consider **La Bourgogne French Restaurant**. This ten-table French country dining room features New York steak with peppercorn sauce, roast saddle of lamb, veal sweetbreads with Madeira sauce, coquilles St. Jacques and fresh fish selections. For appetizers there are escargots, baked brie and lobster cocktail. Round off the meal with cherries jubilee or chocolate mousse and you have a French feast right here in tropical Hawaii. Reservations are highly recommended. Dinner only. Closed Sunday and Monday. ~ Kuakini Plaza on Kuakini Highway, four miles south of Kailua; 808-329-6711; e-mail burgundy@gte.net. DELUXE TO ULTRA-DELUXE.

The less formal of the two restaurants in the Kona Village Resort, the **Hale Moana** is part of the package for resort guests but is open to the general public on a limited basis for lunch and dinner by reservation only. (Without reservations, you won't get through the guarded front gate.) The buffet-style lunch lets you choose from a spread of fresh salads, vegetables and fruits, cold soups, sashimi, shellfish and desserts, along with hot entrées cooked on an open grill. Dinner selections are served from a limited menu on a rotating basis. Among the dinner entrées are herbed macadamia nut–crusted rack of lamb, baked guinea hen breast and stir-fried mako shark. The oceanview setting is spectacular, with outdoor terrace dining and an indoor seating area that, weather permitting, is left open to the sea breezes. ~ Kaahumanu Highway; 808-325-5555, 800-367-5290. ULTRA-DELUXE.

Situated in the posh Four Seasons Resort Hualalai at Historic Kaupulehu, **Pahu I'a** offers romantic indoor and outdoor dining with ocean views around a large saltwater aquarium that forms the restaurant's centerpiece. The changing menu features fine contemporary Pacific cuisine focusing on fresh fish, local produce and locally grown spices and herbs. The emphasis is on nutritionally balanced, healthy fare; vegetarian options are available nightly. ~ 100 Kaupulehu Drive, Kaupulehu-Kona; 808-325-8000. DELUXE TO ULTRA-DELUXE.

**GROCERIES**  The best place to shop anywhere along the Kona Coast is in the town of Kailua. This commercial center features several supermarkets as well as a number of specialty shops. One of the first choices among supermarkets is **Sack 'n Save** in the center of Kailua. It has everything you could possibly need. ~ 75-5595 Palani Road, Lanihau Shopping Center; 808-326-2729.

If you'd prefer another supermarket with a similar selection, try **K.T.A. Super Store**. It's open every day from 5 a.m. to midnight, and is another of the Kailua-Kona area's most convenient and accessible shopping facilities. ~ Kona Coast Shopping Center; 808-329-1677.

**Kona Natural Foods** has an ample stock of vitamins, bathing supplies, grains, fruits and vegetables. By the simple fact that it is the only store of its kind in the area, it wins my recommendation. ~ Crossroads Shopping Center; 808-329-2296.

You might remember that song about how "L.A. is a great big freeway." Well, the Hawaiian version could easily be "Kailua is a great big mall." I have never seen so many shopping arcades squeezed into so small a space. Here are goldsmiths, boutiques, jewelers galore, travel agencies, sandal-makers, knickknack shops, sundries, T-shirt shops and much, much more, all crowded onto Alii Drive.

**SHOPPING**

Personally, I think most items sold along this strip are tacky or overpriced, and in some cases, both. One place I do recommend, however, is **Middle Earth Bookshoppe**. Here you'll find a good selection of Hawaiian books, as well as paperbacks and current bestsellers. ~ Kona Plaza Shopping Arcade, 75-5719 Alii Drive; 808-329-2123.

The **Kona Inn Shopping Village**, which parallels the waterfront, features dozens of shops. Because of its convenient location and variety of stores, it is the center of the visitor shopping scene. ~ Alii Drive.

The **Coconut Grove Marketplace**, on Alii Drive toward the south end of town, features a selection of restaurants and shops. Drop in at the **Rift Zone**, a gallery that features the works of

**event**

**AUTHOR FAVORITE**

In early November Kona comes to life with ten days of activities that include more than 30 community events that are part of the **Kona Coffee Cultural Festival**. Timed with the harvest of Kona's renowned coffee crop (mid-September to January) the festival includes a colorful parade in Kailua and a chance to visit coffee farms for tastings and tours that are both educational and fun. Look for a free copy of the Kona Coffee Country Driving Tour or check www.konacoffeefest.com/drivingtour. ~ 808-326-7820; www.konacoffeefest.com, e-mail info@konacoffeefest.com.

local artists, with a great selection of paintings, ceramics, art glass, woodworks, as well as less pricey art objects. ~ 75-5815 Alii Drive; 808-331-1100.

**Tropical Heat Wave** displays a selection of affordable arts and crafts, some locally made, some imported. ~ 75-5744 Alii Drive; 808-329-4348.

**Kona Marketplace** is another prime shopping destination. Within this complex is the **Kim Taylor Reece Gallery**, which specializes in artistic photographs of classic hula dancers. ~ 75-5729 C Alii Drive; 808-331-2433.

One of the more tastefully designed malls is **Waterfront Row**, a raw-wood-and-plank-floor shopping complex with perhaps a dozen stores and restaurants. ~ 75-5770 Alii Drive.

The **Hulihee Palace Gift Shop**, a small store located behind the palace, specializes in Hawaiian handicrafts and literature. Closed Sunday. ~ 75-5718 Alii Drive; 808-329-1877.

In addition to the centers located along Alii Drive, there are three large shopping malls a couple blocks up from the water. **Kona Coast Shopping Center** and **Lanihau Center** sit on either side of Palani Road near the Kaahumanu Highway intersection. Just south, where the highway intersects with Henry Street, is the **Crossroads Shopping Center**. Across the highway is a **Borders** bookstore. ~ Kaahumanu Highway; 808-331-1668.

The **King Kamehameha Kona Beach Hotel** has a cluster of shops. Several decades back, before the luxury hotels mushroomed along the Kohala Coast, this hotel was a prime stop for shoppers and sojourners alike. Today its glory has faded, but it

**NIGHT RAYS**

For night owls, an adventure in the ocean depths brings you face-to-face with a mesmerizing nocturnal creature—the Pacific manta ray—an imposing specimen with a wing span up to 14 feet. These large rays, closely related to sharks, are also incredible acrobats—I've seen them leap up from the water. Hanging out near the Kona airport or off the Old Kona Surf Hotel, these massive but gentle creatures are attracted to light sources. Several of the waterfront nightspots in Kailua shine spotlights in the water so you can watch manta rays gliding along the shore. Or contact one of these outfitters for night tours: **Manta Ray Dives of Hawaii** (808-325-1687), **Eco Adventures** (808-329-7116) or **Big Island Adventures** (808-329-6068).

still sports some interesting stores. ~ 75-5660 Palani Road; 808-329-2911.

Right next door, between the hotel and the Kona Industrial Area, is the **King Kamehameha Mall**, a small, modern complex with perhaps a dozen shops. ~ 75-5626 Kuakini Highway.

Toward the end of Alii Drive, several miles south of Kailua, stands the **Keauhou Shopping Center**. With several dozen stores, it is one of the largest complexes on the island (though granted, *Big* Island does not mean big shopping malls). ~ Alii Drive and Kamehameha III Road.

What action there is here is near the shorefront on Alii Drive. **NIGHTLIFE** **Huggo's** has stunning ocean views and is usually packed to the gills. Various live bands perform every evening. ~ Alii Drive and Kakakai Road; 808-329-1493.

The **Billfish Bar**, located poolside at the King Kamehameha Kona Beach Hotel, has live Hawaiian contemporary music on weekends. ~ 75-5660 Palani Road; 808-329-2911.

For an evening of slow rhythms and dancing cheek to cheek, there's the **Windjammer Lounge** at the Royal Kona Resort, which has live music and entertainment on weekends. ~ 75-5852 Alii Drive; 808-329-3111.

To sample Hawaii's own designer beers, check out the **Kona Brewing Company**, a brew pub serving an exotic array of local flavors. ~ Kona Shopping Center, Kuakini Highway and Palani Road; 808-334-2739.

Another good bet is the **Big Island Comedy Club**, an ever-moving event that's staged at popular nightspots in Kailua and elsewhere along the coast. Call for the current venue. ~ 808-329-4368.

Catering to both a gay and straight clientele, **The Other Side** offers pool tables, dart boards and recorded sounds. ~ 74-5484 Kaiwi Street; 808-329-7226.

**HALE HALAWAI** This small oceanfront park, fringed with co-    **BEACHES** conut trees, has an activities pavilion but no beach. Its central lo-    **& PARKS** cation in Kailua does make the park a perfect place to watch the sunset, though. ~ Located near the intersection of Alii Drive and Hualalai Road in Kailua.

**OLD KONA AIRPORT STATE RECREATION AREA**    ◄ *HIDDEN*
This white-sand beach parallels Kailua's former landing strip, ex-

tending for a half-mile along a lava-crusted shore. Very popular with Kailuans, this is a conveniently located spot for catching some rays (sun, that is). The water is shallow, with a rocky bottom. There are a few sand channels for entering the water; and there is a sandy inlet good for kids just north of the lighthouse. This area offers excellent diving; lifeguards on duty. Principal catches are threadfin, big-eyed scad, bonefish, *papio* and especially mullet. Facilities include a picnic area, restrooms and showers. ~ Located about one-half mile northwest of the King Kamehameha Kona Beach Hotel on Kuakini Highway in Kailua. The park gate is closed every evening at 8 p.m.

**KAMAKAHONU** 🏃 🏊 🛶 🛥 This snippet of sand hugs the south-most corner of Kailua Bay adjacent to the pier. It's a popular spot with local kids and guests at the adjacent King Kamehameha's Kona Beach Resort. Kayakers and distance swimmers also take advantage of the calm beachside to access the waters of Kailua Bay. The restored Ahuena Heiau provides a great backdrop to a swim. Both the beach and temple were part of Kamehameha's royal compound, called Kamakahonu, "the eye of the turtle." ~ Located at the west end of Alii Drive, adjacent to the pier.

*HIDDEN* ▶ **HONOKOHAU BEACH** 🏊 🛶 🎣 This was once Kailua's nude beach, but prohibitions are in effect. Folks come for miles to soak up the sun on this long narrow strand; it's bordered by a lagoon, backdropped by distant mountains, protected by a shallow reef and highly recommended for the adventurous. Since the water is well-protected, it's good for swimming, although a bit shallow. There are recommended spots for skindiving south of the small-boat harbor but stay away from the harbor itself since sharks are ubiquitous. Surfers enjoy Honokohau's waves. Rather than fish here try Kaloko Pond about one-half mile north. There are no facilities here. ~ Take Kaahumanu Highway a couple miles north from Kailua. Turn onto the road to Honokohau Small Boat Harbor. From the north side of the harbor, walk about 600 yards farther north to the beach.

**MAHAIULA BEACH—KONA COAST STATE PARK** 🏃 🏊 🛶 🎣 A fairly good road, partly paved, partly bumpy leads to beautiful Mahaiula Beach with its white sands and clear blue waters. At the head of a well-protected and deep bay, the swimming

# Kaloko-Honokohau National Historic Park

Designated a National Historic Park in 1969, work is underway on adding a visitor center and walking tour story boards that will identify and explain the **Kaloko-Honokohau National Historic Park**'s concentration of culturally significant sites. Situated just south of Kona International Airport, the park consists of 600 acres on land and 600 acres offshore. At first glance the dry, lava rock landscape seems inhospitable. But Hawaiians took full advantage of its varied resources: fishing coastal waters easily accessed from the sheltered sands of Honokohau Bay, harvesting fishponds made of lava rock walls, growing gourds, coconuts, sweet potatoes, taro and *hau*.

Several unpaved access roads enter the park from Queen Kaahumanu Highway. The northern entry is a mile along a bumpy lava rock road that leads to the impressive **Kaloko Fishpond**. The great fishponds, created by building rock walls that isolated coastal bays and shallows from the open sea, were communal undertakings. The fishpond wall at Kaloko, for example, is 800 feet long, 8 to 10 feet high and about 8 feet wide. Most of its tens of thousands of heavy basalt rocks were brought to Kaloko from places many miles away. While the fishpond remains open, the access road is locked at 3:30 p.m., which means an easy mile-long hike if you want to pay an afternoon visit.

A second point of entry, adjacent to the Honokohau Small Boat Harbor (enter on Kealakehe Parkway) offers easier afternoon access. This leads to the park's south entrance at Honokohau Bay, where the **Aiopio Fish Trap**, the **Aimakapa Fishpond**, and a beautifully crafted oceanside *heiau* platform provide links to the Hawaiian past. There's a white sand beach, and while the bay's waters are shallow, they provide welcome relief from heat that makes a visit to the park an early morning or late-afternoon recommend.

A third access road is marked with signs that lead to the **visitor center** and the **trail** that makes its way past ancient house sites and a large *holua*, a downhill sled run that is a prominent landmark. The trail leads to Honokohau's white sands. For those with ambition and stamina, Kaloko and Honokohau are linked by a beautiful two-mile-long coastal trail (that's four miles round trip) called the **Ala Kahakai**.

Come prepared for the heat at Kaloko, which means bring your own water, sunscreen and sun-sheltering headgear, and wear decent sneakers. There are restrooms at Kaloko and Honokahau. ~ 73-4786 Kanalani Street, #14, Kailua-Kona, HI 96740; 808-329-6881; www.nps.gov/kaho.

is great, as are the snorkeling and diving. In ancient times this coast was (and is) one of the richest in marine resources. There are restrooms, but you should bring your own water. The posted 3:30 p.m. gate closing should be taken seriously. ~ Located 2.6 miles north of Keahole Airport. Drive down an unpaved ocean road about 1.5 miles to the parking lot. Take the turnoff marked State Park, about five miles north of Kona International Airport.

**MAKALAWENA BEACH** Makalawena, the next beach to the north of Mahaiula, is another beautiful stretch of North Kona coast. Sand dunes are the backdrop for this beautiful shoreline made up of intricate caves. If you're a shell collector or birder (Opaeula Pond here is a waterbird sanctuary), this is the place to go. Now and then the modern world intrudes, since the beaches are not far from the jets departing Kona International. It can be reached along the coastal foot trail from Mahaiula Beach (about 30 minutes each way; see listing above).

**KONA COAST STATE PARK** Set at the end of a bumpy lava-bed road, this beach park is certainly secluded. You'll drive in a mile-and-a-half from the highway to a sand-and-coral beach that is bordered by a small lagoon and young palm trees. You can swim, although the bottom is rocky and the surf is often high—that's when the surfers come out. Anglers also frequent this beach. The only facilities are picnic tables and portable toilets. ~ Located one and a half miles off Kaahumanu Highway, about ten miles north of Kailua near the 91-mile marker.

**DISAPPEARING SANDS BEACH** A small strand studded with volcanic rocks, this spot is also called Magic Sands.

### ROYAL GROUNDS

Reminders of the royal past can be found between Kailua and Keauhou Bay, where Kauikeauoli, later to rule as Kamehameha III, was born on March 17, 1814. A bronze **plaque** marks the site. As the story is told, the stillborn infant was brought to life by Keauhou's spring-fed waters and the soulful prayers of the priest officiating at the birth. To the north of Keauhou Bay, the rebuilt cottage on the grounds of the Ohana Keauhou Beach Hotel was a Kailua getaway for King Kalakaua. Nearby are the remains of two badly damaged *heiau* and the waters of the **King's Pool**, one of several sheltered bathing areas along a rocky coastline.

It seems that the white sand periodically washes away, exposing a lava shoreline. When still carpeted with sand, this is a very crowded place. This is a favorite area for swimming and body-surfing. Kona's best surfing spot is just north of here at "Banyans," with breaks year-round over a shallow reef. There are right and left slides. The major catches include mullet, threadfin, big-eyed scad, bonefish and *papio*. Restrooms and showers are the only facilities. ~ Located on Alii Drive, four miles south of Kailua.

**KAHALUU BEACH PARK** Set along the south shore of Kahaluu Bay, this county park is fringed with palm trees. The salt-and-pepper beach is small and often crowded. Swimming is excellent here since the cove is partially protected by outlying rocks. Tropical fish abound, making this a recommended place for snorkeling, especially for beginners. Surfing is good near the reef during periods of high surf. Anglers fish for mullet, threadfin, big-eyed scad, bonefish and *papio*. The bay is also a good spot for throw-netting and surround-netting. Facilities include picnic areas, pavilions, showers and restrooms. ~ Located on Alii Drive, five miles south of Kailua.

# FIVE

# Kohala Coast

Stretching from the northern boundary of Kona to the north-western tip of the Big Island are the districts of South and North Kohala. One element that comes as a visual shock to many first-time visitors to the Big Island's west coast is the endless stretch of black lava that blankets this dry terrain. Standing in the windshadow of both Mauna Loa and Mauna Kea, this region projects the bald unreality of a moonscape. But the ragged shoreline has been trimmed with stands of palm trees and sections along the roadways are splashed with bougainvillea.

During the last several decades South Kohala, which includes some of the island's prettiest beaches, has seen the building of one upscale resort after another. Farther north, where Kohala Mountain forms a 5000-foot-high spine, the territory remains much as it has for decades. As the Kaahumanu Highway (Route 19) gives way to the northerly Akoni Pule Highway (Route 270), the landscape eventually changes from dry and barren to tropical and luxurious.

Geologically, the Kohala Coast was the section of the island that first rose from the sea. Later, as the volcanoes that formed Kohala Mountain became extinct, the region evolved into a center of historical importance. Kamehameha I was born and raised along this wind-blasted coastline and it was here that he initially consolidated his power base. The region is filled with ancient *heiaus* as well as more recent cemeteries that date to the era when sugar plantations dominated the local economy.

Exploring this region from Kailua-Kona you will find that Kaahumanu Highway cuts across a broad swath of lava-crusted country. There are views of Maui to the north, Mauna Kea to the east and Hualalai to the south.

The site of the Puukohola *heiau* and the main harbor for this stretch of coast, Kawaihae, also offers several shops and restaurants and makes a good stop en route to North Kohala or Waimea.

**SOUTH KOHALA**   Waikoloa's Anaehoomalu Bay provides a dividing line between the districts of North Kona and South Kohala, which runs from Anaehoomalu to a border with North Kohala 20 miles beyond Kawaiahae. Old lava flows, mostly from Hualalai, dominate the landscape, with grasses the primary groundcover. The Waikoloa, Mauna Lani, Hapuna and Mauna Kea resorts take advantage of the dry, sunny climate, incorporating most of the coasts few beaches. Hapuna Beach State Park and Spencer Beach State Park are the two exceptions. Numerous archeological remains point to South Kohala's significance, with the Puukohola *heiau*, overlooking the Kawaiahae coastline the last of the great temple complexes of old Hawaii.

For evidence of Kohala's historic significance you need look no farther than **Waikoloa**, located between Honokaa and Waimea. While the area is now heavily developed with tourist resorts, it is also the site of the **Waikoloa Petroglyph Field**. Here you can wander amidst a forbidding lava field etched with ancient symbols. The contrast, with a modern golf course on one side and primitive rock carvings on the other, is ironic to say the least. The path to the petroglyphs is .3-mile in length and begins at the Kings' Shops Mall in Waikoloa. This rough lava course is part of the King's Trail, a mid-19th-century trail built for horseback riders making the 32-mile trip from Kailua to Puako.

Not exactly a hidden destination, the **Hilton Waikaloa Village** is worth a look-see if you are staying on the Kohala Coast. The Hilton Waikoloa, the closest thing to a theme park you'll find on the island, offers a four-acre swimming and snorkeling lagoon, an interactive dolphin guest program, waterfalls, lush gardens and numerous dining spots. You can ride a monorail or hop onto a teak motorboat (you'll feel like you're on the jungle ride at Disneyland, but without the hippos coming up for air) to tour the facility. Better yet, stroll around and gaze at the stunning artworks that adorn the lobbies and gardens of this massive facility. (Reservations are required for the dolphin encounters.) ~ 425 Waikoloa Beach Drive, Waikoloa; 808-886-1234, fax 808-886-2900.

Next door, the Outrigger Waikoloa fronts one of Hawaii's most beautiful beaches, **Anaehoomalu Beach**. This area, with its sheltered cove and natural ponds, was once a gathering place for

Hawaiian royalty. Sea turtles and other marine life call this bay home. (See "Beaches & Parks" below.)

The highway continues north past a desolate desert of black lava to the community of Puako. A short spur off Mauna Lani resort's main road takes you to an easy walk on the Malama Petroglyph Trail that leads to the extensive **Puako Petroglyph Field**. There are hundreds of examples of this Hawaiian art form at Puako, with warriors and outriggers, surfers and sailing ships some of the numerous themes. (It is not permitted to do stencil work on either the old petroglyphs or the contemporary examples that line the trail.)

From Puako, the highway moves north past **Hapuna Beach State Park** (see "Beaches & Parks" below) and the luxurious **Mauna Kea Beach Hotel**. Built by Laurence Rockefeller, it was the first of the five-star resorts to mushroom along the Kohala coastline.

Continuing north lies the harbor of **Kawaihae**, one of the island's busiest ports and the locale of two major *heiaus*, Mailekini and Puukohola, which have been dedicated as the **Puukohola National Historic Site**. Kamehameha built the impressive triple-tiered Puukohola in 1791 after a prophet related that doing so would ensure his victory over his rivals. At the temple dedication, the ambitious chief aided the prophecy by treacherously slaying his principal enemy. Measuring 224 feet by 100 feet, it was built of lava rocks and boulders that were fitted together using no mortar.

Only one-third of **Pua Mau Place Botanic & Sculpture Garden**'s 45 acres has been planted, but the results are already colorfully spectacular, highlighted by an impressive selection of showy hibiscus, towering hedges of bougainvillea, and giant plumeria interspersed with giant bronze insect sculptures with a sci-fi appeal. Take the book describing Pua Mau's plants for a self-guided walking tour. Closed Monday, Tuesday and holidays. ~ 10 Ala Kahua Drive, Kawaiahae; 808-882-0888; www.puamau.org, e-mail mulchedpaths@aol.com.

**NORTH KOHALA**   North Kohala includes much of the mountainous peninsula that provides the Big island with its northernmost lands. The landscape rises from a coastal plain to the lushly forested slopes of the Kohala Mountains. Sugar plantations once flourished here, watered by an irrigation system that diverted the mountain streams of North Kohala's isolated valleys, with Pololu accessible on foot or horseback. Grassy upcountry slopes continue to provide pastureland for cattle. The scenic landscape, historic sites like the Mookini *heiau*, and small towns like Kapaau and Hawi provide Kohala with an distinctive and appealing sense of place.

Just 12 miles to the north along Akoni Pule Highway (Route 270) is **Lapakahi State Historical Park**, where a preserved village provides a unique glimpse into ancient Hawaiian ways. This is definitely worth a leisurely look-see. Dating back 600 years, this

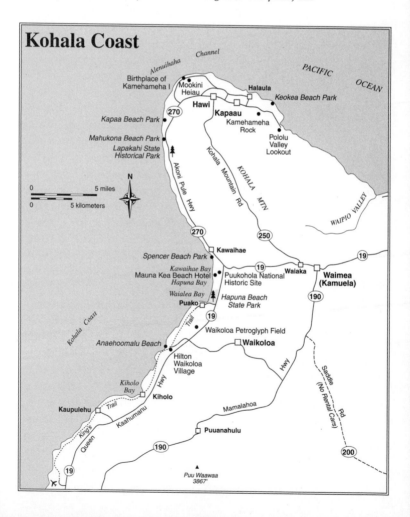

# Kohala Coast

one-of-a-kind site includes fishing shrines, canoe sheds, house sites and burial plots. ~ 808-882-6207.

The old plantation town of **Hawi**, with its trim houses and freshly painted storefronts, harkens back to an earlier era. Back in the 1980s, when the sugar cane industry was in decline, the town looked rather forlorn. But by the beginning of this century it had been completely restored by artists and entrepreneurs. Like neighboring **Kapaau**, it shows its new face in the form of small galleries and local shops. Both are charming enclaves adorned with small churches and relics from the days when sugar was king.

Pride of Kapaau is the original **Kamehameha Statue**, a nine-ton creation cast in bronze. The more famous Honolulu monument is actually only a replica of this gilt figure. Crafted in Florence around 1879 by an American sculptor, the original disappeared at sea on its way to Hawaii but was later recovered and installed here.

The courthouse behind the statue is equally historic, providing a glimpse of small-town life enhanced by informational signs. Senior citizens often man an information desk and "talk story" with those with questions or aloha to share.

HIDDEN ►

A marked side road off Route 270 just east of Kapaau leads through a macadamia orchard to the **Bond Estate**. One of Hawaii's best preserved missionary estates, it dates back to 1841, when it was built by Reverend Elias Bond and his wife, Ellen. Their Maine background is reflected in the New England–style architecture of the stone house, church, school and plantation buildings. Bond designed the property as a self-sufficient farm to

**sights**

**AUTHOR FAVORITE**

Make sure you visit the **Mookini Heiau**, one of the oldest (possibly as old as A.D. 800) and most historically significant archaeological sites from old Hawaii, linked by legend to the arrival of the priest Paao from Tahiti. This holy place measures 250 feet by 130 feet and is reached by taking a left at the Upolu airfield, then following the dirt road for a mile and a half. The **Birthplace of Kamehameha I**, marked with a plaque, lies one-third mile (and two gates) farther west along the same road. The boulders here are reputed to be the original birthstones. The isolated setting is seldom visited, which adds to the spiritual sense of discovery the site offers.

sustain his family, his parishioners and the school where Ellen educated teachers for the 32 one-room schoolhouses the Bonds would eventually establish around the Kohala district. The family eventually converted the farm into a sprawling sugar cane plantation, which became the largest employer in the area and flourished for 100 years. A 1973 earthquake damaged the buildings, and two years later the sugar operation shut down for good. Today Boyd Bond, great-great-grandson of Elias and Ellen, gives tours of the land and the buildings, which are on the National Register of Historic Places, as he works toward restoring the estate as a museum. ~ Off Route 270, Kapaau; 808-889-0883.

The 1886 **Tong Wo Society Building**, a two-story bamboo structure embodying classic Chinese architecture, is listed on the National Register of Historic Places. Because the tong still uses the building for meetings, visitors are not allowed through the ornate red front door, but you can walk through the adjacent Tong Wo Society cemetery and get a palpable sense of the Big Island's Chinese heritage from the inscriptions on the stones, mostly in Chinese characters. ~ Route 70, mile-marker 25, Halawa.

Along this lush, rainy side of the peninsula are taro patches and pandanus forests. Past the **Kamehameha Rock** (a large boulder that the mighty conqueror reputedly carried from the sea), the road ends at **Pololu Valley Lookout**. The view here overlooking Pololu Valley extends along the monumental cliffs that guard Hawaii's north coast. A half-mile trail leads down to a lovely beach, but watch out for the treacherous riptides.

From this cul-de-sac you must backtrack to Hawi, where you can climb the back of **Kohala Mountain** along Route 250 (Kohala Mountain Road), completing a loop tour of North Kohala. Rising to 3564 feet, the road rolls through cactus-studded range country and offers startling views down steep volcanic slopes to the sea. En route are cattle ranches, stands of Norfolk pine and eucalyptus, and curving countryside covered with sweet grasses and wildflowers.

◄ HIDDEN

For years the Kohala district was a placid region strewn with lava and dotted by several pearly beaches. A single resort stood along its virgin coastline. Today a series of upscale resorts is to be found.

**LODGING**

**SOUTH KOHALA**    The **Mauna Lani Bay Hotel and Bungalows**, a 3200-acre resort, rests on a white-sand beach. Designed in the shape of an arrowhead and boasting 350 rooms, this luxurious facility offers two golf courses, ten tennis courts and five restaurants, several of which are award winners. With brilliant green gardens set against black lava, the landscape combines curving lawns and palm-ringed fishponds. Each guest room is spaciously laid out and designed in a pastel motif. ~ 68-1400 Mauna Lani Drive, Kawaihae; 808-885-6622, 800-367-2323, fax 808-885-1484; www.maunalani.com, e-mail reservations@maunalani.com. ULTRA-DELUXE.

Equally elegant, although a bit bigger and flashier, is the 539-room **The Fairmont Orchid, Hawaii**. With grounds that are spacious, beautifully landscaped and maintained, the Orchid sits on a lovely crescent of white sand that provides swimming, snorkeling, and outrigger canoeing. Rooms are spacious, with subtly tinted walls that highlight Hawaiian-themed art and accessories. There are a large oceanside a swimming pool, 11 tennis courts, three restaurants, fitness center, with the resort's two 18-hole golf courses adjacent. ~ 1 North Kaniku Drive, Kohala; 808-885-2000, 800-845-9905, fax 808-885-8886; www.fairmont.com/orchid, e-mail orchid@fairmont.com. ULTRA-DELUXE.

The sprawling **Hapuna Beach Prince Hotel** is nestled into the bluffs above a wide expanse of sandy beach. The posh Hapuna features beautifully landscaped grounds and offers a golf course, tennis courts and its own white-sand beach. The 350 rooms are decorated in shades of peach and beige, and all have large lanais and ocean views. ~ 62-100 Kaunaoa Drive, Kohala Coast; 808-880-1111, 800-882-6060, fax 808-880-3142; www.princeresorts hawaii.com. ULTRA-DELUXE.

The **Mauna Kea Beach Hotel,** built by Laurence Rockefeller, set the standard for resort luxury when it opened in 1965. The 310 rooms are spacious, with lanais that offer ocean or mountain views. The hotel descends to Kaunaoa Beach, one of the Big Island's best. The beautifully landscaped grounds, supplemented by the hotel's art collection, are adjacent to the resort's renowned golf course. ~ 62-100 Mauna Kea Beach Drive, Kohala; 808-882-7222, 800-882-6060, fax 808-882-5700; www.maunakea beachhotel.com. ULTRA-DELUXE.

**NORTH KOHALA**   In the small rustic town of Hawi near Hawaii's northwestern tip, the **Kohala Village Inn** and an adjacent restaurant are the hottest spots around. But there's still privacy and quiet aplenty out back in the sleeping quarters. Rooms in this refurbished establishment feature tin roofs and handsome hardwood floors, and face a small courtyard. The place is tidy, if less than elegant. There are also rooms in an adjacent building. ~ 55-514 Hawi Road, Hawi; 808-889-0404; www.kohala villageinn.com, e-mail info@kohalavillageinn.com. BUDGET TO MODERATE.

**SOUTH KOHALA**    **Waikoloa Villas** is a collection of over 100 condos on the lower slopes of Mauna Kea. Located inland from the South Kohala coast, Waikoloa is a self-contained village with a store, a post office, a pool, a restaurant, tennis courts, a golf course and riding stables. One-bedroom units price at $189, two-bedroom units at $209 and three-bedroom units at $269. ~ 808-883-9144, 800-535-0085, fax 808-883-8740; www.marcre sorts.com, e-mail wkr@aloha.net.

**CONDOS**

Located within the Waikoloa Beach Resort, the **Vista Waikoloa** is a three-story, 50-unit condominium complex along Waikoloa Beach that offers air-conditioned two-bedroom luxury suites with large windows, bright white decor with bamboo accents and kitchens complete with dishwashers. The dining areas are on private 380-square-foot lanais with full ocean views and gas grills. There's a heated outdoor pool as well as whirlpools, an exercise room, and complimentary laundry service. Three-night minimum stay. Prices range from $220 to $240 a night. ~ 69-1010 Keana Place, Waikoloa Village; 808-886-0412, 800-822-4252, fax 808-886-1199.

**AUTHOR FAVORITE**

One way to avoid the high cost of the five-star Kohala Coast resorts is to rent a condominium in one of the many complexes. **Mauna Lani Point** is a collection of villa-style condominiums spread across 19 oceanfront acres, close to a white-sand beach. Luxuriously appointed, the condos have access to Mauna Lani's beaches, jogging trails and a 27-acre historic preserve. Some of the units can fit up to four people; prices range from $305 to $395 a night for one-bedroom units; two-bedroom units run from $405 to $505 a night. Three-night minimum stay required. ~ 68-1050 Mauna Lani Point Drive, Kohala Coast; 800-642-6284, fax 808-661-1025; www.classicresorts.com, e-mail info@classicresorts.com.

The only condominium complex in the secluded beachfront community of Puako, **Puako Beach Condominiums** is a long four-story structure located next to the Puako Store, across the street from the beach and one mile from the luxuriant white sands of Hapuna Beach State Park. All 38 units are air-conditioned, mostly three-bedroom, two-bath units designed to sleep up to six, with a king-size bed, a queen-size bed and two twins. Most units have views of the ocean in front and Mauna Kea in back. The grounds are nicely landscaped with flower gardens, and there are a round swimming pool and a children's wading pool. Weekly rates only. ~ Puako Beach Drive, Puako; 808-965-9446. ULTRA-DELUXE.

**DINING**

**SOUTH KOHALA**   Dining out in South Kohala means resort dining, which includes a wide range of upscale hotel restaurants, with additional restaurants, including inexpensive fast food options like pizza and tacos at the Queen's Court at the Kings' Shops at Waikoloa.

The same fusion menu that made Roy's on Oahu a big success draws crowds to **Roy's Waikoloa Bar & Grill**. Roy's is worth a visit, with specialties like misoyaki butterfish, seared *ahi* and cheese and garlic-sauce shrimp. Located in the Kings' Shops complex, it's best to make reservations for dinner seating, which includes indoor and outdoor seating. ~ Kings' Shops at Waikoloa; 808-886-4321; www.roysrestaurant.com, e-mail waikoloa@roys restaurant.com. DELUXE.

The **Big Island Steak House** menu supplements steaks and ribs with salads, seafood and other specialties. There's something

**BED DOWN AT ANAEHOOMALU BEACH—LUXURY STYLE**

The **Outrigger Waikoloa Beach**, a sprawling 545-unit resort, stands along the golden strand of Anaehoomalu Beach, one of Hawaii's most beautiful beaches. An airy lobby decorated with teak furnishings and a stunning century-old *koa* canoe offers a warm island welcome. Guest rooms with rattan furnishings and neutral tones are quite roomy and comfortable, and you can wander the 15 acres of lovely gardens and discover ancient petroglyph fields and a royal fishpond. ~ 69-275 Waikoloa Beach Drive, Waikoloa; 808-886-6789, 800-922-5533, fax 808-886-7852; www.out rigger.com. ULTRA-DELUXE.

for everyone on the menu. The atmosphere is lively, with a setting heavy with Hawaiian memorabilia. Dinner only. ~ Kings' Shops at Waikoloa; 808-886-8805. MODERATE TO DELUXE.

The **Grand Palace Chinese Restaurant** offers a menu with plenty of choices, with seafood the specialty of the house. ~ Kings' Shops at Waikoloa; 808-886-6668. MODERATE TO DELUXE.

With all the development that occurred along the Kohala Coast, it seems inevitable that gourmet restaurants would become an important part of the landscape. Thus far, few independent dining rooms have opened; most are connected with one of the several resorts now dotting the shoreline.

The Mauna Lani Bay Hotel hosts some well-known, formal and very expensive restaurants. At the **Bay Terrace** there's an ever-changing menu. The offerings may include fresh grilled salmon in an asparagus sauce or mahimahi with feta cheese. Beef dishes include prime rib with a spicy horseradish sauce and Black Angus steak. Breakfast and dinner are served. ~ Mauna Lani Bay Hotel, 68-1400 Mauna Lani Drive, Kawaihae; 808-885-6622, fax 808-885-1478. ULTRA-DELUXE.

Also located at the Mauna Lani Bay Hotel is the **Canoe House**, one of the Big Island's most highly regarded dining rooms. Specializing in Pacific Rim cuisine and offering spectacular sunsets as an appetizer, it delivers fine food and a fine time. The menu, which changes frequently, is a creative mix of island and Asian dishes. Dinner only. ~ 808-885-6622, fax 808-885-1478. ULTRA-DELUXE.

For Continental cuisine with a touch of Provence, try **The Batik** at the Mauna Kea Beach Hotel. This hotel, built on the Kohala Coast by Laurence Rockefeller, is famous for its fabulous feasts. For American-style dishes plus spectacular ocean views, there's also the **Pavilion**. ~ Mauna Kea Beach Hotel, 62-100 Mauna Kea Beach Drive, Kohala; 808-882-7222. ULTRA-DELUXE.

Old Matson menus line the walls at **Village Steak House**, which has plate-glass views of the Waikoloa Village Golf Course. Selections such as filet mignons, porterhouses, New York strips and T-bone steaks are no surprise, but you can also find fresh fish, shrimp and chicken entrées prepared with an Asian twist. Daily specials round out the menu. No dinner Monday. ~ Hilton Waikoloa Village; 808-883-9644. DELUXE.

**NORTH KOHALA**   You'll find an increasing number of note-worthy (or at least affordable) restaurants along Hawaii's north-western shore.

If you cast anchor in the town of Kawaihae, consider **Café Pesto**. Gourmet pizza is the specialty at this simple café. But you'll also find pastas prepared with Asian flair, risottos and fresh fish. ~ Kawaihae Center, Suite 101, Kawaihae; 808-882-1071, fax 808-882-1459; www.cafepesto.com, e-mail palmer@interpac.net. MODERATE TO DELUXE.

The food is Mexican but the theme is surfing at **Tres Hombres Beach Grill**, located in the same complex. There is a great display of surfing memorabilia and some of the bar counters are even fashioned from surfboards. ~ Kawaihae Center, Kawaihae; 808-882-1031. MODERATE TO DELUXE.

Located just across from Kawaihae Harbor, **Kawaihae Harbor Grill & Seafood Bar**'s menu runs from burgers to catch-of-the-day, pastas to steak. Alfresco seating is a pleasant option at this casual restaurant known for its fresh fish. For dessert, try the *lilikoi* (passion fruit) cheesecake. ~ Route 270, Kawaihae; 808-882-1368, fax 808-882-7005. MODERATE TO DELUXE.

The **Blue Dolphin Restaurant** has a comfortable outdoor dining pavilion where plate lunches and hamburgers are served for the noontime meal. In the evening, the menu becomes more formal, with Pacific/Mediterranean cuisine. Call for dinner hours. Closed on rainy days. ~ Across from Kawaihae Harbor, Kawaihae; phone/fax 808-882-7771. MODERATE TO DELUXE.

HIDDEN ►   For a taste of funky, traditional Hawaii there's **The Soda Fountain**. Set in a tinroof plantation building with bare walls and plastic tablecloths, it serves breakfast, lunch and dinner at super-low prices. No dinner from June through August. ~ Just off Akoni Pule Highway about one mile east of Hawi; 808-889-0208. BUDGET.

In the center of Hawi is the **Kohala Coffee Mill**, a café that serves coffee, smoothies and pastries, but especially Tropical Dreams Ice Cream. Created locally, Tropical Dreams whips up exotic flavors like mango, white chocolate ginger and lychee. ~ Akoni Pule Highway, Hawi; 808-889-5577, 877-301-7683, fax 808-889-5062. BUDGET.

**Hula La's Mexican Kitchen & Salsa Factory** starts the day with breakfast burritos, *huevos rancheros* and three-egg omelets. Nachos, soft tacos and green chicken enchiladas are part of the full menu. Food is freshly prepared and delicious. ~ Kohala Trade Center, Hawi; 808-889-5668. BUDGET.

A cheerfully tropical missionary-style facade with pillars shaped like palm trees greets visitors to **Jen's Kohala Café**, a friendly little eatery next door to the biggest art gallery in town. The menu features creative dishes highlighting locally grown ingredients, such as black-bean-and-red-onion chili with corn bread and the house specialty, the Kamehameha—shredded pork, local onions and baby greens wrapped in herbed garlic flatbread. Jen's also serves salads and ice cream. ~ Route 270 at Kapaau Waterworks Road, North Kohala; 808-889-0099. BUDGET TO MODERATE.

**GROCERIES**

**Whaler's General Store** is a moderate-sized grocery market located in the Waikoloa mall complex. ~ Waikoloa Beach Drive, Waikoloa; 808-886-7057.

Up the mountain several miles above Waikoloa, you'll find **Waikoloa Village Market** in the Waikoloa Highlands Center. ~ 808-883-1088.

On the western side of the island, there are several stores on the Kohala peninsula. Between Kawaihae and Kailua is one store in Puako, **Puako General Store**, with a small collection of groceries and dry goods. ~ 7 Puako Beach Drive, Puako; 808-882-7500.

**K. Takata Store** is an old market with an ample stock of groceries. It's the best place to shop north of Kailua. Closed Sunday afternoon. ~ Route 27, between Hawi and Kapaau; 808-889-5261.

**A. Arakaki Store** is conveniently located for campers and picnickers headed out to Pololu Valley. ~ Route 270, Halaula; 808-889-5262.

**AUTHOR FAVORITE**

Up near Kohala's northern tip, in the well-preserved historic town of Hawi, is the **Bamboo Restaurant**. Located in the 1920s-era general store turned gallery, this restaurant is decorated with tropical plants and deep wicker chairs. The menu offers a mix of Pacific regional and "local style" cuisine and includes such items as Thai broiled prawns and grilled fresh island fish in a variety of preparations. All meats and produce served are locally grown. There's Hawaiian music Friday and Saturday nights. Reservations required. Closed Sunday night and Monday. ~ Akoni Pule Highway, Hawi; 808-889-5555; www.thebamboorestaurant. com, e-mail bamrest@interpac.net. MODERATE.

**SHOPPING** Shopping in Kohala was once a matter of uncovering family-owned crafts shops in tiny towns. Now that it has become a major resort area, you can also browse at designer stores in several top-flight hotels. Simply drive along Akoni Pule Highway between Kailua and the Kohala Peninsula; you'll encounter, from south to north, the **Royal Waikoloan, Hilton Waikoloa Village, Mauna Lani Bay Hotel** and the **Mauna Kea Beach Hotel.** Each of these large resort complexes features an array of boutiques, knickknack shops, jewelers, sundries and other outlets.

All along the Kaahumanu Highway, there's a type of graffiti unique to the Big Island. Setting white coral atop black lava, and vice versa, ingenious residents and visitors have spelled out their names and messages.

Also consider the **Kings' Shops at Waikoloa.** Set on the road leading in to the Waikoloa resort complex, this mall contains clothing stores, a sundries shop and several other promising enterprises.

A beautiful and diverse collection of Hawaii's signature instruments are found at the **Ukulele House.** Choices start at under $25 and price upward into the many hundreds. It's fun browsing even if you have no intention of making a purchase. ~ Kings' Shops at Waikoloa; 808-886-8587.

**Indochine** features imports from Asia, including lovely jewelry and a wide variety of arts and crafts. Amidst that which is familiar are pieces that are special. ~ Kings' Shops at Waikoloa; 808-886-8383.

**Arts Pacifica** displays a sophisticated selection of paintings and artworks from an incongruously located gallery. ~ 61-3642 Kawaiahae Road, Kawaiahae; 808-880-1444.

On the other hand, the diminutive town of Hawi, another of the island's clapboard plantation towns, hosts several artist shops. **The Gallery of Bamboo** has a marvelous collection of island clothes, keepsakes and knickknacks. ~ Akoni Pule Highway, Hawi; 808-889-1441. Another lunar landing place just down the road, **Sugar Moon** is a ceramics shop with beautifully crafted works in clay. ~ Akoni Pule Highway, Hawi; 808-889-1441.

The **L. Zeidman Gallery** offers an impressive selection of hand-turned wooden bowls made of a variety of native and exotic woods. ~ 55-3553 Akoni Pule Highway, Hawi; 808-889-1400.

Hawaii's largest used book store isn't located in Honolulu, but in small town Kapaau. The **Kohala Book Shop's** selections includes many hard-to-get classics of Hawaiiana as well as a well-stocked contemporary bookshelf. Leave yourself some time to browse. Closed Sunday and Monday. ~ 54-3885 Akoni Pule Highway, Kapaau; 808-889-6400; www.kohalabooks.com.

Farther along Akoni Pule Highway, in the falsefront town of Kapaau, you'll find **Ackerman Galleries**. Divided into two different stores on opposite sides of the street, Ackerman's features fine art in one location and crafts items in the other. ~ Akoni Pule Highway, Kapaau; 808-889-5971; www.ackermangalleries.com.

Night owls along the Kohala Coast roost at the large resort hotels. The Mauna Kea Beach Hotel has a Hawaiian band at **The Terrace** and features a solo guitarist or a jazz duo in the **Batik Room**. ~ Kaahumanu Highway, Kawaihae; 808-882-7222.     **NIGHTLIFE**

The **Honu Bar** at the Mauna Lani Bay Hotel is one of several places in this spacious resort to dance, listen to Hawaiian music, or imbibe. It swings to life Thursday through Saturday with a live jazz band. Some guests, however, may prefer a game of chess, pool or backgammon. ~ 68-1400 Mauna Lani Drive, Kawaihae; 808-885-6622.

The **Paniolo Lounge** at the Fairmont Orchid hosts a band that plays Hawaiian and contemporary music. ~ 1 North Kaniku Drive, Kohala; 808-885-2000.

The night scene at the **Royal Waikoloan** centers around a watering hole called the **Clipper Lounge** that offers a variety of diversions ranging from live bands to Polynesian revues. ~ Kaahumanu Highway, Waikoloa; 808-886-6789.

On weekends, the **Blue Dolphin Restaurant** features local bands, which draw a lively crowd. Closed on rainy days. ~ Across from Kawaihae Harbor, Kawaihae; phone/fax 808-882-7771.

Also in Kawaihae, there is the **Tres Hombres Beach Grill**, where you can enjoy the original collection of surfing memorabilia that decorates the place. ~ Kawaihae Center, Kawaihae; 808-882-1031.

For Hawaiian music, try the **Bamboo Restaurant** on Friday and Saturday nights. Reservations required. ~ Akoni Pule Highway, Hawi; 808-889-5555.

Due to limited resources (such as water), county campgrounds determine capacity by how many people are camping rather than number of sites. They are on a first-come, first-served basis and close after the allotted number of campers is reached.     **BEACHES & PARKS**

**ANAEHOOMALU BEACH** An enchanting area, this is one of the island's most beautiful beaches. There are palm trees, two ancient fishponds filled with barracuda, and a long crescent of white sand. Turn from the sea and take in the gorgeous mountain scenery. Or explore the nearby petroglyph field and archaeological ruins. This beach is very popular and often crowded since it's fronted by a major resort complex. Swimming is excellent along this partially protected shore; there is no lifeguard on duty. Snorkeling is good for beginners but it lacks the scenic diversity elsewhere. Mullet, threadfin, big-eyed scad, bonefish and *papio* are among the usual catches here. Facilities include picnic tables, restrooms and an outdoor shower; there are restaurants in the adjacent Outrigger Waikoloa Beach. ~ Located a half-mile off Kaahumanu Highway, about 25 miles north of Kailua near the 76-mile marker.

**SECRET POND AT MAUNA LANI** Adjacent to the series of fishponds at the Mauna Lani Resort, Secret Pond's cool fresh waters are reached on the trail that leads past the fishponds to the coast. The pool was created in the 19th century when stream waters were enclosed by a lava rock wall. The crystal blue-green waters are inviting, although the pool is too small for much of a swim.

**HOLOHOLOKAI BEACH PARK** This scenic stretch of coast consists of mostly rocky shoreline, with small intermittent patches of sand. Rocky shallows offshore make for difficult ocean access, but beachcombing offers a natural serenity, complete with blue and turquoise seas in the foreground and the colorful North Kohala Mountains as a distant backdrop. Near the shore is a stand of rare native milo trees. The Mauna Lani Resort maintains restroom and shower facilities at the site. ~ Holoholokai is accessed by a trail that departs the parking lot for the Malama Petroglyph Trail. Well-marked signs direct you there after entering the Mauna Lani Resort.

**MAUUMAE BEACH** A rocky coastline and offshore shallows make for difficult water access. Mauumae does, however, have visual appeal, thanks to the colorful contrast of white coral sands, black lava rock shallows, luminous blue waters, and the green of the distant North Kohala Mountains. Beachcombers can wander the coast with nary a soul to disturb them. ~ Mauumae is part of the Mauna Lani Resort's undeveloped acreage and is accessed by a trail that departs the parking lot for the Malama Petroglyph Field. Well-marked signs direct you there once you've entered the Mauna Lani Resort.

**"69" BEACH OR WAIALEA BAY**    No, it's not what ◄ HIDDEN you might think. This lovely beach is named for a numbered utility pole at the road turn-off rather than for licentious beach parties. The white-sand shoreline extends several hundred yards along a rocky cove. Despite houses nearby, the spot is fairly secluded; fallen *kiawe* trees along the beachfront provide tiny hideaways. It's a good place to swim but exercise caution. When the water is calm it's also a good spot for snorkeling. Surfers paddle out to the breaks near the southwest end of the bay and off the northwest point. There are no facilities here. ~ Located near the entrance to Hapuna Beach Park, about five miles south of Kawaihae. From Kaahumanu Highway, turn into the park entrance. Then take the paved road that runs southwest from the park (between the beach and the A-frames). Go about six-tenths of a mile on this road and then turn right on a dirt road (the road at the very bottom of the hill). When the road forks, after about one-tenth mile, go left. Follow this road another one-tenth mile around to the beach.

**HAPUNA BEACH STATE PARK**    Here's one of the state's prettiest parks. A well-tended lawn—studded with *hala*, coconut and *kiawe* trees—rolls down to a wide corridor of white sand that extends for one-half mile, with points of lava at either end. Maui's Haleakala crater looms across the water. This is a popular and generally very crowded place. Unfortunately, a major resort hotel was built at one end of the beach. Swimming is excellent at the north end of the beach but beware of danger-

**KIDS ONLY**

If you're traveling with kids, they'll enjoy the Ocean Sports Hawaii's **Kid's Adventure Day**. Only the escorts are over 14 on this half-day catamaran adventure that departs Waikoloa Resort's Anaehoomalu Bay. ~ At the Hilton Waikoloa Village and the Outrigger Waikoloa Resort; 808-886-6666 ext. 1, 888-724-5234; www.hawaiioceansports.com.

ous currents when the surf is high; lifeguards on duty. Snorkelers enjoy the coral and fish near the rocks and cliffs at the end of the beach. *Papio*, red bigeye, mullet, threadfin and *menpachi* are often caught here. Facilities include picnic areas, restrooms and showers. ~ Located on Kaahumanu Highway, three miles south of Kawaihae.

▲ No tent or trailer camping is allowed. However, screened A-frame shelters, located on a rise above the beach, can be rented. These cottages, which cost $20 per night, are equipped with a table, sleeping platforms and electricity; they sleep up to four people. Bring your own bedding and cooking utensils. Toilet and kitchen facilities are shared among all six A-frames. For reservations, contact Hawaii State Parks. ~ 808-882-7995.

**KAUNAOA BEACH (MAUNA KEA BEACH)** Selected by Laurence Rockefeller as the site for the famed Mauna Kea Beach Hotel, the wide crescent of sand faces a sheltered bay that offers wonderful deepwater swimming and snorkeling. Tall palms line a portion of the beach, with the North Kohala Mountains and Mauna Kea, snow-capped in winter, as a backdrop. ~ Public access to the beach is from the public access parking area adjacent to the hotel's golf shop. Access numbers are limited and entry must be approved at the resort's security gate.

**SPENCER BEACH PARK** Lacking the uncommon beauty of Anaehoomalu or Hapuna, this spacious park is still

## FUN WITH FLIPPER

There's nothing quite like a one-on-one experience with those cute, friendly and intelligent creatures of the ocean—dolphins. **Dolphin Quest**, a marine research and educational program, provides this opportunity to both adults and children. Mammal experts teach guests about the dolphins' captivating abilities while instilling an appreciation for the importance of preserving the world's oceans and its inhabitants for future generations. A variety of programs are available, from a 30-minute "Adult Encounter" to a "Dolphin Family Program," a behind-the-scenes "Animal Training Adventure" to a "Dolphin Twilight Camp" for kids ages 5 to 12. You don't have to be Hilton guest, but you do have to make reservations well in advance. An experience you won't forget. ~ Hilton Waikoloa Village, 425 Waikoloa Beach Drive, Waikoloa; 808-886-2875, fax 808-886-7030; www.dolphin quest.org, e-mail dqhawaii@dolphinquest.org.

lovely. There's a wide swath of white sand, backed by a lawn and edged with *kiawe* and coconut trees. Swimming is excellent here and snorkeling will satisfy beginners and experts alike. Anglers try for *papio*, red bigeye, mullet, threadfin and *menpachi*. There are plenty of facilities: picnic area, restrooms, showers, a large pavilion, volleyball and basketball courts and electricity. This is the only county park with a nighttime security patrol. Also, the gates close you in from 11 p.m. to 6 a.m. ~ Located off Kawaihae Road about one mile south of Kawaihae.

▲ Both tent and trailer camping are allowed; $5 per night/per adult, $1 to $2 for children. County permit and reservations are required. This is a very popular place to camp so reserve early—capacity is limited.

**MAHUKONA BEACH PARK** This now-abandoned harbor village and boat landing lies along a rocky, windswept shore. The lawn is shaded with *kiawe* trees; there's no sandy beach here at all. Nicer areas lie to the south, but if you seek a site far from the frenzied crowd, this is a good retreat. The rocks make for poor access for swimming but snorkeling is good. Frequent catches include threadfin, mullet, *menpachi*, *papio* and red bigeye. Facilities include a picnic area, restrooms, showers and electricity. There's no drinking water. ~ Located off Akoni Pule Highway about 13 miles north of Kawaihae.

▲ Tent and trailer; $5 per night/per adult, $1 to $2 for children. County permit required.

**KAPAA BEACH PARK** Besides a spectacular view of Maui, this rocky, wind-plagued park has little to offer. It does have a miniature cove bounded by *kiawe* trees, but lacks any sand, which is sometimes nice to have on a beach. Swimming is difficult because of the rocks. Kapaa offers good diving but the entrance is rocky and the currents are tricky. Fishing is probably your best bet here since you can stand on the rocks and try for threadfin, mullet, red bigeye, *papio* and *menpachi*. Picnic areas and restrooms are the only facilities. There's no drinking water. ~ Located off Akoni Pule Highway about 14 miles north of Kawaihae.

▲ Tents and trailers are allowed, but the terrain is very rocky for tent camping; $5 per night/per adult, $1 to $2 for children. County permit required.

# SIX

# Waimea

Just 15 miles from the tablelands of Honokaa and ten miles from the Kohala Coast, at an elevation of 2670 feet, sits Waimea. Covered with rolling grasslands and bordered by towering mountains, Waimea (also called Kamuela) is cowboy country. Here, *paniolos*, Hawaiian cowboys, ride the range on one of the world's largest independently owned cattle ranches. Founded by John Palmer Parker, an adventurous sailor who jumped ship in 1809, Parker Ranch extends from sea level to over 9000 feet. In a typical year the 225,000-acre ranch is home to 55,000 head of cattle.

The cool rustic countryside, seemingly incongruous in a tropical retreat like Hawaii, is dotted with carpenter's Gothic houses and adorned with stables, large grassy lawns and picket fences. Like every place that's discovered, and word is out on Waimea, growth has had its impact with lots of in-migration from the mainland and Honolulu and second-home communities for the wealthy in the vicinity. There area lot more houses, served by several small malls. There are several haute cuisine restaurants worthy of lunch or dinner, and plenty of bed-and-breakfasts to make for a cozy stay.

The night sky is one of the visual rewards of a Waimea stay. Star-lit of under the soothing brilliance of a full moon, it is spectacular. Support facilities for the observatory complex atop 13,696-foot Mauna Kea are situated here, but a ranch town energy still helps define Waimea, where three museums with ranch-related themes help preserve that heritage, even as economics make ranching a problematic enterprise.

A stay in Waimea also offers easy access to the natural and historic sites found in North Kohala to the west and Hamakua to the east. The surrounding hills offer great hiking and horse back riding on range land marked by grassy mounds of ancient volcanic craters, lush, steep-walled valleys like Pololu and Waipio, and towering waterfalls, while the beaches at Spencer Beach Park and Hapuna are just a short ride downhill.

**SIGHTS**

The museum at **Parker Ranch Visitors Center** presents a history of the Parker family that will carry you back 155 years with its displays of Victorian-era furniture and clothing. In addition to the artifacts and family momentos, there is a movie that tells the story of the Parker family from its earliest days to the present. Admission. ~ 808-885-7655, fax 808-885-7561; www.parker ranch.com, e-mail info@parkerranch.com.

And at the **Historic Parker Ranch Homes** you can view the family's original 1840s-era ranch house and an adjoining century-old home (which doubles as a museum filled with extraordinary French Impressionist artwork). While the original home was built of *koa* and contains a collection of antique calabashes, the latter-day estate boasts lofty ceilings, glass chandeliers and walls decorated with the work of Pissaro and Corot, among others. Closed Sunday. ~ Mamalahoa Highway, one-half mile west of town; 808-885-5433, fax 808-885-5602; www.parkerranch.com, e-mail dquitiquit@parkerranch.com.

Another fine display is at the **Kamuela Museum**. Founded by J. P. Parker's great-great-granddaughter, this private collection of everything from Royal Hawaiian artifacts to moon-flight relics is fascinating, if poorly organized. Admission. ~ Junction of Kawaihae Road and Kohala Mountain Road (junction of Routes 19 and 250); 808-885-4724.

For a splendid example of *koa* woodworking, visit **Imiola Congregational Church** on the east side of town. Built in 1832, this clapboard church has an interior fashioned entirely from the native timber. ~ Mamalahoa Highway; 808-885-4987.

Established in 1985, **Hakalau Forest National Wildlife Refuge** is divided into two sections. Both segments were chosen for their diversity of endemic species of flora and fauna. There are the 5000-acre Kona Forest Unit, upcountry of Kealakekua Bay, which is closed to the public, and the 33,000-acre preserve at Maulua, on the upper slopes of Mauna Kea. The lower portion of Maulua is open to activities such as birdwatching and hiking. Hawaiian owls, hoary bats, hawks and colorful forest songbirds like *apapane* and *akiapolaau* all make their home here. There are no facilities, and no maintained trails. Access is limited to weekends. ~ To reach this isolated acreage means taking the Saddle Road, following the turnoff to Hale Pohaku and the observatories atop Mauna Kea. Turn right where unpaved Mana/Keanakolu Road intersects the summit road. From here it's 12 miles to Hakalau. For entry approval call the refuge between 8 a.m. and 4 p.m.; those approved are given the combination to the locked gate. Information: Fish & Wildlife, 32 Kinoole Street, Hilo; 808-933-6915.

**SADDLE ROAD**   Cutting across the island, Saddle Road climbs from Hilo to an elevation of over 6500 feet (bring a sweater!). The eastern section is heavily wooded with *ohia* trees and ferns and is often fog-shrouded. The central portion includes stark fields of lava only intermittently broken by *kipuka*, "islands" of trees surrounded by lava but left alive—micro-ecosystems that are home to rare native plants and birds. The western portion traverses rolling pastures. The Saddle is a stark landscape, a mosaic of decades-old flows from Mauna Loa's and Mauna Kea's grass-covered cinder cones. You cross lava flows from 1855 and 1935 while gaining elevation that will provide you with the finest view of these mountains anywhere on the island. Before setting out, pack warm clothing and check your gas gauge—there are no

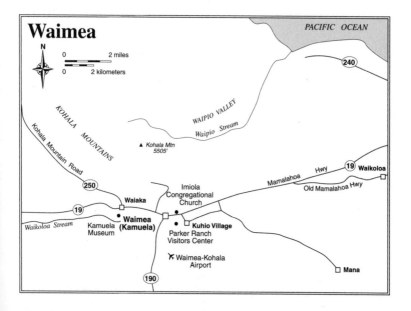

service stations or stores en route. And consult your car rental agency: Some do not permit driving on Saddle Road.

Near the 28-mile marker, the road to Mauna Kea leads 13 miles up to the 13,796-foot summit. The first six miles are passable by passenger car and take in a lookout and the **Onizuka Center for International Astronomy**. This is one stop you will want to make. During the day the **Visitor Information Station** offers videos, exhibits and computers with Mauna Kea and astronomy software running. Sometimes the 11-inch Celestron telescope is set up outside with a solar filter so that you can view the sun and sun spots.

**Summit tours** are held on Saturday and Sunday from 1 to 5 p.m. Visitors must arrive one hour beforehand to get acclimated to the altitude. The tour departs at 2 p.m. on a 4-wheel-drive vehicle. Participants are given the history and details of the summit telescopes on the way up. Once there, an inside tour of one or two of the summit telescopes follows. You'll leave the summit at about 4:30 p.m.

*Note:* Be sure that you have a full tank of gas in your vehicle when driving to Mauna Kea. The steep grade combined with the lower oxygen level makes internal combustion engines run inefficiently. Fuel is not available at the summit—or the road to the volcano.

There's a free **star-gazing program** from 6 to 10 p.m. Four-wheel-drive vehicles are recommended for the trip to the summit, although most cars can handle it without problems. ~ 808-961-2180, fax 808-969-4892.

At the summit you'll find the **Mauna Kea Observatory complex**, one of the finest observatories in the world, but be prepared for freezing temperatures. You'll also be treated to some of the most otherworldly views imaginable. (See "A Window in the Sky" on page 52 for more information about the telescopes on Mauna Kea.)

**Mauna Kea State Recreation Area**, with cabins and recreation area, lies about midway along the Saddle Road. Situated on the tableland between Mauna Kea and Mauna Loa at 6500-feet elevation, this is an excellent base camp for climbing either mountain.

The road continues past a United States military base, then descends through stands of eucalyptus windbreaks into Waimea cat-

# Mana / Keanakolu Road

If you are interested in a scenic drive with an idyllic landscape of grasslands accentuated by rounded cinder cones and slow-moving herds of cattle follow **Mana Road**, which makes a circuit of towering Mauna Kea. Easily reached from Waimea turn right on Mana Road (by the 55-mile marker on Route 19), then turn left where the paved road ends. From here, Mana Road winds a narrow red-dirt path though scenic pastureland before heading higher up the mountain's slopes to **Keanakolu**, a forested site. There are numerous gates along the way, which remain unlocked, allowing visitors to circumnavigate Mauna Kea. This is private land, and those using the road should be attentive to the joggers, hikers, bicyclists and off-road vehicles that may also be taking advantage of the wild, expansive beauty of the setting. The gates serve to keep cattle in the right pastures, so make sure to close all gates behind you.

The full circuit can be done as a full-day excursion. If a full circuit is too much to handle, it's easy to backtrack after the first 10–12 miles. While most of the road does not require four-wheel-drive, if the weather has been rainy, portions of the road may be impassable. (Keep in mind that most car rental contracts forbid off-road travel.)

tle country. Here you can pick up the Mamalahoa Highway (Route 190) southwest to Kailua, only 87 miles from Hilo. Passing through sparsely populated range country over 2000 feet in elevation, this road has sensational views of the Kona Coast and Maui.

**LODGING**

Set amid the Kohala Mountains in the cowboy town of Waimea are two hotels, both within walking distance of local markets and restaurants. **Waimea Country Lodge** is a modern multi-unit motel with exposed-beam ceilings and furniture of knotty pine. Guest rooms are large, carpeted and equipped with telephones, shower-tub combinations and color televisions; some have small kitchenettes. ~ 65-1210 Lindsey Road; 808-885-4100, 800-367-5004, fax 808-885-6711; www.castleresorts.com. MODERATE.

**Kamuela Inn**, a neighbor just down the street, has modest one- and two-room units, and suites in a newer wing. These are clean and bright with private baths. All of the 30 units are equipped with cable TV and some have refrigerators. Guests are served a continental breakfast. ~ Kawaihae Road; 808-885-4243, 800-555-8968, fax 808-885-8857. MODERATE.

Situated at the foot of the Kohala Mountains, **Waimea Gardens Bed and Breakfast** offers another lodging option with its three distinctive studios: one with a fireplace, another with a hot tub and private garden, and a third with a private deck and garden. Benches, which dot the water's edge along the stream out back, are perfect for an afternoon of relaxation. Tropical fruit, breads and pastries start each day. ~ 65-1632 Kawaihae Road; 808-885-8550, fax 808-885-0473; e-mail campbell@hawaii.rr. com. DELUXE.

HIDDEN ►     The cabins at **Mauna Kea State Recreation Area** are convenient for hikers or skiers headed up to Mauna Kea. With its stunning mountain views, sparse vegetation and chilly weather, this rarefied playground hardly seems like Hawaii. For remoteness and seclusion, you can't choose a better spot. A picnic area and restrooms are the only facilities. No tents or trailers are allowed. The cabins can be rented from the Division of State Parks, 75 Aupuni Street, Hilo, Hawaii, HI 96721; 808-974-6200. The individual cabins, each accommodating up to six people, have two bedrooms, bath, kitchenette and an electric heater. Cabins have loads of cooking utensils and sufficient bedding. Rates are $45 for four people and $5 for each additional person. There are also fourplex cabinettes that rent for $55 for eight people and $5 for each additional person. These aren't nearly as nice as the individual cabins. They are one-bedroom units crowded with eight bunks; cooking is done in a community dining and recreation area next door. ~ On the Saddle Road about 35 miles west of Hilo.

**DINING**     With all the fine-dining possibilities here, Waimea is short on short-order restaurants. There is not much in the way of inexpensive ethnic restaurants. You will find two in Waimea Center (Mamalahoa Highway): **Great Wall Chopsui** has steam-tray Chinese food for lunch and dinner but serves an American breakfast. ~ 808-885-7252. BUDGET. **Yong's Kalbi** serves Korean dishes. Closed Sunday. ~ 808-885-8440. BUDGET TO MODERATE.

Waimea's oldest frame house, built in 1852 and still owned by the same Hawaiian family, is the setting for **Maha's Cafe**. This breakfast and lunch restaurant is a labor of love for "Maha," a former chef at the Mauna Lani Resort who chose to get back to her roots with Hawaiian cuisine featuring local ingredients such as taro, sweet potatoes and locally grown produce. Among the light breakfast selections are poi pancakes with coconut syrup. Lunch options include broiled fish and smoked *ahi* with *lilikoi* (passion fruit) salsa, and, for vegans, the "Lalamilo vegie," a double-decker club-style sandwich of fresh-picked cucumbers, tomatoes, avocado, Kahua lettuce and Kohala clover sprouts with green olive pesto. Don't pass up one of the traditional Hawaiian desserts such as bread pudding with guava-ginger sauce. Closed Tuesday. ~ 1 Waimea Center; 808-885-0693, fax 808-889-5755. BUDGET TO MODERATE.

The pungent scent of garlic soup rolls out the doorway of **Aioli's**, an eat-in or take-out deli, bakery and catering service that doubles as a small gourmet restaurant at dinner hour. Lunch features custom-made sandwiches on homemade bread, from hamburgers to fresh-catch fish, and always includes two vegetarian entrées. The dinner menu spans the ethnic spectrum and changes constantly. Typical dinner specials are herb-crusted prime rib, mahimahi and *langostinos en papillote*, walnut-stuffed pasta and herb-marinated grilled shrimp. Closed Monday. ~ Opelo Plaza, Kawaihae Road; 808-885-6325. MODERATE TO DELUXE.

A cutesy rendition of the little fish taco shacks that line the beaches in Baja California, **Tako Taco Taqueria** has a couple of tables and a booming take-out business. The fare includes salads

**AUTHOR FAVORITE**

Waimea's first contribution to Hawaii regional cuisine is **Merriman's**, a very highly regarded restaurant that has received national attention. The interior follows a neo-tropical theme and the menu is tailored to what is fresh and local. Since the locale is not simply Hawaii, but upcountry Hawaii, the cuisine combines the seashore and the cattle ranch. You might find fresh fish with spicy *lilikoi* sauce or steak with *kiawe*-smoked tomato sauce; gourmet vegetarian dishes round out the fare. I highly recommended it. No lunch Saturday and Sunday. ~ Opelo Plaza, Kawaihae Road; 808-885-6822, fax 808-885-8756; www.merrimanshawaii.com, e-mail goodfood@lava.net. DELUXE TO ULTRA-DELUXE.

and assorted Mexican standbys such as big, two-fist bean burritos, but the claim to fame here is the fresh fish tacos with tomatillo and pineapple salsa. ~ 65-1271 Kawaihae Road; 808-887-1717. BUDGET.

If you're hankering for a steak up here in cowboy country, then ride on in to **Paniolo Country Inn**. There are branding irons on the walls and sirloins on the skillet. The booths are made of knotty pine and dishes have names like "Lone Ranger" and "bucking bronco." You can order barbecued chicken, baby back ribs or a "south of the border" special. ~ 65-1214 Lindsey Road; 808-885-4377. MODERATE TO DELUXE.

**Koa House Grill** takes its name from the walls—dark *koa* panels accented with cowboy gear and photos of *paniolos*. The cuisine is steak and seafood with a few additional pasta dishes for good measure. ~ 65-1144 Mamalahoa Highway; 808-885-2088, fax 808-885-5590. MODERATE TO ULTRA-DELUXE.

HIDDEN ►

*Paniolos* and other locals hang out at the counter of the **Hawaiian Style Café**, a funky little diner where the portions are huge and the prices ridiculously low. Breakfast might be an omelet bigger than your plate or a stack of buttermilk pancakes 12 inches in diameter. For lunch, you can fill up on cholesterol with a big, fat, juicy hamburger and a heaping pile of fries. The place is justly known for its Friday-only *luau* plate featuring *laulau*, *kalua* pig, *lomi* salmon, chicken long rice and pickled vegetables. "All-you-can-eat" might be an understatement; it's likely to be all you'll need to eat for your entire stay on the island. Breakfast and lunch only. ~ Kawaihae Road; 808-885-4295. BUDGET.

## YEE HAW

Saddle up at **Dahana Ranch**, a 600-acre cattle spread near Waimea. Hawaiian "horse whisperer" Harry Nakoa offers several options for would-be *paniolos* (Hawaiian cowboys and girls). At this 140-head cattle operation and quarter horse farm you can opt for a "Range Station Ride," where you are taught wrangling techniques—then drive the cattle from one pasture to another. Or you can gallop across the range, mingling with the sheep, horses and cattle that call this ranchland home. ~ P.O. Box 1293, Kamuela, HI 96743; 808-885-0057, 888-399-0057, fax 808-885-7833; www.dahanaranch.com.

One of my favorite Waimea dining spots is the **Edelweiss** restaurant, a cozy club with a knockout interior design. The entire place was fashioned by a master carpenter who inlaid *sugi* pine, *koa* and silver oak with the precision of a jeweler. Run by a German chef who gained his knowledge at prestigious addresses like Maui's plush Kapalua Bay Hotel, Edelweiss is a gourmet's delight. The dinner menu includes wienerschnitzel, roast duck and a house specialty—sautéed veal, lamb, beef and bacon with *pfifferling*. For lunch there is bratwurst, sauerkraut and sandwiches. Closed Sunday and Monday, and the month of September. ~ Kawaihae Road; 808-885-6800. DELUXE TO ULTRA-DELUXE.

Chef Daniel Thiebaut blends his French training with local foods and Asian flavors to create exceptional Pacific Rim cuisine at his namesake restaurant, **Daniel Thiebaut**. Artfully presented entrées such as miso-glazed salmon, wok-fried sea scallops and Hunan-style rack of lamb fill the menu. Located in a former general store, the interior retains much of its old warmth and feel with polished hardwood floors and period furnishings. No lunch on Saturday and Sunday. ~ 65-1259 Kawaihae Road; 808-887-2200, fax 808-887-0811; www.danielthiebaut.com, e-mail reservations@danielthiebaut.com. ULTRA-DELUXE.

**GROCERIES** The one supermarket located along this route is **K.T.A. Super Store**, open daily from 6 a.m. to 11 p.m. ~ Mamalahoa Highway; 808-885-8866.

**Kona Healthways** has a large supply of vitamins, baked goods, cosmetics and so on. ~ 67-1185 Mamalahoa Highway; 808-885-6775.

**SHOPPING** **Waimea Center** is *the* shopping complex in Waimea's cattle country. This modern center features boutiques, knickknack shops and more. You'll find the mall located in the center of Waimea.

**The Quilted Horse** has quilts (without the horse) and decorative items for the home like candles, woodcarvings and wallhangings. ~ Kawaihae Road.

**Parker Square** specializes in "distinguished shops." Particularly recommended here is the **Gallery of Great Things**, a store that fulfills the promise of its name. Look for locally made arts and crafts as well as contemporary and tribal art and work representing Polynesia, Indonesia and the Pacific Rim. ~ 808-885-7706.

**Bentley's Home Collection,** in the same complex, offers everything from clothing to greeting cards. ~ Kawaihae Road; 808-885-5565.

Hawaiian and Polynesian art, antiques and artifacts are featured at **Mauna Kea Galleries.** They have a fascinating collection of ceramics, hula dolls, graphics and quilts. ~ 65-1298 Kawaihae Road; 808-969-1184; www.maunakeagalleries.com.

**Dan Deluz's Woods** has beautifully handcrafted bowls, boxes and carvings. The owner, in the business for decades, is a master of his trade. ~ 64-1013 Mamalahoa Highway; 808-885-5856.

Things Hawaiian, which means everything from books to Hawaiian quilt patterns, bric-a-brac to collectible Hawaiiana, and clothing to artworks, can be discovered at **Cook's Discoveries.** ~ 64-1066 Mamalahoa Highway; 808-885-3633.

**NIGHTLIFE**    There's not much to do at night in *paniolo* country except listen to the cows moo. If you're lucky, something will be happening at the 490-seat **Kahilu Theatre,** which offers dance performances, concerts, plays and current movies. ~ Parker Ranch Center; 808-885-6017.

# SEVEN

# Kona/Kau District

South of Kailua lies the Kona/Kau district, a region often overlooked by Big Island visitors. The land at this end of the island was formed from the lava flows of Hualalai and Mauna Loa. Black- and green-sand beaches hug the rugged coastline, while coffee trees and windswept grasslands cling to the ragged hillsides. Small towns, unspoiled by tourism, sit along the highway, lost in a time warp of tropical reveries. The southernmost point in the United States is here, as are coffee plantations, historic landmarks and other gems to discover.

South Kona was heavily populated in pre-contact Hawaii and home to the island's most important temples (*heiau*). Kau was more of a backwater, still largely a wilderness, isolated from the centers of population and often under the rule of high chiefs of neighboring districts. In the lee of Mauna Loa's immense rain shadow desert conditions prevail along much of the Kau coast, where isolated green sand, black sand, and beige sand beaches are to be found. Kau's Ka Lae, or South Point, is the southernmost land in the United States, closer to the equator than Key West. If the land was dry, Kau's seas were rich with fish. Some of the earliest archeological remains from Polynesian times are canoe huts and fishermen's shelters not far from South Point.

Small plantation towns dot the two-lane Mamalahoa Highway, which links Kailua to Hawaii Volcanoes National Park. Most of these villages are suffering the loss of sugar cane, which was the staple of the Kau economy until the mills closed and the fields were abandoned in the 1990s. In South Kona on the other hand, coffee has seen a boom-time expansion in cultivation, with dozens of upcountry farms producing world-renowned Kona brews. Colorful flowers abound along the upcountry stretch of the Mamalahoa Highway that winds its way through South Kona's coffee country, adding vibrant color to scenic vistas of the lowlands and coast. The town of Holualoa, five miles uphill from Kailua is the capital of coffee country, with a sprinkling of tasting houses and shops.

**SIGHTS**

*HIDDEN* ▶

Along the lower slopes of Hualalai just above Kailua lies **Kona coffee country**. This 20-mile-long belt, located between the 1000- and 2000-foot elevation and reaching south to Honaunau, is an unending succession of plantations glistening with the shiny green leaves and red berries of coffee orchards. If you prefer your vegetation decaffeinated, there are mango trees, banana fronds, macadamia nut orchards and sunbursts of wildflowers. To make sure you remember that even amid all the black lava you *are* still in the tropics, old coffee shacks and tinroof general stores dot the countryside.

So rather than heading directly south from Kailua, make sure you take in the full sweep of Kona's coffee country. Just take Palani Road (Route 190) uphill from Kailua, then turn right onto Route 180. This winding road cuts through old Kona in the heart of the growing region—watch for orchards of the small trees. Before the coast road was built, this was the main route. Today it's somewhat off the beaten track, passing through funky old country towns like Holualoa before joining the Mamalahoa Highway (Route 11) in Honalo.

In the heart of coffee country, **Holualoa** retains its small-town feel, even with its trendy collection of galleries along Mamalahoa Highway, a two-lane road that winds through the three-block-long heart of town. Make time to visit **Kona Blue Sky** at the south end of town for a free coffee tasting and specialties like chocolate-covered macadamia nuts and coffee beans. If you're interested, you can wander among coffee trees after viewing an informative video on coffee growing. ~ 76-973A Hualalai Road, Holualoa; 808-322-1700, 877-322-1700, fax 808-322-1473; www.konablueskycoffee.com, e-mail kbsky@aloha.net.

On Mamalahoa Highway, you'll also encounter the old Greenwell Store, a lava stone building that dates to 1875, and a perfect place to combine shopping with museum browsing. The **Kona Historical Society Museum and Gift Shop** has taken over this former general store (now on the National Register for Historic Places). Today it's filled with artifacts from Kona's early days plus contemporary postcards, calendars and other items. Of particular interest are the marvelous collections of photos and an-

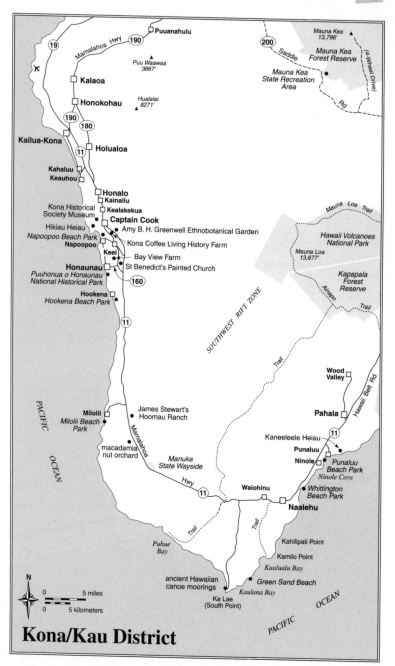

# Kona/Kau District

tique bottles. Closed Saturday and Sunday. ~ Mamalahoa Highway, Kealakekua; 808-323-3222, fax 808-323-2398; www.kona historical.org, e-mail khs@konahistorical.org.

This main route continues south along the western slopes of **Hualalai**. Located on an ancient Hawaiian agricultural site, the **Amy B. H. Greenwell Ethnobotanical Garden** spreads across 12 acres of upland countryside. The land is divided into four vegetation zones, varying from seaside plants to mountain forests, and is planted with hundreds of Polynesian and native Hawaiian species. On a self-guided tour, you can wander through fields cleared by Hawaiians in pre-contact days and view the plants that were vital to early island civilizations. Guided tours are offered the second Saturday of every month at 10 a.m. or by appointment. Closed Saturday and Sunday. ~ Off Mamalahoa Highway, Captain Cook; 808-323-3318, fax 808-323-2394; www. bishopmuseum.org/greenwell.

HIDDEN ▶

Across the road from the Greenwell Garden is the Kona Historical Society's **Kona Coffee Living History Farm**. Known locally as Uchida Farm, this seven-acre working coffee farm depicts the daily life of immigrant farmers from the 1920s to the 1940s, when small family farms dominated the rural Kona landscape and life in the district revolved around the annual coffee cycle. Access to the grounds is by guided tour only, where you can view the orchards, a Japanese-style farmhouse, gardens and old processing mills. Closed Saturday and Sunday. Fee. ~ Mamalahoa Highway, Captain Cook; 808-323-2006, fax 808-323-9576; www. konahistorical.org, e-mail khs@konahistorical.org.

HIDDEN ▶

Near the town of Captain Cook, Napoopoo Road leads down to Kealakekua Bay. First it passes the UCC **Hawaii Coffee Factory Outlet**. I don't know about you, but I'm a confirmed "caffiend," happily addicted to java for years. So it was mighty interesting to watch how the potent stuff goes from berry to bean to bag, with a few stops between. If you haven't tried Kona coffee, one of the few brews grown in the United States, this is the time. ~ 160 Napoopoo Road, Captain Cook; 808-322-3789, fax 808-324-1528; www.ucc-hawaii.com, e-mail info@ucc-hawaii.com.

**Kealakekua Bay** is a marine reserve and outstanding snorkeling spot with technicolor coral reefs and an array of tropical fish species. Spinner dolphins swim close to shore in this area. Here you can also check out the reconstructed temple, **Hikiau Heiau**, where Captain James Cook once performed a Christian burial service for one of his crewmen.

Captain Cook himself had little time left to live. Shortly after the ceremony, he was killed and possibly eaten by natives who had originally welcomed him as a god, his divinity questioned when he returned to Kealakekua Bay to repair a broken ship's mast after a regal departure. A stolen cutter was the cause, with Cook and a number of marines going ashore to demand its return on threat of taking the high chief hostage. Cook was attacked as he came ashore. His body was taken and ceremonially dismembered. A portion of Cook's remains were eventually returned and were taken back to England. Some say portions of the flesh were eaten and the bones preserved in an effort to take possession of Cook's *mana*, his life force, or spiritual energy. A white obelisk, the **Captain Cook Monument**, rises across the bay where the famous mariner fell in 1779. The cliffs looming behind the Captain Cook marker in Kealakekua Bay are honeycombed with **Hawaiian burial caves**.

En route to Napoopoo, drop in on the **Kahikolu Congregational Church**, a beautifully preserved example of 19th-century Hawaiian architecture. The church, built in 1854 of *koa* wood, lava rock, and limestone mortar of crushed coral, is still an active a congregation. Its size reveals the large Hawaiian population that once lived along this stretch of South Kona coast. Henry Opukahaia, the first Hawaiian missionary who worked to convert his people to Christianity in the mid-19th century, is buried here. ~ 808-328-8110.

**Puuhonua o Honaunau National Historical Park** sits four miles south of Kealakekua Bay on Route 160. This ancient holy

**RIDE TO BRITAIN**

Located on the Kealakekua shoreline, on a stretch of coastline that forms the Bay's northern arm, the Captain Cook Monument (on land given to the British government) is reached by a long, strenuous trail that climbs hillsides before descending to the coast. It's far easier on horseback, with **Kings' Trail Rides O'Kona**, in the upcountry town of Kealakekua, offering daily horseback excursions to the site that include lunch and time for snorkeling and a swim. ~ P.O. Box 1366, Kealakekua, HI 96750; 808-323-2388; www.konacowboy.com.

ground, also known as the Place of Refuge, was one of the few places to which *kapu* breakers and refugees could flee for sanctuary. Once inside the Great Wall, a lava barricade ten feet high and 17 feet wide, they were safe from pursuers. Free booklets are available for self-guided tours to the royal grounds, *heiaus* and menacing wooden images of Native Hawaiian gods that made this beachfront refuge one of Hawaii's most sacred spots. The *heiaus*, dating back to the 16th and 17th centuries, are among the finest examples of ancient architecture on the Big Island. Also explore the house models, built to traditional specifications, the royal fishpond and the displays of ancient arts and crafts. Picnic tables and a sandy sunbathing area offer a place to relax—and don't miss the fascinating tidepools along the lava shoreline. (There's also great snorkeling here in the area just offshore from the boat ramp.) If you can, time your visit to Puuhonua o Honaunau for late afternoon and stay long enough to enjoy the sunset. Facing west, the setting sun silhouettes the rebuilt Hale o Keawe in vibrant color. You may be the only one there, which adds to a marvelous sense of the past that comes to life with serenity and power. Admission. ~ 808-328-2288, fax 808-328-8251.

At **Bay View Farm** you can tour a mill that produces Kona coffee. The trees here, like many you'll see along the roadside, are pruned to six or eight feet. Each will produce about 10 to 12 pounds of berries, which, after being picked by hand, will eventually produce two pounds of beans. Like peas in a pod, there are two beans per berry. A pulping machine squeezes them out of the red berry skin. Next, the beans are dried for up to a week and are turned every hour during daylight. Finally, the outer husks

**AUTHOR FAVORITE**

St. Benedict's, my favorite church in all the islands, lies just up the hill from Bay View Farm. An imaginative Belgian priest, hoping to teach his parishioners through color and imagery, transformed this rickety wooden chapel into a **Painted Church** by covering the interior walls with murals. He depicted several religious scenes and painted a vaulted nave behind the altar to give this tiny church the appearance of a great European cathedral. The charming exterior is carpenter's Gothic in style with a dramatic spire. ~ 84-1540 Painted Church Road, Honaunau; 808-328-2227, fax 808-328-8482.

are removed and the beans are graded and bagged for shipping. Small amounts of the premium beans are roasted on the premises (you can watch) and served as free samples (you can also buy more, of course). ~ Painted Church Road, Honaunau; 808-328-9658, 800-662-5880, fax 808-328-8693; www.bayviewfarmcof fees.com, e-mail bayview@aloha.net.

There is little except you, alternating bands of greenery and dark lava, and the black macadam of the Mamalahoa Highway as you proceed toward the southern extremities of the Big Island. Here along the lower slopes of Mauna Loa, lifeless lava fingers cut across lush areas teeming with tropical colors. The contrast is overwhelming: Rounding a bend, the road travels from an overgrown land of poinsettias and blossoming trees to a bleak area torn by upheaval, resembling the moon's surface. Once past the lava flows that have ravaged the countryside, you'll discover a terrain that, though dry and windblown, is planted with macadamia nut orchards and fields of cattle-range grasses.

About 30 miles south of Kailua, take the turnoff to the quaint Hawaiian fishing village at **Milolii**. It's quiet and remote, offering a glimpse of life as it once was in Hawaii. (See "Beaches & Parks" section below for more information.)    ◄ HIDDEN

Continuing south, Mamalahoa Highway passes the late **James Stewart's Hoomau Ranch** (87-mile marker), then a sprawling **macadamia nut orchard**. Eventually, the road arrives at the **South Point** turnoff. South Point Road leads through 11 miles of rolling grassland burned dry by the summer sun to the nation's southernmost point. En route you'll pass a cluster of windmills that draw energy from the trades that blow with ferocity through this region. Fishermen have built **platforms** along the sea cliff here to haul their catches up from the boats that troll these prime fishing grounds.

Located downslope on the Southwest Rift of Mauna Loa near South Point, **Kula Kai Caverns** consists of several miles of thousand-year-old braided lava tube systems through which experienced spelunkers guide tours by reservation only. Visitors can choose among various trips, from an easy half-hour walking tour to a half-day expedition deep into the side of the world's most massive mountain, where they will encounter cave-adapted insects and other creatures as well as fantastic root zones and lava formations. The guides provide all required equipment, including helmets, lights, gloves and kneepads. Tour fee. ~ P.O. Box 6313, Oceanview, HI 96757; 808-929-7539 or 808-929-9725; www.kulakaicaverns.com, e-mail caver@kulakaicaverns.com.

There are also **ancient Hawaiian canoe moorings** in the rocks below, and the remains of a *heiau* near the light tower. Some archaeologists believe that South Point was one of the places where **HIDDEN ▶** Polynesian discoverers first settled. Another local feature, **Green Sand Beach**, is a two-mile hike along the waterfront from the Kaulana boat ramp. Olivine eroding from an adjacent cinder cone has created a beach with a decidedly greenish hue. It's a hot hike, so if you go, make sure you take water. A rough shorebreak may make swimming risky.

Back on the highway continue on to **Naalehu**, the nation's southernmost town, and then on to **Punaluu Beach Park**. With its palm trees and enchanting lagoon, Punaluu's black-sand beach is simply gorgeous. The tourist complex detracts from the natural beauty, but to escape the madding mobs the explorer need wander only a couple of hundred yards east to the rocky remains of **Kaneeleele Heiau**. Or venture about one-third mile south to **Ninole Cove**. Although there's a condominium complex nearby, this spot is a bit more secluded. Many of the stones along Ninole's pebbly beach are filled with holes containing "baby" stones that are said to multiply.

From Punaluu to Volcanoes National Park, the highway passes through largely uninhabited grassland and sugar cane areas. **Pahala**, the only town along this stretch, is a plantation colony. **HIDDEN ▶** For an interesting side trip, go through Pahala to **Wood Valley Temple**, where a Tibetan Buddhist monk and his followers have taken over an old Japanese temple. Situated on 25 acres, the temple was dedicated in 1980 by the Dalai Lama. A tranquil yet dynamic place, it is painted in floral colors and adorned with a gilded statue of the Buddha. A donation of $5 per person to visit the temple and grounds is requested. ~ P.O. Box 250, Pahala, HI 96777; 808-928-8539.

**LODGING**  For a funky country place high in the mountains overlooking the Kona Coast, try the **Kona Hotel**. Catering primarily to workers, this 11-unit hotel remains a real sleeper. It might be difficult to book a room during the week, but on weekends, the lunchpail crowd heads home and you can rent a small place at an unbelievably low rate. Shared bathroom facilities. It's five miles to the beaches and action around Kailua, but if you're after an inexpensive retreat, this is the place. ~ Route 180, Holualoa; 808-324-1155. BUDGET.

Down the road, **Teshima's Inn** has small, cozy rooms at similar rates. These are set in an L-shaped structure fronting a small garden. The rooms have linoleum floors and wood-paneled walls decorated with Japanese art. Here you're 1300 feet above sea level and nine miles from Kailua. This charming inn is run by Mrs. Teshima, a delightful Japanese woman who has operated the establishment for years. Rooms are offered on a monthly (and yearly) basis only, so you're sure to meet plenty of locals here. For a real taste of basic, backcountry Hawaii, this is your place. ~ Mamalahoa Highway, Honalo; 808-322-9140. BUDGET.

One of the more unique places to stay on the Big Island is the **Dragonfly Ranch**. Spread across two acres, the Dragonfly is billed by owner Barbara Moore as a "healing-arts retreat." The grounds are luxurious and the atmosphere is decidedly New Age. The "honeymoon suite" has an outdoor bed complete with mirrored canopy, a sunken bath and shower. Three of the five units have partial kitchen facilities, or, for a small fee, you can participate in the family-style dinner. Don't expect condo-style living, but do prepare yourself for an experience. ~ Route 160, Honaunau; 808-328-2159, 800-487-2159, fax 808-328-9570; www.dragonfly ranch.com, e-mail dfly@aloha.net. MODERATE TO ULTRA-DELUXE.

◄ HIDDEN

### SLEEP UNDER THE BIG TOP

If camping is your idea of vacation fun, check out **Margo's Corner**. Margo's guests are generally bicyclists looking for refuge from highrise hotels and staid inns. Hot showers, breakfast and dinner are provided, and sleeping quarters consist of a number of tent sites situated in a large yard filled with pine trees and organic gardens. Some visitors sleep out in the open under the canopy of trees. For the less adventurous, a guest cottage with a queen-size bed, a private bath and a view of the garden is available, or try the "Adobe Suite" that sleeps six and includes a sauna. Also on the premises are a health food store and a community room. Ask about the art retreats. No smoking. Closed Thursday and Sunday except with reservations. ~ P.O. Box 447, Naalehu, HI 96772; phone/fax 808-929-9614; e-mail margos.corner@mailcity.com. BUDGET TO MODERATE.

Upcountry Honaunau has several noteworthy bed and breakfasts that cater to gays. The **Horizon Guest House** has 40 acres of privacy with spectacular views from rooms and the pool and jacuzzi. There are four suites to choose from. On Highway 11 near the 100-mile marker and the Hookena Beach turnoff. ~ P.O. Box 957, Honaunau, HI 96726; 808-328-2540, 888-328-8301, fax 808-328-8707; www.horizonguesthouse.com, e-mail contact@horizonguesthouse.com. MODERATE.

**Hale Aloha Guest House** is a nearby alternative, with a studio, four guest rooms and a deluxe suite. At 1600 feet elevation, the views are spectacular and the setting private. ~ 84-4780 Mamalahoa Highway, Honaunau HI 96726; phone/fax 808-328-8955, 800-897-3188; www.halealoha.com, e-mail vacation@hale aloha.com. MODERATE TO DELUXE.

With manicured grounds leading to a tiled-roof villa, **Kealakekua Bay Bed and Breakfast** combines picture-perfect views of Kealakekua Bay with its assortment of accommodations. Three light and airy suites are available. The Alii includes a jacuzzi tub to relax in, but all rooms have private entrances, private baths and refrigerators. Native Hawaiian prints, wicker furniture and ceiling fans adorn each room, including the lounge and dining room. The Ohana Kai cottage has two bedrooms, two-and-a-half baths, a kitchen, laundry, and a private lanai and garden, sleeping up to six. ~ P.O. Box 1412, Kealakekua, HI 96750; 808-328-8150, 800-328-8150, fax 808-328-8866; www.keala.com, e-mail kbaybb@aloha.net. MODERATE TO DELUXE.

At **H. Manago Hotel,** you'll have a varied choice of accommodations. Rooms in the creaky old section have communal baths. The battered furniture, torn linoleum floors and annoying street noise make for rather funky living here. Rooms in the newer section rise in price as you ascend the stairs. First-floor accommodations are the least expensive and rooms on the ethereal third floor are the most expensive, but all reside in the budget range. The only advantage for the extra cost is a better view. All these rooms are small and tastelessly furnished—somehow orange carpets don't make it with naugahyde chairs. But you'll find visual relief in the marvelous views of mountain and sea from the tiny lanais. There's also a restaurant and television room in the old section. ~ Mamalahoa Highway, Captain Cook; 808-323-2642, fax 808-323-3451. BUDGET.

**Shirakawa Motel**, the country's southernmost hotel, sits on ◄ *HIDDEN*
stunningly beautiful grounds. Once when I stopped by, a rainbow lay arched across the landscape and birds were loudly riot-
ing in the nearby hills. Located 1000 feet above sea level, this
corrugated-roof, 12-room hostelry offers quaint rooms with faded
furniture and functional kitchenettes. Without cooking facilities,
the bill is even less. A spacious two-room suite with a kitchen is
also available. ~ Mamalahoa Highway, Waiohinu; phone/fax 808-
929-7462; www.shirakawamotel.com, e-mail shirak@hialoha.net.
You can also write P.O. Box 467, Naalehu, HI 96772 for reservations. BUDGET.

**Wood Valley Temple**, a Buddhist retreat, has dormitory-style ◄ *HIDDEN*
and private rooms. Set on 25 landscaped acres, it provides a
serene resting place. The guest rooms are pretty basic but have
been pleasantly decorated and are quite comfortable. Baths are
shared and guests have access to the ample kitchen
facilities. Call for reservations; two-night minimum. ~ Four miles outside Pahala; 808-928-8539;
www.nechung.org, e-mail nechung@aloha.net. BUDGET.

> The nene, Hawaii's state
> bird, can be found nest-
> ing on the desolate
> slopes of Mauna Loa,
> Mauna Kea and
> Hualalai.

**Sea Mountain at Punaluu** is a welcome contradiction in terms—a secluded condominium. Situated in the
arid Kau District south of Hawaii Volcanoes National Park,
it rests between volcanic headlands and a spectacular black-sand
beach. A green oasis surrounded by lava rock and tropical vegetation, the complex contains a golf course, pool, tennis courts
and jacuzzi. The several dozen condos are multi-unit cottages
(moderate to deluxe). The condos are well-decorated and include
a bedroom, sitting room, kitchen and lanai; slightly larger units
are available (deluxe to ultra-deluxe). ~ Off Mamalahoa Highway, Punaluu; 808-928-8301, 800-488-8301, fax 808-928-8008;
www.seamtnhawaii.com, e-mail seamtn@mymailstation.com.
MODERATE TO ULTRA-DELUXE.

From Kailua south, the Mamalahoa Highway heads up *mauka*    **DINING**
into the mountains above the Kona Coast. There are numerous
restaurants in the little towns that dot the first 15 miles. All sit
right on the highway.

At the north end of Holualoa is the **Holuakoa Cafe**, where
the sandwiches and baked goods make a great alfresco breakfast
or lunch. The changing menu also includes salads, soups and

quiche. ~ 76-5900 Mamalahoa Highway, Holualoa; 808-322-2233. BUDGET.

**Teshima's** is a pleasant restaurant modestly decorated with lanterns and paintings. It's a good place to enjoy a Japanese meal or a drink at the bar. This café is very busy at lunch. Dinner features several Japanese and American entrées. Breakfast is also served. ~ Mamalahoa Highway, Honalo; 808-322-9140. MODERATE.

*Ohia trees, with their red pompom flowers, are often the first spots of life in a newly formed lava flow. Maybe that's why Madame Pele deems their flowers sacred.*

There's a different mood entirely at the **Aloha Café**. Here in the lobby of the town's capacious movie house, a young crew serves delicious breakfasts as well as sandwiches, salads and seafood during lunch and dinner. So if for some bizarre reason you've always longed to dine in the lobby of a movie theater . . . . If not, you can eat out on the oceanview lanai. Dinner on Thursday, Friday and Saturday. ~ Mamalahoa Highway, Kainaliu; 808-322-3383; www.alohacafe.com, e-mail thalohat@aloha.net. MODERATE TO DELUXE.

**Manago Hotel** has a full-size dining room. Primarily intended for the hotel guests, the menu is limited and the hours restricted to "meal times" (7 to 9 a.m., 11 a.m. to 2 p.m., and 5 to 7:30 p.m.). Lunch and dinner platters consist of a few daily specials. Sandwiches are also available. Closed Monday. ~ Mamalahoa Highway, Captain Cook; 808-323-2642; www.managohotel. com, e-mail manago@lava.net. BUDGET.

HIDDEN ►

The **Keei Café** used to be a fish market, and its concrete floors and plastic chairs aren't the sort of ambiance you'd expect of a fine-dining establishment, but the Hawaiian-American and eclectic fusion cuisine served here ranks among the best in the area. From Thai curry, Brazilian seafood chowder, pork chops in peppercorn gravy and catch-of-the-day fish specials to peanut-miso salad, vegetarian black beans and tofu fajitas, everything is made from scratch using local ingredients. Leave room for the heavenly coconut flan. Closed Monday. ~ 83-4587 Mamalahoa Highway, Captain Cook; 808-328-8451. MODERATE.

In Kealakekua Ranch Center, a shopping center on Mamalahoa Highway in Captain Cook, there is one low-priced eatery, **Hong Kong Chop Suey**. It is one of those Chinese restaurants that have (literally) over 100 items on the menu. Closed Tuesday.

~ Mamalahoa Highway, Captain Cook; 808-323-3373. BUDGET TO MODERATE.

**Canaan Deli** comes recommended by several readers, who like the hoagies and the pastrami sandwiches and their specialty, Philly cheesesteak sandwiches. They also have pizzas and hamburgers at this friendly stopping place, as well as a breakfast menu. Personally, I go for the bagels with cream cheese and lox. ~ Mamalahoa Highway, Kealakekua; 808-322-6607. BUDGET.

On the road down to Puuhonua o Honaunau, there's a great lunch stop—**Wakefield Gardens & Restaurant**. You can wander the tropical preserve, then dine on a papaya boat, sandwiches, a fresh garden salad, or a "healthy burger" (made with natural grains), then try a slice of homemade pie. Lunch only. ~ Route 160, Honaunau; 808-328-9930. BUDGET TO MODERATE.

From the outside, the **Coffee Shack** may look something like a brownish mobile home teetering on the brink of a cliff, but the view from hundreds of feet above the surf is part of what makes this roadside diner south of Captain Cook so special. The breakfast menu features eggs benedict and poi-bread french toast among its offerings. Lunch and dinner selections include pizzas and fish sandwiches on homemade bread. ~ 85-5799 Mamalahoa Highway, Honaunau; 808-328-9555. BUDGET.

In the Kau district, **Cafe Ohia** serves Mexican food and a few local favorites at breakfast, lunch and dinner. No dinner on Sunday. Closed Monday. ~ Mile marker 77, Mamalahoa Highway; 808-929-8086. BUDGET.

For something more comfortable, try **Mister Bill's**. At this small dining room, the menu includes steak, prawns and chicken. In an area lacking in full-service dining facilities, this restaurant is a welcome oasis. Breakfast but no dinner on Sunday. ~ Mile marker 78, Mamalahoa Highway; phone/fax 808-929-7447. MODERATE TO DELUXE.

Down in Naalehu, the nation's southernmost town, you'll find the **Shaka Restaurant**. There are full-course breakfasts; at lunch they serve sandwiches, plate lunches and salads; the dinner menu has beef, seafood and chicken dishes. Closed Monday. ~ Mamalahoa Highway, Naalehu; 808-929-7404. BUDGET TO MODERATE.

Along the lengthy stretch from Naalehu to Hawaii Volcanoes National Park, one of the few dining spots you'll encounter is the

**Seamountain Golf Course & Lounge** in Punaluu. Situated a short distance from the black-sand beach, this restaurant serves a lunch menu consisting of hamburgers, chicken wings and cold sandwiches. Topping the cuisine are the views, which range across the links out to the distant volcanic slopes. ~ Punaluu; 808-928-6222, fax 808-928-6111. BUDGET.

**GROCERIES**    Strung along Mamalahoa Highway south of Kailua is a series of small towns that contain tiny markets.

The only real supermarket en route is **Choice Mart**. ~ Kealakekua Ranch Center (upper level), 82-6066 Mamalahoa Highway, Captain Cook; 808-323-3994.

**Pineapple Park**, about ten miles south of Kailua, has fresh fruits and vegetables. ~ Mamalahoa Highway, Captain Cook; 808-323-2224.

**Kahuku Country Market**, in the Kau district, has an ample inventory of groceries and drugstore items. ~ Mile marker 78, Mamalahoa Highway; 808-929-9011.

Down at the southern end of the island, the **Naalehu Island Market** is the prime place to stock up. ~ Mamalahoa Highway, Naalehu; 808-929-7527.

**SHOPPING**    After escaping the tourist traps in Kailua, you can start seriously shopping in South Kona. Since numerous shops dot the Mamalahoa Highway as it travels south, I'll list the most interesting ones in the order they appear.

Holualoa offers shoppers some interesting options along downtown's main drag. Check out **Sam Rosen Goldsmith** for artful designs in gold and silver. ~ Old Holualoa post office, Mamalahoa Highway; 808-324-1688. **Cinderella's Antiques** features antiques and collectibles. ~ Mamalahoa Highway; 808-322-2474. This enclave is also a center for art galleries. Among the most noteworthy is **Studio 7 Gallery**, a beautifully designed multiroom showplace that displays pottery, paintings, sculpture and prints. Closed Sunday and Monday. ~ Mamalahoa Highway; phone/fax 808-324-1335. Artist Matthew Lovein creates *raku*-style wishing jars from a Holualoa workshop; his elegant pottery artwork is for sale at the **Holualoa Gallery**. ~ 76-5921 Mamalahoa Highway; 808-322-8484. A few doors down, housed in an old coffee mill, is the **Kona Arts Center**, where local artists gather to create their wares. ~ Mamalahoa Highway.

For hats and baskets woven from pandanus and bamboo, and sold at phenomenally low prices, turn off the main road onto Route 18 (Hualalai Road) and check out **Kimura Lauhala Shop**. Closed Sunday. ~ Mamalahoa Highway, Holualoa; 808-324-0053.

**Blue Ginger Gallery** displays an impressive array of crafts items produced by local artisans. There are ceramics, custom glass pieces, woodwork and hand-painted silk scarves. ~ 79-7391 Mamalahoa Highway, Kainaliu; 808-322-3898.

Another recommended store is **Paradise Found**, which features contemporary and Hawaiian-style clothes. ~ Mamalahoa Highway, Kainaliu; 808-322-2111. **Knick-Knacks & Paddy-Whacks** is the place for things old and aging. ~ Mamalahoa Highway, Kealakekua; 808-323-2239.

**Kahanahou Hawaiian Foundation**, an apprentice school teaching Hawaiians native arts, sells hand-wrought hula drums and other instruments, as well as masks and other crafts. It also serves as an introduction to Hawaiian music as you view bamboo nose flutes, musical bows, dancing sticks and ceremonial drums. ~ Mamalahoa Highway, Kealakekua; 808-322-3901.

◀ HIDDEN

Not to be bypassed is **Big Island Art Farm**, a shop specializing in *koa* and other exotic hardwoods. The shop was born when two local woodworkers, alienated by the high prices demanded for their pieces by galleries, decided to go into business for themselves. The result is a shop where the work is not only exquisite but also financially accessible to all. Among the many items, you'll find bowls and boxes, as well as larger, more elaborate creations. Closed Sunday. ~ 82-6156 Mamalahoa Highway, beside the Manago Hotel, Captain Cook; 808-323-2247, fax 808-323-3495.

**AUTHOR FAVORITE**

One of my favorite shops is **Kealakekua's Grass Shack**. This place is crowded with Hawaiiana, not just from native Polynesians, but from the island's late arrivals as well—Americans, Chinese, Japanese, Portuguese. As a former owner once explained, "We go all the way from poi to tofu." There are *milo* and *koa* wood pieces, handwoven baskets and much more. Most interesting of all, to me at least, are the antique tools and handicrafts. Ask for a tour of the mini-museum. It'll be an education in things Hawaiian. ~ Konwena Junction, Kealakekua; 808-323-2877.

**Omodt Art Designs** sells jewelry and decorative pieces fashioned from a unique polymer clay technique. The process begins with cylinders of clay that have multiple colors and designs running their length; the cylinder is then sliced like a sushi roll, each segment revealing the same design. If this doesn't make sense to you, check it out for yourself. The studio does not keep specific hours; call ahead for an appointment. ~ 84-5222 Mamalahoa Highway, Honaunau; 808-937-2543; www.omodtart.com.

Given their catchy moniker, it was probably inevitable that the Bong Brothers Coffee Company, a long-established Kona coffee growing and roasting operation, would open a retail location. Bong, the Chinese coffee growers' family name, has nothing to do with *pakalolo* paraphernalia, but don't tell that to the folks who have made Bong Brothers (and Bong Sistah) T-shirts a hot Big Island souvenir. You'll find them on sale at **Bong Brothers** on Route 11 in Honaunau, along with local fruits such as cherimoya, star fruit and sugarloaf pineapples. The shop also serves fresh-squeezed juices and smoothies, as well as homemade soups and, of course, coffee straight from their own roasting room. ~ 84-5227 Manaloa Highway, Honaunau; 808-328-9289, fax 808-328-8112; www.bongbrothers.com. BUDGET.

**NIGHTLIFE**    The **Kona Association for the Performing Arts** produces an ongoing series of theatrical performances. In addition to plays, it periodically schedules concerts. ~ 808-322-9924.

**BEACHES & PARKS**    **NAPOOPOO BEACH PARK**    Small boats occasionally moor off this black-rock beach on Kealakekua Bay. Set amidst cliffs that rim the harbor, it's a charming spot, drawing caravans of tour buses on their way to the nearby Hikiau Heiau and Captain Cook Monument. Kealakekua Bay, one mile wide and filled with marine life, is an underwater preserve that attracts snorkelers and glass-bottom boats. In the bay there are good-sized summer breaks. Just north, at "Ins and Outs," the surf breaks year-round. Mullet, *moi*, bonefish, *papio* and big-eyed scad are the common catches. Napoopoo's gray-sand beach was washed away by a storm in 1992, leaving a bouldered beach in its place. The steep incline makes ocean access risky. A picnic area, showers and restrooms are the only facilities. There's a soda stand just up from the beach. ~ In the town of Captain Cook, take Napoopoo

Road, which leads four miles down to Kealakekua Bay; turn right at the end of the road.

**MANINI BEACH** 🏃 🦞  This is more a rocky point of land than a sandy beach. The rocky coast combined with occasional rough waters make swimming a challenge, but hiking along the coast offers scenic views while the green slopes of Mt. Hualalai tower overhead. Offshore diving is decent, not great. There are no facilities at the park, with the nearest restrooms at Puuhonua O Honaunau or Napoopoo. ~ Turn toward the coast on Manini Street, just to the south of Napoopoo. At the end of the road, park and take the short walk to the point.

**KEEI BEACH** 🐚 🦞 🛶  This salt-and-pepper beach extends for a quarter-mile along a lava-studded shoreline. Situated next to the creaky village of Keei, this otherwise mediocre beach offers marvelous views of Kealakekua Bay. It is far enough from the tourist area, however, that you'll probably encounter only local people along this hidden beach. Darn! The very shallow water makes swimming safe, but limited. Try the north end. Plenty of coral makes for good snorkeling. Mullet, threadfin, bonefish, *papio* and big-eyed scad are common catches here. There are no facilities. ~ Take the Mamalahoa Highway to Captain Cook, then follow Napoopoo Road down to Kealakekua Bay. At the bottom of the hill, go left toward the Puuhonua o Honaunau National Historical Park. Take this road a half-mile, then turn right onto a lava-bed road. Now follow this extremely rough road another half-mile to the beach.

◄ HIDDEN

**SACRED SHORES**

**Kealakekua Bay,** "the way of the gods," was viewed as the endpoint of a sea route linking Hawaii with other god-inhabited lands. In keeping with this sacred link, there were several important temples on the shoreline. To the north was Hikiau Heiau, to the south the Puuhonua o Honaunau. The Captain Cook Monument, built in the 19th century, also graces the shore. A trail makes it possible to reach the isolated site on foot or on horseback. The trail is long, hot and dusty, with numerous uphill and downhill segments, and is best enjoyed in the cool morning hours.

**HOOKENA BEACH PARK** Popular with adventurous travelers, this is a wide, black-sand beach, bordered by sheer rock walls. Coconut trees abound along this lovely strand, and there's a great view of the South Kona coast. This is a recommended beach for swimming. Near the cliffs south of the beach are some good dive spots. Mullet, threadfin, bonefish, *papio* and big-eyed scad are among the most common catches. A picnic area and restrooms are the only facilities. There is no drinking water, but cooking and bathing water is available. ~ Take the Mamalahoa Highway south from Kailua for about 21 miles to Hookena. Turn onto the paved road at the marker and follow it four miles to the park.

▲ Tent camping is allowed; $5 for adults, $1 to $2 for children. A county permit required.

On the Big Island, you can experience 11 of the 13 climatic regions—all in one day.

HIDDEN ► **MILOLII BEACH PARK** Even if you don't feel like a character from Somerset Maugham, you may think you're amid the setting for one of his tropical stories. This still-thriving fishing village is vintage South Seas, from tumbledown shacks to fishing nets drying in the sun. Unfortunately, however, new houses have been springing up in the last few years. There are patches of beach near the village, but the most splendid resources are the tidepools, some of the most beautiful I've ever seen. This area is fringed with reefs that create safe but shallow areas for swimming, and great spots for snorkeling. Exercise extreme caution if you go beyond the reefs. This beach is a prime area for mullet, bonefish, *papio*, threadfin and big-eyed scad. Facilities include restrooms, picnic area and a volleyball court. There's no running water. ~ Take the Mamalahoa Highway south from Kailua for about 33 miles. Turn off onto a well-marked, winding, one-lane, macadam road leading five miles down to the village.

▲ Permitted only in the seaside parking lot. Get there early and you can park a tent beneath the ironwood trees with the sea washing in just below; $5 for adults, $1 to $2 for children. County permit required.

**MANUKA STATE WAYSIDE** This lovely botanic park, almost 2000 feet above sea level, has a beautiful ocean view. The rolling terrain is planted with both native and imported trees and carpeted with grass. The only facilities are restrooms and a picnic area. ~ On Mamalahoa Highway, 19 miles west of Naalehu.

▲ No tent and trailers are allowed here, but you can park your sleeping bag in the pavilion. No electricity. A state permit is required.

**WHITTINGTON BEACH PARK** This pretty little park features a small patch of lawn dotted with coconut, *hala* and ironwood trees. It's set on a lava-rimmed shoreline near the cement skeleton of a former sugar wharf. There are some marvelous tidepools here. Access to the water over the sharp lava rocks is pretty rough on the feet. But once you're in the snorkeling is very good and there's a good surf break in summer with a left slide. Mullet, *menpachi*, red bigeye, *ulua* and *papio* are the most frequent species caught. Facilities consist of picnic area, restrooms and electricity. ~ Across from the abandoned sugar mill on Mamalahoa Highway, three miles north of Naalehu.

▲ Tent and trailer camping are allowed; a county permit is required.

**PUNALUU BEACH PARK** A black-sand beach fringed with palms and bordered by a pleasant lagoon, this area, unfortunately, is regularly assaulted by tour buses. Still, it's a place of awesome beauty, one I would not recommend bypassing. One reason for the hubbub is the appearance of the endangered green sea turtles, which should not be disturbed. For more privacy, you can always check out **Ninole Cove**, a short walk from Punaluu. This attractive area has a tiny beach, grassy area and lagoon, which is a good swimming spot for children in calm conditions. Exercise caution when swimming outside the lagoon. The snorkeling is only mediocre. Surfers attempt the short ride over a shallow reef (right slide). Principal catches are red bigeye, *menpachi*, *ulua* and *papio*. Facilities include a picnic area, restrooms, showers and electricity. ~ Located about a mile off Mamalahoa Highway, eight miles north of Naalehu.

▲ Tents and trailers are allowed; county permit required.

# EIGHT

# Hawaii Volcanoes National Park

Covering 344 square miles and extending from the Puna shoreline to the 4090-foot summit of Kilauea to the summit crater of Makuaweoweo atop 13,677-foot Mauna Loa, this incredible park is deservedly the most popular attraction on the Big Island. Its two live volcanoes, still-young Kilauea (the world's most active volcano) and towering Mauna Loa (said to be inflating with a possible result of resurgence in 2003) make the region as elemental and unpredictable as the next volcanic eruption.

Currently, the 20-year-long eruption of Kilauea, which resulted in the loss of several hundred homes and the coastal town of Kalapana in 1991, continues unabated. As a result, a visit to the coast when lava is flowing into the sea has been an experienced enjoyed by millions under the watchful eye of National Park Service rangers.

Unlike Washington's Mt. St. Helens or Mt. Pinatubo in the Philippines, Hawaii's volcanic eruptions are generally less dangerous, their lava released in rivers that flow, largely underground, to the sea, where lava erupts in tall fountains, the release of cinder and ash creates cone-shaped craters called cinder cones.

In addition to the coastal fireworks, the Park offers extensive hiking trails that access craters volcanically active in the '70s and '80s when Kilauea's summit crater, Halemaumau was active. There are also gentler hikes to fern forests alive with native birds, lava tubes to explore, a visitor center with films and displays that graphically tell Hawaii's story.

Overnight options include an appealing selection of cottages and bed-and-breakfasts found in sprawling Volcano Village, an outpost of artists and escapists who appreciate the lush abundance of flowers and greenery, the fragrant air, the cool temperatures and an often-misty climate. Don't make the park a day trip; it's worth as much time as you can spare.

Contained within this singular park are rainforests, black-sand **SIGHTS**
beaches, rare species of flora and fauna, and jungles of ferns. If
you approach the park from the southwest, traveling up the Mamalahoa Highway (Route 11), the points of interest begin within
a mile of the park boundary.

Here at the trailhead for **Kau Desert Trail**, you can follow a
short (1.5 miles round trip) path that leads to **Footprints**, an area
where, according to legend, Halemaumau's hellish eruption over-
whelmed a Hawaiian army in 1790. The troops, off to battle Kamehameha for control of the island, left the impressions of their
dying steps in molten lava—or so the story goes. According to
Park officials, the tracks were left in hot mud by travelers, not
warriors. Either way, the tracks can still occasionally be seen in
the very fragile hardened ash layers.

Continuing along the highway, turn up Mauna Loa Road to
the **Tree Molds**. Lava flowing through a *koa* forest created these
amazing fossils. The molten rock ignited the trees and then cooled,
leaving deep pits in the shape of the incinerated tree trunks.
(Bring mosquito repellent.) It's a little farther to **Kipuka Puaulu**
or **Bird Park**, a mile-long nature trail leading through a densely
forested bird sanctuary. *Kipuka* means an "island" surrounded by
lava and this one is filled with more than 30 species of Hawaiian
trees, including *koa*, *kolea* and *ohia*. If the weather's clear, you
can continue along this narrow, winding road for about ten miles
to a **lookout** perched 6662 feet high on the side of Mauna Loa.

Back on the main road, continue east a few miles to **Kilauea
Visitor Center**, which contains a museum, a film on recent eruptions, a bookstore and a information desk. ~ 808-985-6000, fax
808-985-6004; www.nps.gov/havo.

Across the road on the rim of Kilauea at **Volcano House**,
there's a hotel and restaurant. An earlier Volcano House, built in
1877, currently houses the **Volcano Art Center**, right next to the
visitor complex. Here you'll find notable exhibits and gallery
works by local artists whose creations relate to the Hawaiian environment and heritage. They also host classes in the Hawaiian
language and Hawaiian arts such as hula and lei making, as well
as painting, ceramics, glass and photography. ~ P.O. Box 104,
Hawaii National Park, HI 96718; 808-967-7565, fax 808-967-
7511; www.volcanoartcenter.org.

Not far from the Volcano Art Center are the **Sulphur Banks**. You can either walk the ten-minute trail or drive along Crater Rim Drive to get to this odoriferous sightseeing spot. Here, green, red, brown and yellow hues are painted by deposits of crystal that form on the rocks when the gas reaches the surface. Other minerals, including opal, earthy hematite and gypsum, form by the weathering of the rock. These solfataras, or fumaroles, are vents that issue steam, hydrogen sulfide and other gases. Kilauea releases tons of sulphuric gases every day. *Take note*: People with heart conditions, pregnant women and those with breathing problems should avoid this area, since these gases are unhealthy for them.

Just beyond the Sulphur Banks are the less smelly **Steam Vents**. Here you can take a steam bath just by approaching the railing of the vent. The steam is caused by groundwater hitting the heated lava. On cooler days you'll find more steam. Steam vents are located on the edge of Kilauea Caldera. A meadow is formed by alterations to the soil that prevent the growth of trees and shrubs. Be careful around the steam vents; they can actually burn you. You'll find larger vents around the crater if you hike around it.

From the art center you can pick up Crater Rim Drive, one of the islands' most spectacular scenic routes. This 11-mile loop passes lava flows and steam vents in its circuit around and into **Kilauea Caldera**. It also takes in everything from a rainforest to a desert and provides views of several craters.

Proceeding clockwise around the crater, the road leads near **Thurston Lava Tube,** a well-lit cave 450 feet long set amid a lush tree-fern and *ohia* rainforest. The tube itself, created when outer layers of lava cooled while the inner flow drained out, reaches heights inside of ten feet. You can walk through the tunnel and along nearby **Devastation Trail**, a half-mile paved asphalt trail that cuts through a skeletal forest of *ohia* trees regrowing after being devastated in a 1959 eruption.

Another short path leads to **Halemaumau Crater**. This pit, which erupted most recently in 1982, is the traditional home of Pele, the goddess of volcanoes. Even today steam and sulfurous gas blast from this hellhole, filling the air with a pungent odor and adding a sickly yellow-green luster to the cliffs. Halemaumau is actually a crater within a crater, its entire bulk contained in Kilauea's gaping maw. (People with sulfur sensitivity or heart

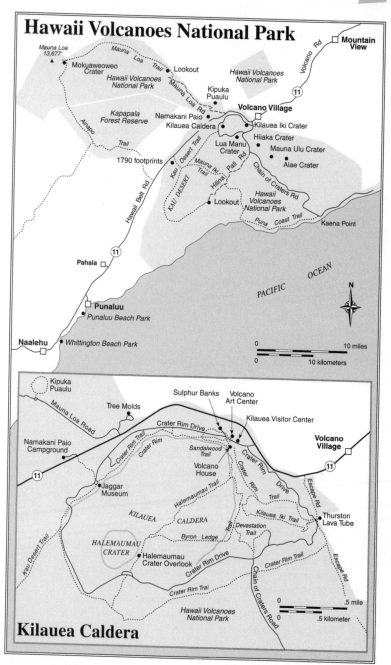

# Hawaii Volcanoes National Park

Mauna Loa
13,677'

Mokuaweoweo
Crater

Hawaii Volcanoes
National Park

Mauna Loa Trail

Lookout

Mauna Loa Rd

Kipuka
Puaulu

Hawaii Volcanoes
National Park

Volcano Rd

Mountain
View

11

Kapapala
Forest Reserve

Namakani Paio

Kilauea Caldera

**Volcano Village**

Kilauea Iki Crater

Ainapo

Trail

Lua Manu
Crater

Hiiaka Crater

Mauna Ulu Crater

Alae Crater

1790 footprints

Mauna Iki
Trail

Kau Desert Trail

Pali Rd

Hawaii Belt Rd

KAU DESERT

Hilina

Lookout

Chain of Craters Rd

Hawaii
Volcanoes
National Park

Puna Coast Trail

Kaena Point

11

**Pahala**

OCEAN

PACIFIC

N

**Punaluu**

Punaluu Beach Park

**Naalehu**

Whittington Beach Park

0          10 miles

0          10 kilometers

Kipuka
Puaulu

Tree Molds

Sulphur Banks

Volcano
Art Center

Kilauea Visitor Center

Mauna Loa Road

Crater Rim Drive

Namakani Paio
Campground

Crater Rim Trail

Crater Rim

Sandalwood
Trail

Volcano House

**Volcano
Village**

11

Crater Rim

Drive

Escape Rd

11

Jaggar
Museum

Halemaumau Trail

KILAUEA     CALDERA

Crater Rim

Trail

Kilauea Iki Trail

Thurston
Lava Tube

HALEMAUMAU
CRATER

Byron Ledge

Trail

Devastation
Trail

Kau Desert Trail

Halemaumau
Crater Overlook

Crater Rim Drive

Crater Rim Trail

Escape Rd

Crater Rim Trail

Chain of Craters Road

Hawaii Volcanoes
National Park

0          .5 mile

0          .5 kilometer

# Kilauea Caldera

or breathing problems should probably avoid this site, as should infants, children and pregnant women.)

Around the southern and western edges of the caldera, the road passes part of the **Kau Desert**, a landscape so barren that astronauts bound for the moon were brought here to train for their lunar landing. At the **Jaggar Museum**, adjacent to the U.S.G.S. park observatory, you can catch an eagle's-eye glimpse into Halemaumau Crater and take in a series of state-of-the-art displays on volcanology. Then the road continues on to a succession of steam vents from which hot mists rise continually.

The highway zips into Hilo from the Kilauea Crater area. Until several years ago you could take a more interesting and leisurely route by following **Chain of Craters Road** down to the Puna district. At present a lava flow several miles wide has closed part of the road. The 20-mile-long section that is still open skirts several pit craters, traverses miles of decades-old lava flows, and descends 4000 feet to the coast. Near the sea, a two-mile trail leads to an excellent collection of **petroglyphs at Puuloa**. The Chain of Craters Road then hugs the cliffs of the shoreline until it abruptly ends, buried for ten miles under lava flows as much as 75 feet deep.

While many other landmarks along this volcanically active coast have been lost to Pele's advances, the **Holei Sea Arch** remains. Located near the place where lava has covered the coastal portion of the Chain of Craters Road (near mile marker 19), the

**ERUPTION UPDATE**

The East Rift Zone eruption of Kilauea Volcano entered its 20th year in 2003, a record for longevity since records began in the 19th century. The Puna coast near Kamoamoa, where lava has blocked the Chain of Craters Road, remains the most active zone, attracting thousands of viewers daily. Since you're in Hawaii Volcanoes National Park, the eruption zone if carefully monitored by Park Service Rangers who position rope barriers for viewing the flow into the ocean. Dawn and dusk provide the best viewing, providing the contrast that makes the glowing lava vibrantly stand out. Dusk attracts large crowds, which detracts from the spiritual intensity of the experience. At dawn you're likely to be alone and undistracted. The **Eruption Update**, a 24-hour recorded message, provides information on the latest eruptions. ~ 808-985-6000.

arch was carved from a lava rock promontory by the battering power of the sea.

**Volcano Village**, a small rural enclave, lies one mile Hilo-side of the main entrance to Hawaii Volcanoes National Park. The village itself includes a few shops and restaurants on Old Volcano Road, which parallels Route 19 for about one mile. The rest consists of a grid of country roads fronting homes nestled amidst lush vegetation of endemic fern and *koa* forest interspersed with flowering ginger, hydrangea, camellia and other flowering exotics that prosper in the wet, temperate climate.

The village population includes both Native Hawaiians and an assortment of mainland escapists, including many artists and other creative types who revel in Volcano's rural isolation and spiritual energy. Ira Ono, one of Volcano's long-term residents and a key multimedia artist-in-residence, operates **Volcano Garden Arts**, a working gallery, in the vintage 1908 Hopper Estate. The workshop-cum-gallery-cum-sculpture-garden offers special classes in various arts throughout the year. Closed Monday. ~ 19-3834 Old Volcano Road; 808-967-7261; www.volcanogarden arts.com.

**Volcano House**, a 42-room hotel, perches 4000 feet above sea **LODGING** level on the rim of Kilauea Crater. Situated in Hawaii Volcanoes National Park, this hotel provides a unique resting place. You can watch the steam rise from Halemaumau Crater or study the rugged contours of slumbering Kilauea. Standard rooms are unfortunately located in a separate building behind the main hotel. For a view of Kilauea, ask for a "crater view," from a superior or deluxe room on the volcano side. The rooms are small and decorated in an ever tidy and cozy fashion. There's wall-to-wall carpeting but no TV or radio. And you certainly won't need an air conditioner at these breathless heights. ~ Near the entrance to Hawaii Volcanoes National Park; 808-967-7321, fax 808-967-8429; e-mail volcanohouse@earthlink.com. MODERATE TO ULTRA-DELUXE.

There are quite a number of lovely bed and breakfasts along the Puna/Kau coast in Volcano Village, which plays host to those *akamai* (smart) enough to plan a dusk visit to the eruption site, about 40 to 45 minutes from park headquarters. Since you want to be there at dusk to see the lava at its most awesome, a stay in

Volcano is the right choice. (The volcano isn't a good day trip.) It's more than two hours on dark, twisting, country roads to Kona and Kohala hotels. Besides, the night sky, undimmed by civilization, is a spectacle of brilliant stars and fragrant breezes, which makes an evening walk something memorable.

HIDDEN ►    The **Volcano Rainforest Retreat** is a Zen-perfect cluster of buildings linked by pathways that wind through one and a half acres of lush fern forest. There is nothing rustic about the lodging, however. Handcrafted by owners Peter and Kathleen Golden, the four stylish cottages are constructed of cedar and redwood and individually decorated with touches such as *shoji* doors, fresh-cut flowers and Hawaiian prints. A soak in the communal hot tub is a welcome treat after a long day of sightseeing. ~ P.O. Box 957, Volcano, HI 96785; phone/fax 808-985-8696, 800-550-8696; www.volcanoretreat.com, e-mail volrain@bigisland.net. MODERATE TO DELUXE.

Scattered around a seven-acre estate, **My Island Bed & Breakfast Inn** offers a variety of lodging choices. The historic 1886 Connecticut farmhouse, once the missionary home of the Lyman family, has three rooms with shared and private baths. There's even a Franklin fireplace (circa 1868) to keep you warm when there's a chill in the air. Be sure to check out the "handpoured" glass windows and *koa* branches used as handrailings. Separate garden units with private entrances overlook the lush grounds, and a number of guesthouses around the area sleep from two to eight people. A casual, family-style breakfast is served every morning. ~ P.O. Box 100, Volcano, HI 96785; 808-967-7216, fax 808-967-7719; www.myislandinnhawaii.com, e-mail myisland@ilhawaii.net. BUDGET TO DELUXE.

The wood-shingled buildings at the 1931 **Hale Ohia Cottages** are conveniently located just outside park headquarters on beautifully landscaped grounds. Hale Lehua, Ihilani and #44 cottages are freestanding structures with fireplaces and kitchenettes. There are also five suites (two in the main house and three in another cottage), all with private baths and entrances. The spacious two-story, three-bedroom Hale Ohia suite is well-suited to family travelers, with three bedrooms, a large living space, a full kitchen and a covered lanai with room for barbecuing. ~ P.O. Box 758, Volcano, HI 96785; 808-967-7986, 800-455-3803, fax 808-967-

# Camping
## near the Caldera

The main campground at Hawaii Volcanoes National Park, **Namakani Paio Campground** is situated in a large, open grassy area dotted with eucalyptus and *ohia* trees at an elevation of 4000 feet. Although there are a handful of designated campsites, it's mostly a matter of simply picking a clear spot, first-come, first-served, and pitching your tent there. The campground has water and restrooms, and there are fire grills and picnic tables in a central pavilion. Bring your own firewood—none is available on-site. There are no reservations, no reservations and no check-in. Open year-round; seven-day maximum stay. ~ Off Route 11, 31.5 miles southwest of Hilo; 808-967-7321.

Located just above the campground of the same name, **Namakani Paio Cabins** are ten extremely basic cabins operated by the Volcano House hotel. Each sleeps up to four people, with one double bed and twin-size bunk beds, all bare-mattress. Amenities include a picnic table and an outdoor barbecue grill. Cabin occupants use the campground restrooms and drinking water supply. Showers are available at the hotel. Rates are $40 a night for two people, $8 per additional person, plus $20 for optional linen rental and a $12 key deposit. Reservations are required; make them through the reception desk at the Volcano House. ~ Off Route 11, 31.5 miles southwest of Hilo; reservations—Volcano House, Hawaii Volcanoes National Park, HI 967128; 808-967-7321.

The national park's recently opened **Kulanaokuaiki Campground** has three campsites so far, with more under construction. Located in the middle of the Kau Desert at an elevation of 2700 feet, it offers the remote feel of wilderness camping without the hike. There is a vault toilet but no water; bring plenty. The developed campsites have picnic tables and barbecue grills; bring your own firewood. There are no reservations and no check-in. Open year-round. ~ Five miles southwest from Chain of Craters Road on Hilima Pali Road; 808-967-7321.

8610; www.haleohia.com, e-mail information@haleohia.com. MODERATE TO DELUXE.

Hostess Conard Eyre adds to the charm of **Green Goose Lodge**, a plush B&B fronting the Volcano Golf Course, just to the west of Volcano Village proper. A single master suite means privacy for guests, who share Eyre's lovely home, complete with fireplace for chilly Volcano nights and mornings and a spacious deck that overlooks the fairways of the Volcano Country Club golf course. The suite features a four-poster bed complemented by an eclectic collection of antiques that adds to the pleasure of a stay. The suite sleeps up to four, with a full gourmet breakfast (Eyre is an accomplished chef) served daily. ~ 99-1798 Painiu Loop, Volcano; 808-985-7172; www.greengooselodge.com, e-mail information@greengooselodge.com.

Host Jim Grigg's bed and breakfast is a separate one bedroom cottage surrounded by native forest, also in the vicinity of the golf course. Built in 1950, the redwood cottage has a warm country feel. There's cable TV and VCR, and a video library for a diversion on a cool, quiet evening. ~ 23 Golf Links Road, Volcano; 808-985-8861.

**Volcano Accommodations**, a central agency, can help book reservations at a variety of area B&Bs. ~ 808-967-8662, fax 808-985-7028; www.hawaii-volcano.net, e-mail info@hawaii-volcano.net. You can also contact **Volcano Places** for cottage rentals. ~ 808-967-7990, 877-967-7990; www.volcanoplaces.com.

**AUTHOR FAVORITE**

**Kilauea Lodge** does not rest on the lip of the crater, but that doesn't prevent it from being the finest place in the area to stay. Set on tropically wooded grounds, this hideaway nevertheless conveys a mountain atmosphere. Some guest rooms have fireplaces; all have private baths. This coziness carries over into an inviting common room shared by guests and furnished with rocking chairs and a tile fireplace. The lodge, built in 1938 as a YMCA camp, rests at the 3700-foot elevation and combines the best features of a Hawaiian plantation house and an alpine ski lodge. It also provides a memorable contrast to the ocean-oriented places that you'll probably be staying in during the rest of your visit. A two-bedroom cottage with a hot tub is also available. ~ Old Volcano Road, Volcano Village; 808-967-7366, fax 808-967-7367; www.kilauealodge.com, e-mail stay@kilauealodge.com. MODERATE TO DELUXE.

If you're looking for a vista, **Volcano House Restaurant**—perched on the rim of Kilauea Crater—affords expansive views. Located at 4000-foot elevation in Hawaii Volcanoes National Park, this spacious dining room looks out on sheer lava walls and angry steam vents, and on a clear day, the imposing bulk of Mauna Loa. If you can tear yourself away from the stunning scenery, there's buffet-style breakfast and lunch, and an ample dinner menu highlighted by fresh fish, prime rib, linguini marinara and a variety of seafood dishes. ~ 808-967-7321. DELUXE TO ULTRA-DELUXE.

In L.A. there's the Hard Rock Café; in Volcano Village, it's the **Lava Rock Café**. Breakfast, lunch and dinner feature "magma mini meals," but only at dinner can you get a "full eruption." The lasagna, T-bones and fajitas are, presumably, burning hot. The Lava Rock also serves as an internet café for you e-mail junkies. No dinner on Sunday or Monday. ~ Old Volcano Road, Volcano Village; 808-967-8526, fax 808-967-8090; www.volcanovillage.com. BUDGET TO DELUXE.

And for those languorous evenings when time is irrelevant and budgets forgotten, there is **Kilauea Lodge**. You can sit beside a grand fireplace in an atmosphere that mixes tropical artwork with alpine sensibility. The exposed-beam ceiling and elegant hardwood tables comfortably contrast with a menu that features "prawns Mauna Loa," catch of the day and chicken Milanese. Dinner only. ~ Old Volcano Road, Volcano Village; 808-967-7366; www.kilauealodge.com, e-mail stay@kilauealodge.com. DELUXE TO ULTRA-DELUXE.

**Thai Thai Restaurant** brings the best of Thai cuisine to the quiet of Volcano Village. The diverse menu has seafood, meat and vegetarian specialties, all fresh and delicious, with generous portions. Reservations recommended. Dinner only. ~ 19-4084 Volcano Road (next to the TruValue store); 808-967-7969. MODERATE TO DELUXE.

The **Volcano Golf & Country Club Restaurant** serves breakfast and lunch overlooking the golf course, where flocks of *nene* geese gather among rare golden blossom *lehua* trees. Start your day with a breakfast burger on a bagel, a breakfast burrito or a more conventional option such as an omelette or french toast. Besides hamburgers, sandwiches and salads, the luncheon menu features house specialties that include garlic pepper chicken, teriyaki beef, mahimahi, *ahi* tuna and stir-fry dishes. Or simply stop in for coffee and a slice of the club's scrumptious macadamia nut cheesecake. ~ Pii Mauna Drive, Hawaii Volcanoes National Park; 808-967-8228; www.volcanogolfandrestaurant. com. BUDGET TO MODERATE.

**GROCERIES**  The Volcano Store, located just outside the national park, has a limited stock of groceries and dry goods. ~ Old Volcano Road, Volcano Village; 808-967-7210.

**PARKS**  **NAMAKANI PAIO** Situated in a lovely eucalyptus and *koa* grove in the middle of Volcanoes National Park, this campground offers both outdoor and cabin camping. There is a picnic area and restrooms. ~ On Mamalahoa Highway (Route 11) about three miles west of park headquarters and 31 miles southwest of Hilo.

▲ Tent and trailer camping. No permit required but, as always, campers should note that there is a seven-day limit.

Cabins are rented from the Volcano House (808-967-7321). Each cabin has one double and two single beds, plus an outdoor grill. No firewood or cooking utensils are provided. The units rent for $40 a day for two people, $8 for each additional person up to four. Sheets, blankets and towels are provided, but it's recommended that you bring a sleeping bag. Showers are not available for campers.

**NINE**

# Puna District

The bulging triangle in the southeast corner of the Big Island is the Puna District. Puna preserves a hint of the feel of old Hawaii, in part because it is still home to a fair number of Native Hawaiians, and also because the feel is rural and tropical. Puna's ragged shoreline of red-black lava rock shelters a series of small bays. There are also thermal pools to be enjoyed, evidence that Pele is at work beneath the lushly green and forested landscape. At Mackenzie Park, lava tubes provide further evidence, as does Lava Trees State Park.

The East Rift Zone, Kilauea's most active, makes its way through Puna's fertile landscape. There's plenty in evidence of past flows, including the fast-advancing lava that in 1991 covered the village of Kalapana and a subdivision on the forested slopes of Kilauea. With force to spare, Puna is home to Hawaii's only experiment with geothermal energy, a project that has languished since a much-anticipated debut in the 1970s that drew the opposition of those who considered it an affront to Madame Pele.

Pele has not been modest in her recent efforts, advancing Puna's coastline 700 feet seaward, forming a new black sand beach at Kalapana to replace the famous palm-lined shores of Kaimu Beach Park, once a Puna landmark. Hundreds of community-planted coconut palms lie ashore of black sands formed when hot lava splattered at contact with the surging sea. The palms are a symbol of the bonds that still link people to Puna.

**SIGHTS**

Now that Chain of Craters Road has been covered in a layer of black lava, the only way to visit the area is by following Route 130, which will carry you through the tumbledown plantation town of **Keaau** and near the artistic little community of **Pahoa**, or along Route 137, an enchanting country road that hugs the coast.

Herbalist Barbara Fahs offers tours of her one-acre **Hiiaka's Healing Hawaiian Herb Garden** on Tuesday, Thursday and Saturday afternoons and by appointment. She introduces visitors to her 80 species of healing plants such as *noni*, kava kava, *mamaki* and *kookoolau*, tells about their folklore, history and uses, and shares professional tips for growing your own herb garden. She also operates a gift shop selling products from her garden, gives herbal treatments, and offers classes and quarterly three-day retreats. ~ HCR 2, Box 9620, Keaau, HI 96749-9339; 808-966-6126; www.hiiakas.com, e-mail goddess@hiiakas.com.

Dating back to 1918, the **Akebono Theater** in Puna had the distinction of being the oldest operating motion picture theater in the Hawaiian islands. The rickety old wooden building served as a community center, hosting amateur theatrical productions and showing old movies, until it closed down for much-needed repairs a couple of years ago. It continues to serve as a village landmark, though, and the parking lot is the scene of a **farmers' market** on Saturday and Sunday mornings. As this book goes to press, the theater is in the process of reopening on a limited basis, showing vintage movies on Saturday nights and housing a vegetarian snack bar called Huna Ohana. ~ Puna; 808-965-9661.

In 1990, **lava flows** poured through Kalapana, severing Routes 130 and 137 (which have since been reconnected) and covering many houses. Kalapana, once home to more than 400 people, was largely destroyed. Today, a few isolated houses form oases in a desert of black lava. Just above the town, where the roadway comes to an abrupt halt, you can see how the lava crossed the road.

HIDDEN ►

The former **Star of the Sea Painted Church** in Kalapana used to be my favorite church in all the Hawaiian Islands. An imaginative Belgian priest, hoping to add color and imagery to the mass, covered the interior walls of this tiny, spired carpenter's Gothic chapel with murals depicting religious scenes and painted a vaulted nave behind the altar to give the little church the appearance of a European cathedral. In 1990, when a slow-moving lava flow destroyed much of Kalapana, villagers lifted the church off its foundation and trucked it to safety just hours before the lava would have engulfed it. The Catholic Church decommissioned it and sold it to the Kalapana Ohana Association for "$1 and love," and it was moved to a three-acre site leased from the state along the Kalapana-Pahoa Highway. The association was awarded a small government grant to convert it into a Native Hawaiian cultural center, but the *hoolaulea*, or celebration, they organized to raise matching funds was scheduled for September 15, 2001—and cancelled at the last minute because of tragic events half a world away. Today, it still stands forlorn by the roadside as volunteers from the 40-member Kalapana Ohana Association work to keep it from deteriorating. As this book goes to press, the association's president says the painted interior is "kind of closed," but check as you pass by and see whether the villagers' dream has come true yet.

After exploring the area of recent volcanic action, you can backtrack along the coast via Route 137, which proceeds northeast through jungly undergrowth and past dazzling seascapes to

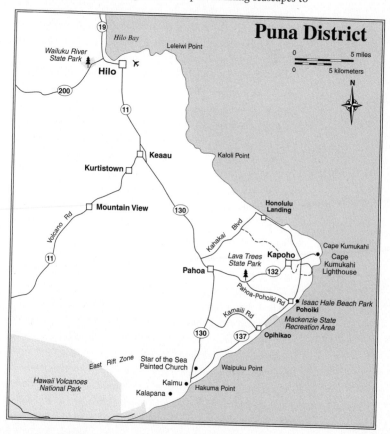

the tiny villages of **Opihikao** and **Pohoiki** or continue on Route 137 past Kapoho where the paved road ends. Now you're on a red dirt and cinder road, appropriately named **Red Road**. At times the coastline is in sight, at times it is hidden by tall iron-woods and lush vegetation. The road undulates, following the contour of the landscape, giving the drive a roller coaster feel. The rural landscape provides an away-from-it-all feeling, which characterizes Puna's rustic appeal.

HIDDEN ►

At the intersection of Route 137 and Route 132, take a right onto the dirt road and follow it seaward toward the site of a truly eerie occurrence. When the 1960 lava flow swept down to destroy this entire region, it spared the **Cape Kumukahi Lighthouse** on the state's easternmost point. Today you can see where the wall of lava parted, flowed around the beacon, then closed again as it continued to the sea. In the process, it added about 500 yards of land to the point—an awesome demonstration of how young this Big Island really is. It is rumored that the lighthouse keeper at the lighthouse had given an old woman a meal just before the lava flowed down to the sea. Could it be that Madame Pele spared the lighthouse after enjoying a satisfying dinner?

HIDDEN ►

Another natural phenomenon worth taking a detour for are the **Kapoho Tide Pools**, situated at the lush, easternmost point of the Big Island. Landscaped by nature, they offer a magical sense of place, with sheltered waters offering some of the best snorkeling, even for novices. To get there head south on Route 137. Some of the pools are adjacent to residences in Kapoho, but Wai-opea Pools are in a public area. The trick is getting there. The pools are located near the end of Kapoho-Kai Road. It's about a half-mile walk to the ocean.

Now return to Route 132 and head west back toward Pahoa. The road passes more of the **1960 lava flow**, which covered almost 2000 acres and totally leveled the small village of Kapoho.

The **Pohoiki Road**, the shortest link between the Puna coast and the rough-and-tumble town of Pahoa, traverses rolling terrain, much of it a grid of streets carved into the rainforest, accessing pseudo-agricultural subdivisions that are rural Puna's version of affordable housing. **Lava Trees State Park**, recently cleared of alien plant species in an effort to restore the native Hawaiian ecosystem, is about halfway between Pahoa and the coast at Pohoiki. An eruption, circa 1790, caused the grotesque formations at Lava Tree State Park. Here the molten rock swamped a grove of *ohia* trees, then hardened around the skeletons to create a fossil forest. When fissures in the earth drained the molten lava, these petrified trees were left as a lonely legacy. In strange and exotic fashion, these giant skeletons, mixed with fresh growth, loom above huge cracks in the landscape.

In the beautiful Puna District, a volcanic region fringed with black-sand beaches, there's a marvelous place called the **Kailani Eco-Resort and Adventures**. Situated on Route 137, 13 minutes from Pahoa, it sits just above the ocean on 113 acres. In addition to lodging, this New Age resort provides a lifestyle. There are weekly classes in hula, weaving and lei making; lectures on the history and culture of Hawaii; plus programs in dance, aerobics, yoga and massage. The facilities include a Japanese health spa with two jacuzzis and a sauna, a swimming pool and volleyball and tennis courts. Guests stay in multi-unit lodges, sharing a spacious living room, or in private cottages; treehouse units with ocean views are also available. Sleeping accommodations are basic but appealing, with pine walls; the room decorations are crafted at the center. Campsites are available at budget prices. Special events for gays are planned during the year. Meals are $30 a day per person, or you can cook for yourself. ~ RR 2, Box 4500, Pahoa, HI 96778; 808-965-7828, 800-800-6886, fax 808-965-0527; www.kalani.com, e-mail kalani@kalani.com. MODERATE TO ULTRA-DELUXE.

**LODGING**

◄ HIDDEN

Located in Keaau, just off the road to Pahoa and within 15 minutes of Hilo, is **Rainforest Retreat**, a lovely B&B on the slopes of Kilauea. Three rooms, each with full kitchen, are nestled among *ohia* trees and wild orchids. The property's proximity to Hawaii Volcanoes National Park is evident in the evenings when the vol-

**BLACK HEAT**

Since the latest series of volcanic eruptions began on the Big Island in 1983, the Puna District has been in constant turmoil. During one phase, an average of 650,000 tons of lava a day was spewing from the earth. In all, it has covered 40 square miles of the Big Island, creating 525 acres of new land masses along the ocean, destroying nearly 200 houses and fashioning several new black-sand beaches.

cano's fiery glow is often visible from the back porch. Guests are given free tours of the adjacent one-acre orchid nursery. ~ HCR-1 Box 5655, Keaau, HI 96749; 808-961-4410, 888-244-8074, fax 808-966-6898; www.rainforestretreat.com, e-mail info@rain forestretreat.com. MODERATE.

**GAY LODGING**    After a long day traversing the dense growth of tropical flowers and macadamia and fruit trees, guests are grateful for a soak in a hot tub, a stint in the steam house or a minute with the masseuse. All this and more are obtainable at the **Butterfly Inn**, an all-women bed and breakfast located between Hilo and the village of Volcano. Rooms are cozily decorated, and in the morning a breakfast of assorted fruits, juices and breads may be taken onto the enclosed deck. ~ P.O. Box 6010, Kurtis-town, HI 96760; 808-966-7936, 800-546-2442; www.thebutter flyinn.com, e-mail hiwomen@ilhawaii.net. MODERATE.

**DINING**    In the rustic town of Pahoa, there's **Luquin's Mexican Restaurant**, a friendly Mexican eatery serving a variety of dishes from south of the border. You'll find all the familiar favorites on the menu, from *huevos rancheros* to enchiladas, as well as fish tacos smothered in deliciously *picante* red chili salsa. There's a cantina bar, and the old-time Pahoa-style atmosphere is enhanced by a colorful paint job. ~ Old Government Road, Pahoa; 808-965-9990. MODERATE.

Pahoa has more to offer in the way of Italian food than you might expect. One good choice is the **Godmother Restaurant**, a clean and bright little eatery that serves all the familiar stand-bys—lasagna, fettuccini, ravioli, spaghetti and meatballs—as well as scampi and special parmigiana-style pork chops. Etched-glass windows are the highlight of the simple decor. Takeout is

**WATCH WHERE YOU WANDER**

While in Puna, visitors should not wander off-road. This was, and likely still is, a prime locale for growing *pakalolo*, as marijuana is known in Hawaii. (*Paka* translates as "weed," *lolo* as "crazy.") Ill-conceived State and Federal drug eradication efforts have made for some bad energy concerning marijuana cultivation. The end result has been counterproductive, driving up prices without stopping the flow, pushing more money into an illegal pipeline.

available. ~ 15-2969 Government Road, Pahoa; 808-965-0055. MODERATE.

Another entry in Pahoa's Italian restaurant scene, **Paolo's Bistro** specializes in Tuscan-style cuisine, highlighting fish dishes and freshly made pasta with pesto or olive oil and garlic. The short menu is supplemented by daily specials. Ingredients are straight from the farm, and the emphasis is on quality rather than quantity. The atmosphere is family-friendly. ~ 333 Pahoa Road, Pahoa; 808-965-7033. MODERATE.

An open-air design accented with overhead fans and bamboo panels gives **Sawasdee Thai Cuisine** an easy, friendly ambience of the East. Serving a full array of curry, rice and noodle dishes, this cozy restaurant is a comfortable fit for lunch or dinner. Closed Wednesday and Sunday. ~ Old Government Road, Pahoa; 808-965-8186. BUDGET TO MODERATE.

For more traditional fare consider **Black Rock Cafe**. This booth-lined shrimp-and-steak eatery offers a half-dozen different beef dishes as well as spaghetti, baby back ribs and a catch-of-the-day fish entrée. ~ Old Government Road, Pahoa; 808-965-1177. MODERATE.

**GROCERIES** A **farmers' market** in the clapboard town of Pahoa convenes every Sunday morning. Otherwise, there are a few small markets. The junction town of Keaau has a **Sure Save**. ~ Old Volcano Road and Keaau–Pahoa Road, Keaau; 808-966-9316.

Also in Pahoa, there's **Da Store**. ~ Route 130; 808-965-9411. For health foods, consider **Pahoa Natural Groceries**. ~ 15-1403 Nanawale Homesteads, Pahoa; 808-965-8322.

**SHOPPING** Out in the volcano region, on the road down to the Puna District, you'll pass through the tiny town of **Pahoa**. Either side of Route 130, the main drag, is lined with falsefront buildings. Each one seems to contain yet another ingenious craft shop run by a local resident.

**BEACHES & PARKS** **ISAAC HALE BEACH PARK** This small park on the Puna coast is pretty but run-down. There's a patch of black sand here and some hot springs nearby. A boat landing ramp makes this a popular park with local folks. Swimming is okay when the sea is calm. There are both summer and winter breaks in the center of the bay. The most common catches here are *papio*, *moi*, mountain bass, *menpachi*, red bigeye, *ulua* and goatfish. A picnic area and restrooms are the only facilities. ~ Route 137, about two miles northeast of MacKenzie State Recreation Area.

▲ Tent and trailer camping. County permit required. I much prefer nearby MacKenzie State Recreation Area for overnighting.

**MACKENZIE STATE RECREATION AREA** ⤙ This beautiful 13-acre park lies in an ironwood grove along a rocky coastline. King's Highway, an ancient Hawaiian trail, bisects the area. There is no swimming, snorkeling or surfing because a sea cliff borders the park. However, there's good shore fishing from rock ledges. Picnic area and pit toilets are the only facilities. There's no drinking water. ~ Route 132, nine miles northeast of Kaimu.

▲ Tent camping; a state permit is required.

**AHALANUI BEACH PARK** Volcanically heated thermal springs are the attraction at this coastal stopover, providing a natural hot tub with relaxing views. ~ Ahalanui is just off Route 137, about one mile north of the intersection of Pohoiki Road.

**KEHENA BEACH** 🏃 ⚓ 🏄 Gray to black sands formed by lava cinders grace this clothing-optional beach, which lures gays and straights alike. There is good swimming offshore and the location, at the base of a wooded hillside, makes for privacy. There are no facilities. ~ Park at the lot by the 19-mile marker on Route 137. A short trail leading to Kehena's black sands. Cars should be locked with nothing tempting in sight since theft has been a problem.

# TEN

# Hilo

There's one thing you'll rarely miss in this tropical city—rain. Hilo gets about 130 inches a year. The Chamber of Commerce will claim it rains mostly at night, but don't be deceived. It's almost as likely to be dark and wet at midday. There is a good side to all this bothersome moisture—it transforms Hilo into an exotic city crowded with tropical foliage, the orchid capital of the United States.

Hilo is the closest you will approach in all Hawaii to a Somerset Maugham–style South Seas port town. With its turn-of-the-20th-century stores, many badly needing a paint job, and old Chinese shops, it's a throwback to an era when tourists were few and Hawaii was a territory. Thanks to a broad shallow bay, its coastal sands provided an active place of entry for the fishermen who harvested Hilo's rich coastal waters. Hilo was one of the largest settlements in the islands, a center of trade and a meeting place of chiefs. It has long-served as capital of the Big Island, a headquarters for the sugar plantations that ran to the north along the Hamakua Coast.

The 20th century would bring devastation to the bustling town of Hilo in the form of destructive tsunamis in the '40s and '60s. The '70s followed with the accelerating decline of sugar, a century-long era brought to an end in the late 1990s when the last of Hamakua's plantations closed. Victims of third world competition. Downtown further suffered from the exodus of business to inland shopping malls that came with the '80s, and the Big Box retailers who followed in the 1990s.

Sections of town, especially around Waianuenue Avenue, have been refurbished and dabbed with 1990s flash, but much of the downtown still feels like the 1950s, with a collection of small-town shops and restaurants. The gutters are rusty, the rain awnings have sagged, and an enduring sense of character overhangs the place with the certainty and finality of the next downpour.

**SIGHTS**

Hilo is a tropical wonderland, a rainforest with hotels, shops and great places to visit. A visit to one of the city's many flower nurseries is an absolute must. These gardens grow orchids, anthuriums and countless other flowers. There are two that I highly recommend. **Orchids of Hawaii** specializes in *vanda* orchids, birds of paradise and anthuriums. Closed Saturday and Sunday. ~ 2801 Kilauea Avenue; 808-959-3581, 800-323-1449, fax 808-959-4497; www.alohaorchids.com, e-mail orchidhi@gte.net. **Nani Mau Gardens** is a 20-acre visual feast that houses a wide variety of tropical flowers and plants. It also has a gift shop. Admission. ~ Several miles south of Hilo near Route 11 at 421 Makalika Street; 808-959-3541, fax 808-959-3152; www.nanimau.com, e-mail garden@nanimau.com.

Banyan Drive is another green thumb's delight. Sweeping past Hilo's nicest hotels, this waterfront road is shaded with rows of giant banyan trees. Plaques proclaim the dignitaries who planted them, including Franklin D. Roosevelt, Babe Ruth and Amelia Earhart. Next to this verdant arcade are the **Liliuokalani Gardens**, 19 acres exploding with color. These Japanese gardens, featuring both Hawaiian and Asian trees, are dotted with pagodas and arched bridges. ~ Banyan Drive and Lihiwai Street.

From Banyan Drive, a short footbridge crosses to **Coconut Island**, a palm-studded islet in Hilo Bay. This old Hawaiian sanctuary presents a dramatic view of Hilo Bay and, on a clear day, of Mauna Kea and Mauna Loa as well.

It's not far to **Wailoa River State Park**, where grassy picnic areas surround beautiful **Waiakea Fishpond**. Across one of the pond's arching bridges, at Wailoa Visitors Center, there are cultural exhibits and an information desk. ~ Off Kamehameha Avenue; 808-933-0416.

In downtown Hilo, the **Lyman House Memorial Museum** is a fascinating example of a 19th-century missionary home. Built in 1839, the house is furnished with elegant period pieces that create a sense of this bygone era (the house is open to guided tours only). Also on the property is a Hawaiian history museum focusing on Hawaiian culture and the islands' many ethnic groups, and an excellent collection of rocks and minerals. Among the

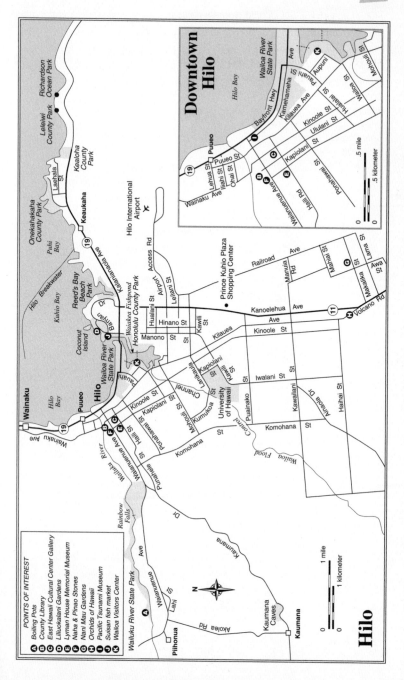

**POINTS OF INTEREST**

- Ⓐ Boiling Pots
- Ⓑ County Library
- Ⓒ East Hawaii Cultural Center Gallery
- Ⓓ Liliuokalani Gardens
- Ⓔ Lyman House Memorial Museum
- Ⓕ Naha & Pinao Stones
- Ⓖ Nani Mau Gardens
- Ⓗ Orchids of Hawaii
- Ⓘ Pacific Tsunami Museum
- Ⓙ Suisan fish market
- Ⓚ Wailoa Visitors Center

**Downtown Hilo**

Hilo Bay

Wailoa River State Park

**Hilo**

Onekahakaha County Park

Richardson Ocean Park

Leleiwi County Park

Kealoha County Park

Keaukaha

Hilo International Airport

Prince Kuhio Plaza Shopping Center

Wainaku

Puueo

Hilo Bay

University of Hawaii

Wailuku River State Park

Rainbow Falls

Kaumana Caves

Kaumana

Pihonua

museum's highlights is a 3-D map of the entire Hawaiian chain, from ocean floor to mountain top. Closed Sunday. Admission. ~ 276 Haili Street; 808-935-5021, fax 808-969-7685; www.lymanmuseum.org, e-mail info@lymanmuseum.org.

A self-guided tour from the Hilo Mainstreet Program Office leads you to 17 sites of historic and architectural significance in this tropical enclave. ~ 329 Kamehameha Avenue; 808-935-8850.

The **Pacific Tsunami Museum** recaptures in photos, videos and interactive displays the tidal waves that periodically wreak havoc on Hilo. Most notorious was the 1946 tsunami, which swept a half-mile inland and killed 94 people on the Big Island. Computers lead visitors through the history and physics of these infamous phenomena and survivors present first-hand accounts in the museum's videotaped oral histories. Closed Sunday. ~ 130 Kamehameha Avenue; 808-935-0926, fax 808-935-0842; www.tsunami.org, e-mail tsunami@tsunami.org.

The **East Hawaii Cultural Center Gallery** displays the work of local and international artists in a series of exhibits that change monthly. The building itself, an old police station that has achieved historic landmark status, is a work of art. Closed Sunday and the last week of every month. ~ 141 Kalakaua Street; 808-961-5711, fax 808-935-7536.

Fronting the library on nearby Waianuenue Avenue are the **Naha** and **Pinao Stones**. According to legend, whoever moved the massive Naha Stone would rule all the islands. Kamehameha overturned the boulder while still a youth, then grew to become Hawaii's first king.

Continue up Waianuenue Avenue to **Rainbow Falls**, a foaming cascade in Wailuku River State Park. Here, particularly in the morning, spray from the falls shimmers in spectral hues. It's another two miles to **Boiling Pots**, where a series of falls pours turbulently into circular lava pools. The rushing water, spilling down from Mauna Kea, bubbles up through the lava and boils over into the next pool.

Kaumana Drive, branching off Waianuenue Avenue, leads five miles out of town to **Kaumana Caves**. A stone stairway leads from the roadside down to two fern-choked lava tubes, formed during Mauna Loa's devastating 1881 eruption. Explore the lower tube, but avoid the other—it's dangerous.

HIDDEN ►    Also be sure to visit the **Panaewa Rainforest Zoo**. Located in a lush region that receives over 125 inches of rain annually, this modest facility houses numerous rainforest animals as well as other species. There are colobus monkeys, pygmy hippos and tigers, plus an array of exotic birds that include crowned cranes, pueos, parrots, Hawaiian coots, laysan ducks and nenes. ~ One mile off the Mamalahoa Highway several miles south of town; 808-959-7224, fax 808-981-2316; www.hilozoo.com, e-mail coh zoo@interpac.net.

**LODGING**

The main hotel district in this rain-plagued city sits astride the bay along Banyan Drive. Most hotels offer moderately priced accommodations, while a few are designed to fit the contours of a more slender purse.

Near the far end of tree-lined Banyan Drive lies the **Hilo Seaside Hotel**. This charming place is actually on a side street fronting Reed's Bay, an arm of Hilo Bay. Owned by the Kimis, a Hawaiian family, it has the same friendly ambience that pervades their other hotels. There's a large lobby decorated with tile, *koa* wood and bamboo. A carp pond complete with footbridges dominates the grounds. The rooms are small and plainly decorated. Most are wallpapered and equipped with telephone, television and a combination shower-tub (perfect for soaking away a rainy day). The lanais overlook lush gardens and the hotel swimming pool. All in all, for friendly ambience and a lovely setting, the Seaside is a prime choice. ~ 126 Banyan Way; 808-935-0821, 800-367-7000, fax 808-969-9195; www.hiloseasidehotel.com, e-mail sandsea@aloha.net. MODERATE TO DELUXE.

**Hilo Bay Hotel** is another economical oceanfront establishment. The theme here is Polynesian, and proprietor "Uncle Billy" carries it off with flair: wicker furniture, thatch and *tapa* in the lobby, a restaurant/cocktail lounge, a bayside swimming pool and several carp ponds dotted about the tropical gardens. Standard rooms have wall-to-wall carpeting, televisions, telephones and air conditioning. The rooms are plainly furnished, located away from the water and rent for a moderate price. Superior rooms (which overlook the gardens, are larger, more attractive and come with ocean views) can be reserved for slightly more. Oceanfront rooms are also available and rent for deluxe prices. ~ 87 Banyan Drive; 808-935-0861, 800-367-5102, fax 808-935-7903; www.unclebilly.com, e-mail resv@unclebilly.com. MODERATE TO DELUXE.

On a tree-lined residential street just across the Wailuku River sits the **Dolphin Bay Hotel**. This comfortable two-story establishment has 18 units, all equipped with kitchenettes. There are studios, one-bedroom apartments, which can accommodate up to four, and a two-bedroom unit, which houses as many as six. Rooms upstairs have exposed-beam ceilings; all units have cinderblock walls, but personal touches like fresh flowers and fruit, and a garden with a running spring, make this a good choice. ~ 333 Iliahi Street; 808-935-1466, fax 808-935-1523; www.dolphinbayhotel.com, e-mail johnhilo@gte.net. MODERATE.

Not far away at the **Wild Ginger Inn** you'll find inexpensive guest rooms, which are carpeted wall-to-wall, attractively furnished and feature ceiling fans. There's a laundry room, a large garden, a spacious lobby and a full continental breakfast every morning. This vintage-1940s Hawaiian-style inn is surrounded by flowering trees and trimly manicured grounds. It also features an open-air lobby that's tastefully tiled and equipped with a very inviting hammock. ~ 100 Puueo Street; 808-935-5556, 800-882-1887, fax 808-969-1225; www.wildgingerinn.com, e-mail wild gingerinn@usa.com. BUDGET.

HIDDEN ►

The former home of the cattle rancher W. H. Shipman and his wife Mary, the historic **Shipman House Bed & Breakfast Inn** has been lovingly restored by the Shipmans' great-granddaughter Barbara Ann and her husband Gary. Much of the furnishings are original and date back to the monarchy, including a Steinway piano Queen Liliuokalani sometimes played while a guest here. Jack London and wife Charmian also spent time at this gracious

**AUTHOR FAVORITE**

When in Hilo, my family often beds down at the **Hawaii Naniloa Hotel**, a highrise affair located right on the water. Rooms are comfortably furnished and nicely adorned. Restaurants, bars, a lounge and a spa are among the many amenities here, but the most alluring feature is the landscape—the tree-studded lawn is fringed with tidepools and volcanic rock. Add outdoor swimming pools, a spacious lobby and friendly staff and you have the perfect nesting spot in town. Guests also have access to the Naniloa Country Club's nine-hole golf course across the street. ~ 93 Banyan Drive; 808-969-3333, 800-367-5360, fax 969-6622; www.naniloa.com, e-mail hinan@aloha.net. MODERATE TO DELUXE.

Victorian. Nowadays, there are five spacious accommodations (two in the detached guest cottage) that are individually decorated with period pieces and fresh flowers. A hula *halau* practices on the premise, and guests are invited to join in on Wednesday-night classes. ~ 131 Kaiulani Street; phone/fax 808-934-8002, 800-627-8447; www.hilo-hawaii.com, e-mail bighouse@bigisland. com. DELUXE.

**Arnott's Lodge** is a clean, bright attractive hostel. Just one block from the waterfront, it is on the outskirts of Hilo in a low-key residential area. There are dormitory rooms available as well as private singles and doubles. Group activities such as hiking and snorkeling trips are frequently arranged. With low-cost prices, and full kitchen and laundry facilities provided, it's one of the area's best bargains. ~ 98 Apapane Road; 808-969-7097, fax 808-961-9638; www.arnottslodge.com, e-mail info@arnottslodge. com. BUDGET.

Located on the waterfront within walking distance of Reeds Bay Beach, Liliuokalani Gardens, Coconut Island and Wailoa River State Park, the **Country Club Condo Hotel** offers lodging in a modern five-story building with distinctively curved architecture. Guest rooms are air conditioned, with contemporary white-and-beige decor and one or two double beds. Some have kitchenettes, and all have balconies—some overlooking the bay and others with less appealing views of the street in front of the hotel. One bedroom suites—actually two guest rooms with a connecting door and a kitchenette—are available. ~ 121 Banyan Drive; phone/fax 808-935-7171; e-mail cchotel@interpac.net. MODERATE.

The largest resort complex in Hilo when it was built in the 1970s, **Waiakea Villas** has always had a hard time staying full. As a result, some of its 100 units are rented long-term as apartments, and others serve as unofficial student housing for the University of Hawaii at Hilo. The 35 guest rooms and suites that are reserved for tourists are in a three-story building shaped like a classic Polynesian longhouse, with a Japanese restaurant and a karaoke bar on the ground floor. The rooms are bright and spacious, with Asian-style decor, ceiling fans and wicker furnishings. Some have kitchenettes, and all have private lanais. The hotel stands amid 14 acres of lush, landscaped grounds on the shore of Blue Lagoon, an inland waterway connected to Hilo Bay. Facilities include a swimming pool, a fitness center and tennis courts. Close to Hilo International Airport, the hotel is convenient for business travelers and visitors with early departing flights, but less appealing for those who are sensitive to noise. ~ 400 Hualani Street; 808-961-2841, fax 808-961-6767; e-mail waiakea1@aloha.com. MODERATE TO DELUXE.

**DINING**

Scattered throughout Hilo are numerous cafés, lunch counters and chain restaurants serving low-cost meals. This is a great town for ethnic eating on a budget.

Try the lunch menu at **Restaurant Kiku,** near the edge of hotel row, which consists of sandwiches (many at low, low cost) as well as Asian and American platters. The menu's limited and the atmosphere nonexistent, but Gwen's place isn't bad for a quick lunch or breakfast. ~ 96 Kalanianaole Avenue; 808-961-2044. BUDGET.

**Uncle Billy's Fish and Steakhouse** at the Hilo Bay Hotel sports Hawaiian decor. In addition to its rattan furnishings, this cozy restaurant hosts Polynesian dinner shows nightly. The menu is filled with surf-and-turf dishes priced reasonably. There's no lunch here, but they do offer breakfast and dinner daily. ~ 87 Banyan Drive; 808-935-0861; www.unclebilly.com, e-mail resv@unclebilly.com. MODERATE TO DELUXE.

Right next to Suisan fish market, **Nihon Restaurant & Cultural Center,** a Japanese dining establishment, is a bit light on the culture, but the food is well prepared. Scenic views of Hilo Bay are accented by artwork from local artists. Specialties include noodle dishes, tempura, sukiyaki and sushi. Closed Sunday. ~ 123 Lihiwai Street; 808-969-1133. MODERATE TO DELUXE.

Home-style Japanese meals are made fresh daily at **Miyo's.** A selection of vegetarian specialties, sashimi, tempura and sesame chicken are served in a simple setting of wooden tables and shoji screens. The dining room, which overlooks a fishpond, boasts views of Mauna Kea. Closed Sunday. ~ Waiakea Villas Shops, 400 Hualani Street; 808-935-2273, fax 808-959-6859. BUDGET TO MODERATE.

For breakfast or lunch in downtown Hilo consider **Canoes Café.** This informal dining area serves breakfast wraps in the morning and offers a "sandwich board" and fresh soups at lunch. ~ 14 Furneaux Lane; 808-935-4070; www.canoescafe.com, e-mail info@canoescafe.com. BUDGET.

There are more than three dozen dishes on the menu at **Reuben's Mexican Food**, numbered one to thirty-seven, and they cover the entire territory. Whether you're searching for enchiladas, *camarones empanizado*, beef tostadas, carne asada or huevos rancheros, you'll find it here. ~ 336 Kamehameha Avenue; 808-961-2552. MODERATE.

**Bear's Coffee Shop** is Hilo's most popular coffee bar, thanks in part to its location in the center of the art gallery district. Breakfast is the big meal here, with fresh-squeezed juices, yummy pastries and specialties such as egg and spinach soufflé on a muffin. There's also a lunch menu featuring deli sandwiches, salads and a few Mexican dishes, and, of course, espresso, cappuccino and latte made with gourmet Kona coffee (available all day). ~ 110 Keawe Street; 808-935-0708. BUDGET.

For creative Italian cuisine in a colorfully romantic atmosphere, the place to go is **Pescatore**, with its yellow exterior, green tablecloths, red chairs, lace curtains and candles in wine bottles. The menu offers such entrées as marinated lamb chops, sautéed chicken breast in lemon caper sauce and pasta puttanesca with anchovy sauce, but as the name suggests, the specialty is fresh seafood, from a traditional cioppino (fisherman's stew) full of lobster, shrimp, scallops and clams to unique sashimi Italian-style. Breakfast served only on Sunday. ~ 235 Keawe Street; 808-969-9090. MODERATE.

Unique is the word for **Broke the Mouth**, a snack shack near the Hilo Farmer's Market. This vegetarian takeout place with picnic tables out front is the creation of a couple who retired from careers as a travel agent and a documentary filmmaker in

◄ HIDDEN

**AUTHOR FAVORITE**

A local institution, **Ken's House of Pancakes** has to top the list for all-American fare. If you've ever been to a Denny's or Howard Johnson's, you've been in Ken's. Endless rows of naugahyde booths, a long counter next to the kitchen, uniformed waitresses—the classic roadside America motif. The cuisine is on par with the decor, but it's a great place to join locals for breakfast (yummy banana pancakes) and it's a good late-night option—open 24 hours. ~ 1730 Kamehameha Avenue; 808-935-8711, fax 808-961-5124; e-mail khop@interpac.net. MODERATE.

Honolulu to start an organic herb, spice and specialty vegetable farm on the Kohala Coast. The signboard "menu," which seems to change at the chef's whim, features homemade veggie burgers on sour poi bread as well as plate lunches ranging from traditional Hawaiian food to outrageously original versions of Chinese, Japanese and Portuguese dishes, all made with locally grown ingredients from the farmer's market—a kaleidoscope of taro, sweet potato, ginger, banana, star fruit, mango, tomato, macadamia nuts, lemongrass, sugar cane, green onions and more. Broke the Mouth also sells souvenir T-shirts and wonderfully unusual sauces, salad dressings and jams. By the way, "broke da mouth" is Hawaiian slang to describe food that tastes so good you'll break your mouth from eating too much. ~ 374 Kinoole Street; 808-934-7670; brokethemouth.com. BUDGET.

**HIDDEN ►**  A hole-in-the-wall local favorite well-hidden behind a bowling alley, **Nori's Saimin and Snacks** has nonetheless grown so popular over the years that it even has its own line of souvenir T-shirts, hats, beach towels and packaged snacks. The atmosphere is boisterous, and it's open until 2 a.m. or so. Saimin, noodles similar to ramen, comes prepared in assorted ways—green and flavored with wasabi, fried with Spam, or in seaweed soup, to name a few. There are also other choices. Try the ahi tuna burger. ~ 688 Kinoole Street #124; 808-935-9133. BUDGET.

For something a little more conventional in Japanese dining, try **Restaurant Miwa** in the Hilo Shopping Center. The atmosphere is traditional, the waitresses wear kimonos, and visitors from Japan rave that the food is the real thing. There's a full sushi bar, featuring rice rolled with raw rarities such as butterfish, abalone, sea urchin and giant clam. Equally special are the *kaiseki*—dinners served with rice consisting of seven small, consecutive courses such as miso soup, pickled vegetables, sashimi, grilled fish, tempura and a dessert. ~ 1261 Kilauea Avenue; 808-961-4454. MODERATE TO DELUXE.

The owner's South American roots are evident at **Hawaiian Jungle Mexican Restaurant,** where the food shows a flavorful Latin influence. The menu is rich with options including salads, and specialties like gazpacho, catch-of-the-day, enchiladas and quesadillas. Decor is casual with appealing stained woods adding to the warmth of the setting. Music's live and lively on Friday, Saturday and Sunday after 7 p.m. It's jazz on Friday, Hawaiian

music on Sunday, and mixed musical fare on Saturday. ~ 110
Kalakaua Street; 808-934-0700. BUDGET TO MODERATE.

**Don's Grill** is one of those all-American places where dinner ◄ *HIDDEN*
comes with soup or salad, hot vegetables, a fresh roll and your
choice of mashed potatoes or fries. In this case it's Hawaiian all-
American, so the menu switches from pork chops to teriyaki beef,
rotisserie chicken to tofu stir-fry, and barbecued ribs to breaded
calamari. Very popular with the local folk. Closed Monday. ~ 485
Hinano Street; 808-935-9099, fax 808-961-0162. MODERATE.

You can dine or take out at **Café Pesto**, an appealing eatery
located in the historic S. Hata Building. This downtown Hilo gathering place serves wood-fired pizza, calzone, risotto, fresh fish
and organic salads. ~ 308 Kamehameha Avenue; 808-969-6640,
fax 808-969-4858; www.cafepesto.com. MODERATE TO DELUXE.

**Tsunami Grill and Tempura**, a small café downtown, serves ◄ *HIDDEN*
Japanese meals. Several *donburi, udon* and tempura dishes are
on tap as well as special seafood dishes. Closed Sunday. ~ 250
Keawe Street; 808-961-6789. BUDGET.

Thailand is represented by **Royal Siam**, an excellent eatery
with a warm ambience, friendly staff, local crowd and exceptional cuisine. You'll find *pad thai* and traditional curries. Closed
Sunday. ~ 70 Mamo Street; 808-961-6100. BUDGET TO MODERATE.

Hilo's foremost steak-and-seafood restaurant is **Harrington's**,
a waterfront dining room that is particularly popular with locals.
Here you can dine in a congenial atmosphere to the strains of
Hawaiian music in the background. Harrington's also has a relaxing bar scene and can be counted on for good food with a
view. ~ 135 Kalanianaole Street; 808-961-4966, fax 808-961-
4975. MODERATE TO DELUXE.

**CATCH THE FRESH CATCH**

Be sure to check out the **Suisan Company Limited**. Started in 1907 by a
small group of Waiakea fishermen, it is a local institution. Anglers bring their
fresh catches—ahi, mahimahi, reef and bottom fish, whatever's jumping—
here for sale. Great photo ops! If you'd like to sample some of the fresh
fish, buy some tasty *poke ahi* (raw tuna chunks seasoned with chili pep-
pers, seaweed, green onions and soy sauce), a favorite Hawaiian dish. ~
93 Lihiwai Street; 808-935-9349, fax 808-935-2115; www.suisan.com.

**GROCERIES**  The island's largest city, Hilo has several supermarkets. Foremost is **Sack-N-Save**. ~ 250 Kinoole Street; 808-935-3113.

Hilo hosts an excellent natural foods outlet—**Abundant Life Wholefoods & Deli**. It contains healthy supplies of vitamins and juices, as well as a deli and fresh organic fruits and vegetables. ~ 292 Kamehameha Avenue; 808-935-7411.

**Holsum/Oroweat Bakery Thrift Store** offers fresh and day-old baked goods at unbeatable prices. Closed Sunday. ~ 1261 Kilauea Avenue, Suite 260; 808-935-2164.

**SHOPPING**  The most convenient way to shop in Hilo is at **Prince Kuhio Plaza**, a full-facility complex with everything from small crafts shops to swank boutiques to a sprawling department store. The Big Island's largest mall, it's a gathering place for local shoppers and a convenient spot for visitors. But bargains and locally crafted products are probably what you're after. So it's a good idea to window-shop through the centers, checking out prices, then do your buying at smaller shops. ~ 111 East Puainako Street; 808-959-3555.

**The Most Irresistible Shop in Hilo** doesn't quite live up to its bold name but does create a strong attraction with jewelry, clothing, ceramics, books and toys. They also feature works by local artists. ~ 256 Kamehameha Avenue; 808-935-9644.

For beach-reading materials, try **The Book Gallery**. This well-stocked shop has many popular titles. ~ 259 Keawe Street; 808-935-4943. If maps, guidebooks and volumes on Hawaiiana sound more inviting, **Basically Books** is an excellent choice. ~ 160 Kamehameha Avenue; 808-961-0144.

### SAVING HISTORY

Grassroots initiatives have brought about a partial revitalization of what remains of the diminishing number of wood-frame buildings that give Hilo a distinctive look. Luckily there have been some notable successes, including the surprisingly elegant Palace Theater (c. 1925), a landmark now partially restored and home to top-notch live theater and musicals. The old Police Station (c. 1910) is now an arts complex, while the classic Kress Building now houses shops and multiscreen movie theaters, each a hopeful sign for the future.

Following a similar theme, **Hana Hou Encore** is a shop filled with "vintage and contemporary island treasures." Among those keepsakes are old Hawaiian song sheets, Matson menus and aloha shirts. Closed Sunday. ~ 164 Kamehameha Avenue; 808-935-4555; e-mail hanahou@ilhawaii.com.

Specializing in "distinct island wearables, bedding and gifts," **Sig Zane Designs** has its own designer line of island dresses and aloha shirts. ~ 122 Kamehameha Avenue; 808-935-7077.

If it's fine *koa* wood pieces you're after, **Big Island Woodworks Gallery** is waiting for you. They have a finely honed collection of bowls and decorative pieces. ~ 206 Kamehameha Avenue; 808-982-8101; www.volcanogallery.com.

Another great spot for original woodwork is south of Hilo about 12 miles on Route 11 at **Dan DeLuz Woods**. The beautiful pieces are fashioned from banyan, sandalwood, *koa* and *milo*, all priced reasonably. The DeLuzes, the craftspeople who own the shop, do all their carving in a separate workshop. If you'd like a description of how the bowls are made, they're happy to provide an informal tour. ~ Mile marker 12, Route 11; 808-968-6607, fax 808-968-6019.

**NIGHTLIFE**

The main scene centers around the big hotels along Banyan Drive. By far the best place is the Hawaii Naniloa Hotel. This hotel has a nicely appointed nightclub, **The Crown Room**. The lounge usually books local groups, but every once in a while it imports a mainland band for special events. There's usually a cover charge and two-drink minimum. Then there is **Joji's Lounge**, which sometimes provides piano tunes in the evening. ~ 93 Banyan Drive; 808-969-3333; e-mail hinan@aloha.net.

**Harrington's** hosts a Hawaiian guitarist on weekends. ~ 135 Kalanianaole Avenue; 808-961-4966.

The **Waioli Lounge** at the Hilo Hawaiian Hotel has live music on weekends. Usually it's a contemporary duo. ~ 71 Banyan Drive; 808-935-9361.

**BEACHES & PARKS**

**KALAKAUA PARK** Located on the corner of busy Kinoole Street and Waianuenue Avenue, this pretty little park has a grand old banyan tree and a pleasant picnic area. A bronze statue of King Kalakaua adds dignity to the park grounds.

**REED'S BAY BEACH PARK** 🏊 🌴 🚿 Reed's Bay, a banyan-lined cove is a marvelous picnic spot. The bay is actually an arm of Hilo Bay, but unlike the larger body of water, Reed's Bay offers excellent swimming in smooth water (though an underwater spring keeps the water cold). There is also an adjacent body of water popular with the locals. They call it "ice pond" due to its cold waters. Facilities include picnic areas, drinking water, showers and restrooms. ~ Located at the end of Banyan Drive.

**ONEKAHAKAHA, KEALOHA AND LELEIWI COUNTY PARKS** 🏊 🌴 🎣 🚿 None of these three parks have sand beaches, but all possess lava pools or other shallow places for swimming. They also have grassy plots and picnic areas, plus restrooms and showers. If you fish along these shores, chances are good you'll net *papio*, threadfin, mountain bass, mullet, big-eyed scad, mackerel scad, milkfish, bonefish or goatfish. Kealoha Park offers good snorkeling, surfing, spear-fishing and throw-netting. ~ All three parks are located within five miles of Hilo, east along Kalanianaole Avenue.

HIDDEN ► **RICHARDSON OCEAN PARK** 🏊 🌴 🎣 🚿 This black-sand beach, south of Hilo Bay, is without doubt the finest beach in the area. From there you can see Mauna Kea hulking in the background. Coconut palms and ironwood trees fringe the beach, while a lava outcropping somewhat protects swimmers. The protected areas also make for good snorkeling. This is one of the best spots around Hilo for surfing as well as bodysurfing and bodyboarding. Winter break with right slides. Mornings and evenings are the prime times, but at all times beware of currents, riptides and sharp reefs. Park officials warn beginners to learn the sport at a less treacherous location. Lifeguards are on duty every day. Anglers try for *papio*, mountain bass, mullet, big-eyed scad, mackerel scad, milkfish, bonefish and goatfish. Facilities here include restrooms and outdoor showers. ~ Take Kalanianaole Avenue to within a quarter-mile of where the paved road ends; watch for the sign to Richardson Ocean Park. The beach is behind and to the right of the center; 808-961-8695, fax 808-961-8696.

# ELEVEN

# Hamakua Coast

 Route 19, the Mamalahoa Highway, leads north from Hilo along the rainy, windswept Hamakua Coast. Planted with papaya, macadamia nuts, taro and ginger root, among other crops and teeming with exotic plant life, this elevated coastline is as lushly overgrown as Hilo.

When skies are free of clouds the view from the two lane highway that snakes its way north from Hilo includes Mauna Kea, a particularly impressive sight when winter snows cap the summit. Several marked turnoffs allow a more intimate link to the landscape, including the four-mile-long Scenic Route just north of Hilo that hugs the rocky coastline and the upcountry road that leads past the plantation town of Honomu to Akaka Falls State Park.

A softly rolling plateau that edges from the slopes of Mauna Kea to the sea, the region is cut by sharp canyons and deep gulches. Waterfalls cascade down emerald walls and tumbling streams lead to lava-rock beaches. Beautiful is too tame a term for this enchanting countryside. There are stands of eucalyptus, shadowy forests and misty fields of sugar cane. Plantation towns, built between 1900 and 1910, filled with pastel-painted houses and adorned with flower gardens, lie along the route. Route 19 is itself a reminder of those days, built to replace the railroad that first accessed this rugged landscape. A small railroad museum at Laupahoehoe provides an introduction to the days when cane was king and towering wooden trestles supported trains carrying harvested cane to the mills and then on to Hilo for export to California.

At Honokaa Route 19 heads toward upcountry Waimea. Hamakua's scenic rewards continue on Route 240, a nine-mile-long spur that ends at the Waipio Valley overlook. Heavily populated in Polynesian times when free-flowing streams made for abundant harvests of water-hungry taro, Waipio and the series of valleys beyond have reverted to wilderness, awaiting the adventurous traveler.

**SIGHTS**   Several miles outside Hilo, follow the signs to the **Scenic Drive**. This old coast road winds past cane fields and shantytowns before rejoining the main highway. Alexander palms line the road. Watch for Onomea Bay: There you'll see a V-shaped rock formation where a sea arch collapsed in 1956.

You might want to stop by **Hawaii Tropical Botanical Garden**, an exotic nature preserve with streams, waterfalls, rugged coastline and over 2000 plant species. This jungle garden, edged by the Pacific and inhabited by shore birds and giant sea turtles, is a place of uncommon beauty. Admission. ~ On the Four Mile Scenic Route, seven miles north of Hilo; 808-964-5233, fax 808-964-1338; www.hawaiigarden.com, e-mail htbg@ilhawaii.net.

Back on the main road, you'll soon come to a turnoff heading inland to **Akaka Falls State Park**. Don't bypass it! A short nature trail leads past bamboo groves, ferns, ti and orchids to Akaka Falls, which slide 442 feet down a sheer cliff face, and Kahuna Falls, 400 feet high. This 66-acre preserve is covered in a canopy of rainforest vegetation. There are birds of paradise, azaleas and giant philodendrons whose leaves measure as much as two feet.

Countless gulches ribbon the landscape between Hilo and Honokaa. For a unique tour, take the road from Hakalau that

HIDDEN ►   winds down to **Hakalau Gulch**. Literally choked with vegetation, this gorge extends to a small beach. Towering above the gulch is the highway bridge.

Another side road several miles north corkscrews down to

HIDDEN ►   **Laupahoehoe Point**, a hauntingly beautiful peninsula from which 24 students and teachers were swept away by the 1946 tidal wave. Here gently curving palm trees and spreading lawns contrast with the lash of the surf.

Beginning in 1899 and lasting until 1946—when sugar was king—railways were the main source of transportation on the Big Island. Nowadays all that's left of the railroads are relics found in the **Laupahoehoe Train Museum**, housed in a former railroad employee's home. Here you'll find railroad artifacts, photos, memorabilia and a chance to "talk story" with the museum's volunteers, many of whom have spent their lives in the community. (By the way, the Hamakua portion of the railway was washed away by the 1946 tidal wave, but many current highway bridges are built on the original trestle foundations.) There's a small gift shop at the museum, with items hand-crafted by local residents, and the museum grounds are planted with tropical fruit trees and ornamentals, making it a nice place for a picnic. ~ Between mile markers 25 and 26 on Route 19; 808-962-6300, fax 808-962-2221; www.geocities.com/trainmuseum.

It's a jungle out there. But at **World Botanical Gardens** they're trying to make a tropical paradise out of it. Among the features are a football field–sized children's maze, a 300-acre botanical garden, a pathway through a dense and very beautiful rainforest, and a vista point overlooking a triple-tiered waterfall; many more features are under development. Be sure to try the complimentary fruit and juice. Closed Sunday. Admission. ~ Located near mile marker 16 on Route 19 in Umauma; 808-963-5427, fax 808-964-5530; www.wbgi.com, e-mail wbgi@hotmail.com.

The plantation town of **Paauilo** offers a glimpse of vintage Hawaii: decaying storefronts and tinroof cottages. Then it's on to **Honokaa**, a village caught in a lazy-paced time warp and the world center of macadamia nut growing.

◀ HIDDEN

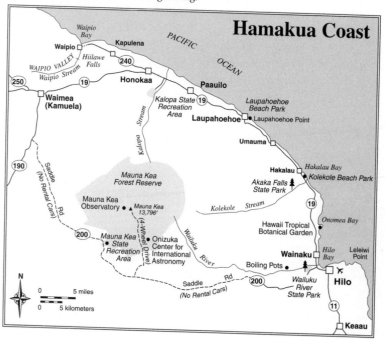

Head out Route 240 to **Waipio Valley**, the island's largest valley. This northcoast gem (see "Waipio Valley—Fertile and Dramatic") is ripe for exploring. Most people get to see Waipio from this scenic lookout where Route 240 comes to an abrupt end. From the lookout you can see the mile-long black sand beach that marks Waipio's border with the sea. Tall ironwoods mark the site that was once a *heiau*, with the taro patches that remain homage to the Hawaiian past. The steep road that makes its way to the Valley floor requires four-wheel drive. It's narrow (in some places only wide enough one vehicle), steep (with up to a 38 degree gradient), with sheer dropoffs that have hosted more than one vehicle.

Taro patches and tumbledown cottages still dot the valley. From the lookout point at road's end, a jeep trail drops sharply into Waipio. Explorers can hike down or take an hour-and-a-half four-wheel-drive tour with the **Waipio Valley Shuttle and Tours**. ~ 808-775-7121. Another agency with tours is **Waipio Valley Wagon Tour**. Its tour is part four-wheel-drive, part mule-drawn, GM shock-equipped wagon. ~ 808-775-9518. Both tours travel several miles up into the valley for eye-boggling views of 1200-foot Hiilawe Falls. Both are closed Sunday. **Hawaiian Walkways** (808-775-0372, 800-457-7759) offers escorted hikes along the valley's south rim with time for a swim in waterfall-fed pool and panoramic valley views.

If you hike in, be prepared for some heavy-duty puffing and panting on the way up, and take heed of no trespassing signs. Camping requires a permit, with unimproved campsites just behind the beach. If you don't have time to explore the valley, be sure to at least take in the vista from the **Waipio Valley Lookout** at the end of Route 240.

*sights*

**AUTHOR FAVORITE**

For the hikers and explorers in the group, the lush **Waipio Valley** is Eden here on Earth. A riot of tropical colors, swimming holes, 600-foot cascades, taro patches and an occasional wild horse are reasons to spend a day or more in this lush and sacred region. For movie buffs, Kaluahina Falls might bring recognition—but only if you were one of the few to see Kevin Costner's landfall in the monumental flop *Water World*. (See "Hiking" in Chapter Two.)

The **Palms Cliff House** is a contemporary take on the Victorian theme, offering five-star elegance with eight oceanview rooms that are this area's most stylish (and pricey) accommodation options. There's a hot tub for relaxing, in-room massage and cooking classes to consider. Shielded from the road by tall palms and dense tropical vegetation, seaside views from the clifftop setting are mesmerizing. A full breakfast is served on the expansive verandah. ~ Route 19, 12 north of Hilo, just before the Honomu turnoff to Akaka Falls State Park, P.O. Box 189, Honomu, HI 96729; 808-963-6076; www.palmscliffhouse.com, e-mail palms cliffhouse@aol.com. DELUXE TO ULTRA-DELUXE.

**LODGING**

**Hotel Honokaa Club**, perched on a hillside above the Hamakua Coast, has a boardinghouse atmosphere. The rooms upstairs are kept thoroughly scrubbed and freshly painted; they're quite adequate. A modest price buys a splendid ocean view, color television plus a tiny private bathroom. Or trade the cable TV away and you can have a small cubicle with community bathroom at even less cost. These rooms are smaller and lack the view, but they're just as clean as the upstairs rooms. Dorm-style hostel accommodations are also available. A continental breakfast is included. ~ Route 240, Honokaa; phone/fax 808-775-0678, 800-808-0678; www.hotelhono.com, e-mail cathy@hotelhono.com. BUDGET TO MODERATE.

◄ HIDDEN

This is prime bed-and-breakfast country that benefits from a rural setting and hosts with plenty of aloha. The five-room **Waipio Wayside**, on Route 240 between Honokaa and Waipio, offers a convenient base for exploring the valley. The century-old home has been nicely updated, preserving the feel of the past. A full breakfast ranging from bacon-and eggs to pancakes is served communally. ~ P.O. Box 840, Honokaa, HI 96727; 808-775-0275, 800-833-8849, fax 808-775-0275; www.waipiowayside.com, e-mail wayside@ilhawaii.net. MODERATE.

At **Mountain Meadow Ranch** in Ahualoa (about five minutes upcountry of Honokaa toward Waimea), you're surrounded by pastureland and tall eucalyptus that scent the air. There are a separate one-bedroom cottage or a two-bedroom suite that can be rented as a one-bedroom booking. Breakfast includes home-brewed coffee, local fruits, breads, pastries and cereal. Rooms are spacious, beds comfortable—fluffy and warm for the cool night air. Owner Gay George is a most pleasant hostess. ~ P.O. Box 1697, Hono-

kaa, HI 96727; phone/fax 808-775-9376; www.mountainmeadow
ranch.com, e-mail bill@mountainmeadowranch.com. MODERATE.

**DINING**

Jolene's Kau Kau Korner has plate lunches, burgers and sandwiches during daylight hours. At dinner, they move on to mahimahi, shrimp and vegetable tempura, stir-fry beef and grilled
chicken with pineapple. It's a simple café but reasonably priced
with good-sized portions and local color. ~ 45-3625 Mamane
Street, Honokaa; 808-775-9498. BUDGET TO MODERATE.

**Mamane Street Bakery and Café** has glass cases full of pies,
pastries, brownies and Hawaiian sweetbread. The tiny café, decorated with old photos and model ships, serves espresso made from
freshly ground local Carter's Farm coffee and features sandwiches
on focaccia bread for lunch. Banana macadamia nut cake is a
specialty here. ~ Mamane Street, Honokaa; 808-775-9478. BUDGET.

When the sun beats down hot on Honokaa's main street, it's
only natural to head for **Simply Natural**, an old-fashioned ice
cream parlor with checkerboard tile floors, rainbow ceiling fans
and homemade ice cream. There is also a vegetarian breakfast
and lunch menu with such items as taro-banana pancakes, tem-
peh sandwiches and gardenburgers. ~ 45-3625 Mamane Street,
Honokaa; 808-775-0119. BUDGET.

HIDDEN ►

Oversize portions, and the fact that on some nights it's the
only restaurant in town, makes **Tex Drive-In & Restaurant** a
Honokaa landmark and gathering place. Local specialties and
standard fare like hamburgers dominate the fast-food menu. ~
Route 19, Honokaa; 808-775-0598. BUDGET.

**GROCERIES**

First you can check out **Jan's Store**. Located in Honomu on the
road to Akaka Falls, it has a limited stock, but you may find
what you need. ~ Honomu; 808-963-6062. Also try **Ti Kane-
shiro Supermarket**, a small-town shop across from the post office in Honokaa. ~ Honokaa; 808-775-0631.

**SHOPPING**

On the road to Akaka Falls in Honomu, you'll happen upon the
**Ohana Gallery**. Here is a wide array of work by local artists and
craftspeople. Of particular note are photographs of the volcano
erupting on the Big Island. The Gallery also serves as an area information center. ~ Honomu; 808-963-5467.

Located two miles from Akaka Falls, the **Woodshop Gallery
and Café** is one of the largest art galleries on the Hamakua Coast,

# Waipio Valley— Fertile and Dramatic

oday it is only lightly inhabited, but at the time Captain Cook reached Hawaii in 1778 it was one of the most heavily populated places in the islands, rich in taro fields and with beach access to the open ocean, Waipio was a breadbasket. By far the largest of the great valleys cut into the North Kohala Mountains, it's walls are creased with several year-round waterfalls and dozens of others that come and go with the rains. The valley walls are steep, with the floor of the valley ranging a half-mile to a mile in width. A stream winds in ways to the ocean, dissecting the valley floor, which for the first two miles inland is was densely populated, home to an estimated 4000 Hawaiians. For perhaps as long as a thousand years Hawaiians lived in Waipio and its sister valleys, linked to the outside world by outrigger canoes.

Legend and history blend in Waipio. It was to Waipio the god Lono came seeking a wife, while the demigod Maui is said to have died here. It was to Waipio that the newborn Kamehameha was taken, to be raised in hiding under threat of death. Here that he returned and declared his allegiance to war god Kukailimoku. It was off Waipio and Waimanu, the next valley to the north, that Kamehameha would return to fight a major sea battle against Maui high chief Kahekili.

By the start of the 20th century, Waipio was greatly depopulated, in part due to foreign-borne illnesses that struck the Hawaiians with epidemic force, and the move to less isolated locales once plantations sent out their call for workers. Many Hawaiians moved to Hamakua's plantation towns or Hilo. The tsunamis that devastated Hilo in the 1940s and 1960s also hit Waipio, further diminishing a population that today likely stands at fewer than 50, with many of these only part time residents.

The wild isolation and tropical landscape made Waipio the choice of the Federal Government when it came to preparing recruits for the Peace Corps in the 1960s. Little remains of the compound, which was in the vicinity of Hiilawe Falls, on Waipio's south walls.

exhibiting fine *koa* wood furniture, collector-quality turned wood bowls, art glass, silks, jewelry boxes and local artworks; its small café serves sandwiches and homemade ice cream. ~ Hakalau; 808-963-6363, 877-479-7995, fax 808-775-0548.

**Kamaaina Woods** in Honokaa has a splendid assortment of handmade bowls and decorations. With items fashioned from *milo*, mango and *koa*, this shop is practically a museum. And if you are interested in learning more about these woods, you can view the factory through the window. ~ Lehua Street, Honokaa; 808-775-7722.

The **Waipio Valley Artworks**, located near the Waipio Valley Lookout, is also cluttered with woodcarvings. Made from several different woods, some of these creations are extremely beautiful. This shop also features paintings, ceramics and other locally crafted items. ~ 48-5416 Government Road; 808-775-0958.

**NIGHTLIFE** The **Honokaa People's Theatre**, a 1930 structure with an Old West–style facade and a portico over the sidewalk, is one of the last motion picture houses in Hawaii with a single big screen. Besides showing first-run films, the renovated theater is used for occasional live dance performances and country music concerts. Each November it is the venue for the Hamakua Music Festival, an extravaganza of jazz, classical and Hawaiian traditional music performances that raises money for music education on the Hamakua Coast. ~ Honokaa; 808-775-0000.

**BEACHES & PARKS** **KOLEKOLE BEACH PARK** Located at the mouth of a wide gulch lush with tropical vegetation, this comfortable park has a large and pleasant grassy area. A stream and waterfall tumble through the park down to the rocky, surf-torn shore. The sandy beach and natural beauty of the place make it very popular among local residents. You can swim in the stream but the

---

**WAIPIO WALKS**

Based in Honokaa, **Hawaiian Walkways** features several walking tour options including the half-day-long Waipio Waterfall Adventure, which includes a waterfall pool swim, lunch and all supplies. The 4.5-mile hike along the rim of Waipio Valley offers spectacular views. You can also arrange special excursions to fit your needs. ~ P.O. Box 1307, Honokaa, HI 96727; 808-775-0372; 800-457-7759; www.hawaiianwalkways.com.

ocean here is forbiddingly rough. Threadfin, *menpachi*, *papio* and *ulua* are the common catches. Facilities consist of a picnic area, restrooms and electricity; there is no drinking water, but spring water is available for cooking and showers. It's one mile to markets and restaurants in Honomu. ~ Located just off Mamalahoa Highway (Route 19) about 12 miles northwest of Hilo.

▲ Tent and trailer; $5 per adult, $1 to $2 per child. County permit required.

**LAUPAHOEHOE BEACH PARK** 🏊 🚻 🏃 ⛵ Set on a low-lying peninsula that was inundated by the 1946 tidal wave, this hauntingly beautiful park is still lashed by heavy surf. A precipitous *pali* and lava-strewn shoreline surround the area. Swimming, snorkeling and surfing are good at times, but usually very dangerous. You can fish for *ulua*, *papio*, *menpachi* and *moi*. Facilities include a picnic area, restrooms, showers and electricity. It's at least 15 miles to restaurants or markets in Honokaa, so bring a lunch. ~ One mile off Route 19 down a well-marked twisting road, about 27 miles northwest of Hilo.

▲ Tent and trailer camping permitted; $5 per adult, $1 to $2 per child. County permit required.

**KALOPA STATE RECREATION AREA** 🏃 A wooded retreat set in the mountains above the Hamakua Coast, this 100-acre park has both untouched expanses ripe for exploring and several beautifully landscaped acres. Ranging from 2000 to 2500 feet elevation, it's a great place for hiking or just for escaping. There are picnic areas, restrooms, showers and cabins. ~ Take Route 19 southeast from Honokaa for about three miles. A well-marked paved road leads from the highway another two miles to the park.

▲ Tent camping is permitted and cabins are also available; call 808-974-6200 for reservations.

**WAIPIO BEACH** 🏃 🏊 Waipio's mile of gray sands are dissected by the waters of Waipio Stream after a journey that begins six miles upstream. With a steep break and often unpredictable currents, swimming requires a careful reading of daily conditions. The setting provides wonderful views of the valley's steep walls. The remains of an ancient *heiau* are situated in an ironwood grove that backs the beach. ~ You can reach the main section of beach by wading the stream, a dangerous task when waters are full. Otherwise it requires a bridge crossing a bit upstream followed by a walk (or drive) to the shore.

▼ ▼ ▼ ▼ ▼ ▼ ▼ ▼ ▼ ▼ ▼ ▼ ▼ ▼ ▼ ▼ ▼ ▼ ▼ ▼ ▼ ▼

# Addresses & Phone Numbers

### HAWAII ISLAND

*County Department of Parks and Recreation* ~ 25 Aupuni Street, Hilo; 808-961-8311; www.hawaii-county.com

*Hawaii Visitors & Convention Bureau* ~ 250 Keawe Street, Hilo; 808-961-5797, and 250 Waikoloa Beach Drive #B15, Waikoloa; 808-886-1655; www.bigisland.org

*Hawaii Volcanoes National Park Headquarters* ~ 808-985-6000; www.nps.gov/havo

*State Department of Land and Natural Resources* ~ 75 Aupuni Street, Hilo; 808-974-6200; www.state.hi.us/dlnr

*Weather Report* ~ 808-935-8555 for Hilo; 808-961-5582 for entire island

### KAILUA-KONA

*Ambulance* ~ 911 or 800-742-5457

*Barber Shop* ~ Hanato's, Kailua Trade Center, 75-5706 Hanama Place #105; 808-329-9119

*Books* ~ Middle Earth Bookshoppe, 75-5719 Alii Drive; 808-329-2123

*Fire Department* ~ 808-961-8297 or 911 for emergencies

*Fishing Supplies* ~ Kona Fishing Tackle, 74-5583 Luhia Street #B7; 808-326-2934

*Hardware* ~ Trojan Lumber Company, 74-5488 Kaiwi Street; 808-329-3536

*Hospital* ~ Kona Community Hospital, 79-1019 Haukapila Street, Kealakekua town; 808-322-9311

*Laundromat* ~ Hele Mai Laundromat, North Kona Shopping Center, behind Firestone; 808-329-3494

*Library* ~ 75-138 Hualalai Road; 808-327-4327

*Pharmacy* ~ Longs Drugs, Lanihau Shopping Center, Palani Road; 808-329-1380

*Photo Supply* ~ Zac's Photo, North Kona Shopping Center, Palani Road and Kuakini Highway; 808-329-0006

*Police Department* ~ 74-5221 Kaahumanu Highway; 808-326-4201 or 911 for emergencies

*Post Office* ~ 74-5577 Palani Road by the Sack 'n Save; 808-331-8307

**HILO**

*Ambulance* ~ 911 or 800-742-5457

*Barber Shop* ~ Modie Barber Shop, 310 Kilauea Avenue; 808-935-4807

*Books* ~ Basically Books, 160 Kamehameha Avenue; 808-961-0144; www.basicallybooks.com

*Fire Department* ~ 808-961-8336 or 911 for emergencies

*Fishing Supplies* ~ Itsu's Fishing Supply, 810 Piilani Street; 808-935-8082

*Hardware* ~ Garden Exchange, 300 Keawe Street; 808-961-2875

*Hospital* ~ Hilo Medical Center, 1190 Waianuenue Avenue; 808-974-4700

*Library* ~ 300 Waianuenue Avenue; 808-933-8888

*Liquor* ~ Kadota Liquor, 194 Hualalai Street; 808-935-1802

*Pharmacy* ~ Longs Drugs, 555 Kilauea Avenue; 808-935-3357

*Photo Supply* ~ Hawaii Photo Supply, 284 Keawe Street; 808-935-6995

*Police Department* ~ 349 Kapiolani Street; 808-935-3311 or 911 for emergencies

*Post Office* ~ 1299 Kekuanaoa Avenue, 808-933-3019; and 154 Waianuenue Avenue, 808-933-3016

# Index

# Lodging Index

## LODGING SERVICES

# Dining Index

## HIDDEN GUIDES

Adventure travel or a relaxing vacation?—"Hidden" guidebooks are the only travel books in the business to provide detailed information on both. Aimed at environmentally aware travelers, our motto is "Where Vacations Meet Adventures." These books combine details on unique hotels, restaurants and sightseeing with information on camping, sports and hiking for the outdoor enthusiast.

## THE NEW KEY GUIDES

Based on the concept of ecotourism, The New Key Guides are dedicated to the preservation of Central America's rare and endangered species, architecture and archaeology. Filled with helpful tips, they give travelers everything they need to know about these exotic destinations.

## PARADISE FAMILY GUIDES

Ideal for families traveling with kids of any age—toddlers to teenagers—Paradise Family Guides offer a blend of travel information unlike any other guides to the Hawaiian islands. With vacation ideas and tropical adventures that are sure to satisfy both action-hungry youngsters and relaxation-seeking parents, these guides meet the specific needs of each and every family member.

Ulysses Press books are available at bookstores everywhere. If any of the following titles are unavailable at your local bookstore, ask the bookseller to order them.

You can also order books directly from Ulysses Press
P.O. Box 3440, Berkeley, CA 94703
800-377-2542 or 510-601-8301
fax: 510-601-8307
www.ulyssespress.com
e-mail: ulysses@ulyssespress.com

## HIDDEN GUIDEBOOKS

____ Hidden Arizona, $16.95
____ Hidden Bahamas, $14.95
____ Hidden Baja, $14.95
____ Hidden Belize, $15.95
____ Hidden Big Island of Hawaii, $13.95
____ Hidden Boston & Cape Cod, $14.95
____ Hidden British Columbia, $18.95
____ Hidden Cancún & the Yucatán, $16.95
____ Hidden Carolinas, $17.95
____ Hidden Coast of California, $18.95
____ Hidden Colorado, $15.95
____ Hidden Disneyland, $13.95
____ Hidden Florida, $18.95
____ Hidden Florida Keys & Everglades,
       $12.95
____ Hidden Georgia, $16.95
____ Hidden Guatemala, $16.95
____ Hidden Hawaii, $18.95
____ Hidden Idaho, $14.95

____ Hidden Kauai, $13.95
____ Hidden Maui, $13.95
____ Hidden Montana, $15.95
____ Hidden New England, $18.95
____ Hidden New Mexico, $15.95
____ Hidden Oahu, $13.95
____ Hidden Oregon, $15.95
____ Hidden Pacific Northwest, $18.95
____ Hidden Salt Lake City, $14.95
____ Hidden San Francisco & Northern
       California, $18.95
____ Hidden Southern California, $18.95
____ Hidden Southwest, $19.95
____ Hidden Tahiti, $17.95
____ Hidden Tennessee, $16.95
____ Hidden Utah, $16.95
____ Hidden Walt Disney World, $13.95
____ Hidden Washington, $15.95
____ Hidden Wine Country, $13.95
____ Hidden Wyoming, $15.95

## THE NEW KEY GUIDEBOOKS

____ The New Key to Costa Rica, $18.95

____ The New Key to Ecuador and the
       Galápagos, $17.95

## PARADISE FAMILY GUIDES

____ Paradise Family Guides: Kaua'i, $16.95
____ Paradise Family Guides: Maui, $16.95

____ Paradise Family Guides: Big Island of
       Hawai'i, $16.95

Mark the book(s) you're ordering and enter the total cost here ➾ [     ]

California residents add 8.25% sales tax here ➾ [     ]

Shipping, check box for your preferred method and enter cost here ➾ [     ]

☐ BOOK RATE              FREE! FREE! FREE!

☐ PRIORITY MAIL/UPS GROUND     cost of postage

☐ UPS OVERNIGHT OR 2-DAY AIR   cost of postage

[     ]

Billing, enter total amount due here and check method of payment ➾

☐ CHECK          ☐ MONEY ORDER

☐ VISA/MASTERCARD _____ EXP. DATE _____

NAME _____ PHONE _____

ADDRESS _____

CITY _____ STATE _____ ZIP _____

MONEY-BACK GUARANTEE ON DIRECT ORDERS PLACED THROUGH ULYSSES PRESS.

## ABOUT THE AUTHOR

**RAY RIEGERT** is the author of eight travel books, including *Hidden San Francisco & Northern California*. His most popular work, *Hidden Hawaii*, won the coveted Lowell Thomas Travel Journalism Award for Best Guidebook as well a similar award from the Hawaii Visitors Bureau. In addition to his role as publisher of Ulysses Press, he has written for the *Chicago Tribune*, *Saturday Evening Post*, *San Francisco Chronicle* and *Travel & Leisure*. A member of the Society of American Travel Writers, he lives in the San Francisco Bay area with his wife, co-publisher Leslie Henriques, and their son Keith and daughter Alice.

## ABOUT THE CONTRIBUTING AUTHORS

**LESLIE HENRIQUES** is the co-publisher of Ulysses Press and has written for several Hidden guides, including *Hidden Hawaii*, *Hidden Oahu* and *Hidden San Francisco & Northern California*. Her travel photographs have been published in *Travel & Leisure* as well as many national newspapers. A member of the Society of American Travel Writers, she lives in Berkeley (though she would rather be in the islands) with husband and partner Ray Riegert, and their two children Keith and Alice.

**ALLAN SEIDEN** is an Oahu-based writer, photographer and cultural historian with a focus on Hawaii. Originally from New York City, he has lived in Honolulu since 1974. Seiden has authored more than 15 books on island themes as well as other award-winning projects, and his work has appeared in numerous publications worldwide. He is currently working on a biography of Queen Liliuokalani. Seiden lives in Honolulu with daughters Martine and Sonyah.

**RICHARD HARRIS** has written or co-written 29 other guidebooks including Ulysses' *Hidden Bahamas*, *Hidden Cancún and the Yucatán* and *Hidden Southwest*. He has also served as contributing editor on guides to Mexico, New Mexico and other ports of call for John Muir Publications, Fodor's, Birnbaum, Access and Globe Pequot Press. He is past president of PEN New Mexico and president of the New Mexico Book Association. When not traveling, Richard writes and lives in Santa Fe, New Mexico.